Nutshell
Hornbook Series
and
Black Letter Series
of
WEST PUBLISHING COMPANY
P.O. Box 64526
St. Paul, Minnesota 55164–0526

Accounting

FARIS' ACCOUNTING AND LAW IN A NUTSHELL, 377 pages, 1984. Softcover. (Text)

Administrative Law

AMAN AND MAYTON'S HORNBOOK ON ADMINISTRATIVE LAW, Approximately 750 pages, 1993. (Text)

GELLHORN AND LEVIN'S ADMINISTRATIVE LAW AND PROCESS IN A NUTSHELL, Third Edition, 479 pages, 1990. Softcover. (Text)

Admiralty

MARAIST'S ADMIRALTY IN A NUTSHELL, Second Edition, 379 pages, 1988. Softcover. (Text)

SCHOENBAUM'S HORNBOOK ON ADMIRALTY AND MARITIME LAW,
Student Edition, 692 pages, 1987 with 1992 pocket part. (Text)

Agency—Partnership

REUSCHLEIN AND GREGORY'S HORNBOOK ON THE LAW OF AGENCY AND PARTNERSHIP, Second Edition, 683 pages, 1990. (Text)

STEFFEN'S AGENCY-PARTNERSHIP IN A NUTSHELL, 364 pages, 1977. Softcover. (Text)

NOLAN–HALEY'S ALTERNATIVE DISPUTE RESOLUTION IN A NUTSHELL, 298 pages, 1992. Softcover. (Text)

RISKIN'S DISPUTE RESOLUTION FOR LAWYERS VIDEO TAPES, 1992. (Available for purchase by schools and libraries.)

American Indian Law

CANBY'S AMERICAN INDIAN LAW IN A NUTSHELL, Second Edition, 336 pages, 1988. Softcover. (Text)

Antitrust—see also Regulated Industries, Trade Regulation

GELLHORN'S ANTITRUST LAW AND ECONOMICS IN A NUTSHELL, Third Edition, 472 pages, 1986. Softcover. (Text)

HOVENKAMP'S BLACK LETTER ON ANTITRUST, Second Edition approximately 325 pages, April 1993 Pub. Softcover. (Review)

HOVENKAMP'S HORNBOOK ON ECONOMICS AND FEDERAL ANTITRUST LAW, Student Edition, 414 pages, 1985. (Text)

SULLIVAN'S HORNBOOK OF THE LAW OF ANTITRUST, 886 pages, 1977. (Text)

Appellate Advocacy—see Trial and Appellate Advocacy

Art Law

DUBOFF'S ART LAW IN A NUTSHELL, Second Edition, approximately 325 pages, 1993. Softcover. (Text)

Banking Law

LOVETT'S BANKING AND FINANCIAL INSTITUTIONS LAW IN A NUTSHELL, Third Edition, 470 pages, 1992. Softcover. (Text)

Civil Procedure—see also Federal Jurisdiction and Procedure

CLERMONT'S BLACK LETTER ON CIVIL PROCEDURE, Third Edition, approximately 350 pages, May, 1993 Pub. Softcover. (Review)

FRIEDENTHAL, KANE AND MILLER'S HORNBOOK ON CIVIL PROCEDURE, Second Edition, approximately 1000 pages, May 1993 Pub. (Text)

KANE'S CIVIL PROCEDURE IN A NUTSHELL, Third Edition, 303 pages, 1991. Softcover. (Text)

KOFFLER AND REPPY'S HORNBOOK ON COMMON LAW PLEADING, 663 pages, 1969. (Text)

SIEGEL'S HORNBOOK ON NEW YORK PRACTICE, Second Edition, Student Edition, 1068 pages, 1991. Softcover. (Text) 1992 Supplemental Pamphlet.

SLOMANSON AND WINGATE'S CALIFORNIA CIVIL PROCEDURE IN A NUTSHELL, 230 pages, 1992. Softcover. (Text)

Commercial Law

BAILEY AND HAGEDORN'S SECURED TRANSACTIONS IN A NUTSHELL, Third Edition, 390 pages, 1988. Softcover. (Text)

HENSON'S HORNBOOK ON SECURED TRANSACTIONS UNDER THE U.C.C., Second Edition, 504

Commercial Law—Continued

pages, 1979, with 1979 pocket part. (Text)

MEYER AND SPEIDEL'S BLACK LETTER ON SALES AND LEASES OF GOODS, Approximately 300 pages, 1993. Softcover. (Review)

NICKLES' BLACK LETTER ON COMMERCIAL PAPER, 450 pages, 1988. Softcover. (Review)

STOCKTON AND MILLER'S SALES AND LEASES OF GOODS IN A NUTSHELL, Third Edition, 441 pages, 1992. Softcover. (Text)

STONE'S UNIFORM COMMERCIAL CODE IN A NUTSHELL, Third Edition, 580 pages, 1989. Softcover. (Text)

WEBER AND SPEIDEL'S COMMERCIAL PAPER IN A NUTSHELL, Third Edition, 404 pages, 1982. Softcover. (Text)

WHITE AND SUMMERS' HORNBOOK ON THE UNIFORM COMMERCIAL CODE, Third Edition, Student Edition, 1386 pages, 1988. (Text)

Community Property

MENNELL AND BOYKOFF'S COMMUNITY PROPERTY IN A NUTSHELL, Second Edition, 432 pages, 1988. Softcover. (Text)

Comparative Law

FOLSOM, MINAN AND OTTO'S LAW AND POLITICS IN THE PEOPLE'S REPUBLIC OF CHINA IN A NUTSHELL, 451 pages, 1992. Softcover. (Text)

GLENDON, GORDON AND OSAKWE'S COMPARATIVE LEGAL TRADITIONS IN A NUTSHELL. 402 pages, 1982. Softcover. (Text)

Conflict of Laws

HAY'S BLACK LETTER ON CONFLICT OF LAWS, 330 pages, 1989. Softcover. (Review)

SCOLES AND HAY'S HORNBOOK ON CONFLICT OF LAWS, Student Edition, 1160 pages, 1992. (Text)

SIEGEL'S CONFLICTS IN A NUTSHELL, 470 pages, 1982. Softcover. (Text)

Constitutional Law—Civil Rights

BARRON AND DIENES' BLACK LETTER ON CONSTITUTIONAL LAW, Third Edition, 440 pages, 1991. Softcover. (Review)

BARRON AND DIENES' CONSTITUTIONAL LAW IN A NUTSHELL, Second Edition, 483 pages, 1991. Softcover. (Text)

ENGDAHL'S CONSTITUTIONAL FEDERALISM IN A NUTSHELL, Second Edition, 411 pages, 1987. Softcover. (Text)

MARKS AND COOPER'S STATE CON-

Constitutional Law—Civil Rights—Continued

STITUTIONAL LAW IN A NUTSHELL, 329 pages, 1988. Softcover. (Text)

NOWAK AND ROTUNDA'S HORNBOOK ON CONSTITUTIONAL LAW, Fourth Edition, 1357 pages, 1991. (Text)

VIEIRA'S CONSTITUTIONAL CIVIL RIGHTS IN A NUTSHELL, Second Edition, 322 pages, 1990. Softcover. (Text)

WILLIAMS' CONSTITUTIONAL ANALYSIS IN A NUTSHELL, 388 pages, 1979. Softcover. (Text)

Consumer Law—see also Commercial Law

EPSTEIN AND NICKLES' CONSUMER LAW IN A NUTSHELL, Second Edition, 418 pages, 1981. Softcover. (Text)

Contracts

CALAMARI AND PERILLO'S BLACK LETTER ON CONTRACTS, Second Edition, 462 pages, 1990. Softcover. (Review)

CALAMARI AND PERILLO'S HORNBOOK ON CONTRACTS, Third Edition, 1049 pages, 1987. (Text)

CORBIN'S TEXT ON CONTRACTS, One Volume Student Edition, 1224 pages, 1952. (Text)

FRIEDMAN'S CONTRACT REMEDIES IN A NUTSHELL, 323 pages, 1981. Softcover. (Text)

KEYES' GOVERNMENT CONTRACTS IN A NUTSHELL, Second Edition, 557 pages, 1990. Softcover. (Text)

SCHABER AND ROHWER'S CONTRACTS IN A NUTSHELL, Third Edition, 457 pages, 1990. Softcover. (Text)

Copyright—see Patent and Copyright Law

Corporations

HAMILTON'S BLACK LETTER ON CORPORATIONS, Third Edition, 732 pages, 1992. Softcover. (Review)

HAMILTON'S THE LAW OF CORPORATIONS IN A NUTSHELL, Third Edition, 518 pages, 1991. Softcover. (Text)

HENN AND ALEXANDER'S HORNBOOK ON LAWS OF CORPORATIONS, Third Edition, Student Edition, 1371 pages, 1983, with 1986 pocket part. (Text)

Corrections

KRANTZ' THE LAW OF CORRECTIONS AND PRISONERS' RIGHTS IN A NUTSHELL, Third Edition, 407 pages, 1988. Softcover. (Text)

Creditors' Rights

EPSTEIN'S DEBTOR-CREDITOR LAW IN A NUTSHELL, Fourth Edition,

Creditors' Rights—Continued
401 pages, 1991. Softcover. (Text)

EPSTEIN, NICKLES AND WHITE'S HORNBOOK ON BANKRUPTCY, Approximately 1000 pages, January, 1992 Pub. (Text)

NICKLES AND EPSTEIN'S BLACK LETTER ON CREDITORS' RIGHTS AND BANKRUPTCY, 576 pages, 1989. (Review)

Criminal Law and Criminal Procedure—see also Corrections, Juvenile Justice

ISRAEL AND LAFAVE'S CRIMINAL PROCEDURE—CONSTITUTIONAL LIMITATIONS IN A NUTSHELL, Fourth Edition, 461 pages, 1988. Softcover. (Text)

LAFAVE AND ISRAEL'S HORNBOOK ON CRIMINAL PROCEDURE, Second Edition, 1309 pages, 1992 with 1992 pocket part. (Text)

LAFAVE AND SCOTT'S HORNBOOK ON CRIMINAL LAW, Second Edition, 918 pages, 1986. (Text)

LOEWY'S CRIMINAL LAW IN A NUTSHELL, Second Edition, 321 pages, 1987. Softcover. (Text)

LOW'S BLACK LETTER ON CRIMINAL LAW, Revised First Edition, 443 pages, 1990. Softcover. (Review)

SUBIN, MIRSKY AND WEINSTEIN'S

THE CRIMINAL PROCESS: PROSECUTION AND DEFENSE FUNCTIONS, Approximately 450 pages, February, 1993 Pub. Softcover. Teacher's Manual available. (Text)

Domestic Relations

CLARK'S HORNBOOK ON DOMESTIC RELATIONS, Second Edition, Student Edition, 1050 pages, 1988. (Text)

KRAUSE'S BLACK LETTER ON FAMILY LAW, 314 pages, 1988. Softcover. (Review)

KRAUSE'S FAMILY LAW IN A NUTSHELL, Second Edition, 444 pages, 1986. Softcover. (Text)

MALLOY'S LAW AND ECONOMICS: A COMPARATIVE APPROACH TO THEORY AND PRACTICE, 166 pages, 1990. Softcover. (Text)

Education Law

ALEXANDER AND ALEXANDER'S THE LAW OF SCHOOLS, STUDENTS AND TEACHERS IN A NUTSHELL, 409 pages, 1984. Softcover. (Text)

Employment Discrimination—see also Gender Discrimination

PLAYER'S FEDERAL LAW OF EMPLOYMENT DISCRIMINATION IN A NUTSHELL, Third Edition, 338 pages, 1992. Softcover. (Text)

Judicial Process—Continued

Approximately 350 pages, 1993. Softcover. (Text)

Juvenile Justice

FOX'S JUVENILE COURTS IN A NUTSHELL, Third Edition, 291 pages, 1984. Softcover. (Text)

Labor and Employment Law— see also Employment Discrimination, Workers' Compensation

LESLIE'S LABOR LAW IN A NUTSHELL, Third Edition, 388 pages, 1992. Softcover. (Text)

NOLAN'S LABOR ARBITRATION LAW AND PRACTICE IN A NUTSHELL, 358 pages, 1979. Softcover. (Text)

Land Finance—Property Security—see Real Estate Transactions

Land Use

HAGMAN AND JUERGENSMEYER'S HORNBOOK ON URBAN PLANNING AND LAND DEVELOPMENT CONTROL LAW, Second Edition, Student Edition, 680 pages, 1986. (Text)

WRIGHT AND WRIGHT'S LAND USE IN A NUTSHELL, Second Edition, 356 pages, 1985. Softcover. (Text)

Legal Method and Legal System—see also Legal Research, Legal Writing

KEMPIN'S HISTORICAL INTRODUCTION TO ANGLO-AMERICAN LAW IN A NUTSHELL, Third Edition, 323 pages, 1990. Softcover. (Text)

REYNOLDS' JUDICIAL PROCESS IN A NUTSHELL, Second Edition, 308 pages, 1991. Softcover. (Text)

Legal Research

COHEN AND OLSON'S LEGAL RESEARCH IN A NUTSHELL, Fifth Edition, 370 pages, 1992. Softcover. (Text)

COHEN, BERRING AND OLSON'S HOW TO FIND THE LAW, Ninth Edition, 716 pages, 1989. (Text)

Legal Writing and Drafting

MELLINKOFF'S DICTIONARY OF AMERICAN LEGAL USAGE, 703 pages, 1992. Softcover. (Text)

SQUIRES AND ROMBAUER'S LEGAL WRITING IN A NUTSHELL, 294 pages, 1982. Softcover. (Text)

Legislation—see also Legal Writing and Drafting

DAVIES' LEGISLATIVE LAW AND PROCESS IN A NUTSHELL, Second Edition, 346 pages, 1986. Softcover. (Text)

Local Government

MCCARTHY'S LOCAL GOVERNMENT LAW IN A NUTSHELL, Third Edition, 435 pages, 1990. Softcover. (Text)

REYNOLDS' HORNBOOK ON LOCAL GOVERNMENT LAW, 860 pages, 1982 with 1990 pocket part. (Text)

Mass Communication Law

ZUCKMAN, GAYNES, CARTER AND DEE'S MASS COMMUNICATIONS LAW IN A NUTSHELL, Third Edition, 538 pages, 1988. Softcover. (Text)

Medicine, Law and

HALL AND ELLMAN'S HEALTH CARE LAW AND ETHICS IN A NUTSHELL, 401 pages, 1990. Softcover (Text)

JARVIS, CLOSEN, HERMANN AND LEONARD'S AIDS LAW IN A NUTSHELL, 349 pages, 1991. Softcover. (Text)

KING'S THE LAW OF MEDICAL MALPRACTICE IN A NUTSHELL, Second Edition, 342 pages, 1986. Softcover. (Text)

Military Law

SHANOR AND TERRELL'S MILITARY LAW IN A NUTSHELL, 378 pages, 1980. Softcover. (Text)

Mining Law—see Energy and Natural Resources Law

Mortgages—see Real Estate Transactions

Natural Resources Law—see Energy and Natural Resources Law, Environmental Law

TEPLY'S LEGAL NEGOTIATION IN A NUTSHELL, 282 pages, 1992. Softcover. (Text)

Office Practice—see also Computers and Law, Interviewing and Counseling, Negotiation

HEGLAND'S TRIAL AND PRACTICE SKILLS IN A NUTSHELL, 346 pages, 1978. Softcover (Text)

Oil and Gas—see also Energy and Natural Resources Law

HEMINGWAY'S HORNBOOK ON THE LAW OF OIL AND GAS, Third Edition, Student Edition, 711 pages, 1992. (Text)

LOWE'S OIL AND GAS LAW IN A NUTSHELL, Second Edition, 465 pages, 1988. Softcover. (Text)

Partnership—see Agency—Partnership

Patent and Copyright Law

MILLER AND DAVIS' INTELLECTUAL PROPERTY—PATENTS, TRADEMARKS AND COPYRIGHT IN A NUTSHELL, Second Edition, 437 pages, 1990. Softcover. (Text)

Products Liability

PHILLIPS' PRODUCTS LIABILITY IN

Products Liability—Continued

A NUTSHELL, Third Edition, 307 pages, 1988. Softcover. (Text)

Professional Responsibility

ARONSON AND WECKSTEIN'S PROFESSIONAL RESPONSIBILITY IN A NUTSHELL, Second Edition, 514 pages, 1991. Softcover. (Text)

LESNICK'S BEING A LAWYER: INDIVIDUAL CHOICE AND RESPONSIBILITY IN THE PRACTICE OF LAW, 422 pages, 1992. Softcover. Teacher's Manual available. (Coursebook)

ROTUNDA'S BLACK LETTER ON PROFESSIONAL RESPONSIBILITY, Third Edition, 492 pages, 1992. Softcover. (Review)

WOLFRAM'S HORNBOOK ON MODERN LEGAL ETHICS, Student Edition, 1120 pages, 1986. (Text)

WYDICK AND PERSCHBACHER'S CALIFORNIA LEGAL ETHICS, 439 pages, 1992. Softcover. (Coursebook)

Property—see also Real Estate Transactions, Land Use, Trusts and Estates

BERNHARDT'S BLACK LETTER ON PROPERTY, Second Edition, 388 pages, 1991. Softcover. (Review)

BERNHARDT'S REAL PROPERTY IN A NUTSHELL, Second Edition, 448 pages, 1981. Softcover. (Text)

BOYER, HOVENKAMP AND KURTZ' THE LAW OF PROPERTY, AN INTRODUCTORY SURVEY, Fourth Edition, 696 pages, 1991. (Text)

BURKE'S PERSONAL PROPERTY IN A NUTSHELL, Second Edition, approximately 400 pages, May, 1993 Pub. Softcover. (Text)

CUNNINGHAM, STOEBUCK AND WHITMAN'S HORNBOOK ON THE LAW OF PROPERTY, Second Edition, approximately 900 pages, May, 1993 Pub. (Text)

HILL'S LANDLORD AND TENANT LAW IN A NUTSHELL, Second Edition, 311 pages, 1986. Softcover. (Text)

Real Estate Transactions

BRUCE'S REAL ESTATE FINANCE IN A NUTSHELL, Third Edition, 287 pages, 1991. Softcover. (Text)

NELSON AND WHITMAN'S BLACK LETTER ON LAND TRANSACTIONS AND FINANCE, Second Edition, 466 pages, 1988. Softcover. (Review)

NELSON AND WHITMAN'S HORNBOOK ON REAL ESTATE FINANCE LAW, Second Edition, 941 pages, 1985 with 1989 pocket part. (Text)

Regulated Industries—see also Mass Communication Law, Banking Law

GELLHORN AND PIERCE'S REGULATED INDUSTRIES IN A NUTSHELL, Second Edition, 389 pages, 1987. Softcover. (Text)

Remedies

DOBBS' HORNBOOK ON REMEDIES, Second Edition, approximately 1000 pages, April, 1993 Pub. (Text)

DOBBYN'S INJUNCTIONS IN A NUTSHELL, 264 pages, 1974. Softcover. (Text)

FRIEDMAN'S CONTRACT REMEDIES IN A NUTSHELL, 323 pages, 1981. Softcover. (Text)

O'CONNELL'S REMEDIES IN A NUTSHELL, Second Edition, 320 pages, 1985. Softcover. (Text)

Sea, Law of

SOHN AND GUSTAFSON'S THE LAW OF THE SEA IN A NUTSHELL, 264 pages, 1984. Softcover. (Text)

Securities Regulation

HAZEN'S HORNBOOK ON THE LAW OF SECURITIES REGULATION, Second Edition, Student Edition, 1082 pages, 1990. (Text)

RATNER'S SECURITIES REGULATION IN A NUTSHELL, Fourth Edition, 320 pages, 1992. Softcover. (Text)

Sports Law

CHAMPION'S SPORTS LAW IN A NUTSHELL,. Approximately 300 pages, January, 1993 Pub. Softcover. (Text)

SCHUBERT, SMITH AND TRENTADUE'S SPORTS LAW, 395 pages, 1986. (Text)

Tax Practice and Procedure

MORGAN'S TAX PROCEDURE AND TAX FRAUD IN A NUTSHELL, 400 pages, 1990. Softcover. (Text)

Taxation—Corporate

SCHWARZ AND LATHROPE'S BLACK LETTER ON CORPORATE AND PARTNERSHIP TAXATION, 537 pages, 1991. Softcover. (Review)

WEIDENBRUCH AND BURKE'S FEDERAL INCOME TAXATION OF CORPORATIONS AND STOCKHOLDERS IN A NUTSHELL, Third Edition, 309 pages, 1989. Softcover. (Text)

Taxation—Estate & Gift—see also Estate Planning, Trusts and Estates

MCNULTY'S FEDERAL ESTATE AND GIFT TAXATION IN A NUTSHELL, Fourth Edition, 496 pages, 1989. Softcover. (Text)

PEAT AND WILLBANKS' FEDERAL ESTATE AND GIFT TAXATION: AN ANALYSIS AND CRITIQUE, 265 pages, 1991. Softcover. (Text)

Taxation—Individual

DODGE'S THE LOGIC OF TAX, 343 pages, 1989. Softcover. (Text)

HUDSON AND LIND'S BLACK LETTER ON FEDERAL INCOME TAXATION, Fourth Edition, 410 pages, 1992. Softcover. (Review)

MCNULTY'S FEDERAL INCOME TAXATION OF INDIVIDUALS IN A NUTSHELL, Fourth Edition, 503 pages, 1988. Softcover. (Text)

POSIN'S FEDERAL INCOME TAXATION, Second Edition, approximately 650 pages, May, 1993 Pub. Softcover. (Text)

ROSE AND CHOMMIE'S HORNBOOK ON FEDERAL INCOME TAXATION, Third Edition, 923 pages, 1988, with 1991 pocket part. (Text)

Taxation—International

DOERNBERG'S INTERNATIONAL TAXATION IN A NUTSHELL, 325 pages, 1989. Softcover. (Text)

BISHOP AND BROOKS' FEDERAL PARTNERSHIP TAXATION: A GUIDE TO THE LEADING CASES, STATUTES, AND REGULATIONS, 545 pages, 1990. Softcover. (Text)

BURKE'S FEDERAL INCOME TAXATION OF PARTNERSHIPS IN A NUTSHELL, 356 pages, 1992. Softcover. (Text)

SCHWARZ AND LATHROPE'S BLACK LETTER ON CORPORATE AND PARTNERSHIP TAXATION, 537 pages, 1991. Softcover. (Review)

Taxation—State & Local

GELFAND AND SALSICH'S STATE AND LOCAL TAXATION AND FINANCE IN A NUTSHELL, 309 pages, 1986. Softcover. (Text)

Torts—see also Products Liability

KIONKA'S BLACK LETTER ON TORTS, 339 pages, 1988. Softcover. (Review)

KIONKA'S TORTS IN A NUTSHELL, Second Edition, 449 pages, 1992. Softcover. (Text)

PROSSER AND KEETON'S HORNBOOK ON TORTS, Fifth Edition, Student Edition, 1286 pages, 1984 with 1988 pocket part. (Text)

Trade Regulation—see also Antitrust, Regulated Industries

MCMANIS' UNFAIR TRADE PRACTICES IN A NUTSHELL, Third Edition, approximately 450 pages, 1993. Softcover. (Text)

SCHECHTER'S BLACK LETTER ON UNFAIR TRADE PRACTICES, 272 pages, 1986. Softcover. (Review)

Trial and Appellate Advocacy—see also Civil Procedure

BERGMAN'S TRIAL ADVOCACY IN A

Advisory Board

CURTIS J. BERGER
Professor of Law, Columbia University

JESSE H. CHOPER
Dean and Professor of Law,
University of California, Berkeley

DAVID P. CURRIE
Professor of Law, University of Chicago

YALE KAMISAR
Professor of Law, University of Michigan

MARY KAY KANE
Professor of Law, University of California,
Hastings College of the Law

WAYNE R. LaFAVE
Professor of Law, University of Illinois

RICHARD C. MAXWELL
Professor of Law, Duke University

ARTHUR R. MILLER
Professor of Law, Harvard University

GRANT S. NELSON
Professor of Law, University of California, Los Angeles

ROBERT A. STEIN
Dean and Professor of Law, University of Minnesota

JAMES J. WHITE
Professor of Law, University of Michigan

CHARLES ALAN WRIGHT
Professor of Law, University of Texas

[XIV]

PERSONAL PROPERTY

IN A NUTSHELL

Second Edition

By

BARLOW BURKE
Professor of Law
Washington College of Law
American University

ST. PAUL, MINN.
WEST PUBLISHING CO.
1993

Nutshell Series, In a Nutshell, the Nutshell Logo and the WP symbol
are registered trademarks of West Publishing Co. Registered in the U.S.
Patent and Trademark Office.

COPYRIGHT © 1983 WEST PUBLISHING CO.
COPYRIGHT © 1993 By WEST PUBLISHING CO.
610 Opperman Drive
P.O. Box 64526
St. Paul, MN 55164–0526

All rights reserved
Printed in the United States of America

Library of Congress Cataloging-in-Publication Data
Burke, D. Barlow, 1941–
    Personal property in a nutshell / by D. Barlow Burke, Jr. — 2nd
ed.
    p.   cm. — (Nutshell series)
    Includes index.
    ISBN 0–314–01700–3
    1. Personal property—United States.   I. Title.   II. Series.
KF705.Z9B83 1993
346.7304'7—dc20
[347.30647]
                                                        92–45700
                                                            CIP

ISBN 0–314–01700–3

Burke, Pers.Prop., 2d Ed. NS

PREFACE

Personal property is a subject which is often the grist for a unit of many required, first-year property courses in law school; it is sometimes taught in advanced elective courses as well. It introduces students to ideas useful in other areas of law study—contracts, commercial transactions, and civil procedure, for example. It helps a student distinguish between title and possession. It permits students to see the origins of substantive rules of law in procedure. The substance of the common law is "secreted in the interstices of procedure." H. Maine, Early Law and Custom 389 (1890) (and if the book has a bias, it lies here!). It has lots of uses for the law teacher and engages the law student in the study of a set of readily understandable situations; in short, a good way of beginning law school.

When set early within the first-year curriculum, the study of personal property also has the advantage of reenforcing some of the lessons learned in civil procedure, another course likely to trouble the sleep of first-year students.

The fact that one begins law school with this study has certain limitations. Students study personal property when they are busy adjusting to a new discipline, types of analyses, language, etc.—in short, to our legal culture. That adjustment is no mean task, and many attorneys would like to forget all about it. Students don't have that option, at least before their examinations, and many would give their eye-teeth to be able to sit through those first weeks of class again.

This book is written in part so that they can do that. It provides not a substitute for the classroom experience but one person's extended analysis of the leading cases—the ones likely to be covered in the first weeks of the term—and thereafter flattens out into a discussion of rules and principles of law on the assumption that the student is later better able to see them applied in particular cases.

This book owes a lot to many people; to my students who help me organize my thoughts; to the editors of the many casebooks I've had the pleasure of using who, with their scholarship, suggest relationships it would otherwise take me years to discover; to my research assistants, Brenda Leahy and Patricia Hamnes, who patiently answered my questions about both the detail and the sweep of the law with solid research.

BARLOW BURKE, JR.

Washington, D.C.
February, 1993

OUTLINE

TABLE OF CASES

References are to Pages

TABLE OF CASES

*

PERSONAL PROPERTY

IN A NUTSHELL

Second Edition

*

CHAPTER I
WILD ANIMALS AND FIRST POSSESSION

The study of the law of property generally commences with the subject of personal property as opposed to real or land-related property. The explanation lies in the students' likely familiarity with personalty as opposed to realty: although some students will come to law school owning land or their own homes, all will own their wristwatch or some other form of personal property. "Owning" a thing is of course an all-encompassing term; what it encompasses, what its features are, is the subject of this book.

The study of the law of personal property in turn often commences with cases involving the hunting of wild animals. Our common law early accepted the Roman law idea that a wild animal (*ferae naturae*) is the common property of all, hence no one's personal property. For this reason, these cases present a unique factual situation because in them the wild animal usually has never previously been anyone's property. No prior possessors claim it. When one stops to think about it, the absence of a prior possessor and a chain of title is really quite unique. Most every chattel (the law's generic term for an object of personal property but

1

etymologically rooted in the word "cattle") has been owned by someone at sometime. Occasionally, a chattel which has once been owned is then abandoned by its owner and reverts to being unpossessed. *Eads v. Brazelton* (1861). It is with previously unpossessed chattels that this chapter first deals.

I. THE LEADING CASE

In *Pierson v. Post* (1805), Post, with hounds and upon uninhabited and unpossessed wasteland, started to hunt a fox; Pierson, knowing Post was in pursuit and in order to prevent Post's capturing the pursued animal, killed and carried it off.

Post was probably livid at having his hunt spoiled by that spoil-sport Pierson. So Post sued Pierson.

He styled his complaint as a request for a writ of trespass on the case. Trespass, applied to personal property, is an action to recover damages for any willful injury or harm done by defendant to a chattel where the plaintiff had a present right to possession and the defendant interfered with this right. Trespass thus covers only willful or forcible acts. Where the acts of the defendant were unaccompanied by direct or immediate force and were the indirect cause of an injury and where defendant was not willful, but negligent in his actions, trespass on the case is the proper cause of action. This common law writ, often abbreviated as "case," covers a much wider area than does simple trespass. It is premised on a defendant's duty to respect the plaintiff's right, a breach of that duty and some subsequent harm caused the plaintiff.

The advantage of this latter writ, from Post's viewpoint, is that he did not have to show that he had possession of the fox, as obviously he did not. But this only allowed Post a bit of breathing space since he still had to define the nature of his claimed "legal right," even if it did not amount to a right of possession. Basically Post still had to plead his case in such a way as to emphasize his rights rather than the wrong committed by Pierson. Alternatively, Post could have pled his case in tort, emphasizing that Pierson interfered with his hunt rather than with Post's own right to the fox. It is reasonable to assert that Post's attorney should have pled his client's case using this alternative or tort basis for his complaint.

Why would Post's attorney plead as he did? Perhaps it was done in an effort to avoid having to show an injury (as would be required in a tort action) or under a commonly-used judicial rule of thumb that if possession were shown, so would an injury to Post's right. Remember that from the facts it would appear that the injury had been to Post's pride, not his pocketbook. His attorney did not want the court to dwell on the petty nature of the suit and so pled that his client's rights were injured.

From Post's perspective, then, interference with the lawful activity of hunting, rather than a legal right to the fox, is the gist of the action complained of. It is also probably what made Post angry enough to bring suit. Pierson, to legitimatize his own actions, is interested in focusing the court's attention on the fact that Post had no right to possession of the fox and, this being so, Pierson had as much right as Post to kill it. The writ sued for (trespass on the case) is broad enough to allow both parties ample play at trial; it after all concerns an infringement of a right and thus contains both tort (infringement) and property (rightful possession) elements.

Post won both a jury verdict and the judgment of the trial court. Pierson, however, sued out a writ of certiorari, thus getting himself listed first in the case name that comes down to us. Certiorari permits an appellate court to review the matters of law involved in the case tried below. Indeed, an appeal using this writ is limited to those matters.

The result of this appeal was a reversal of the judgment obtained by Post. Why? Because, the appellate court said, Post's complaint did not state a cause of action. This legal conclusion was just what Pierson wanted and perhaps could not have been obtained in the forum below because if Pierson had there demurred to Post's complaint, he would have only succeeded in getting Post to amend it. So tactically suing out a writ of certiorari was preferable to demurring below.

The decision of the appellate court could not have been an easy one. As of 1805, there was no case-law binding the court. A decision for neither party was compelled by New York precedents. Indeed, the appellate court cites none; it cites no American cases but does cite and distinguishes some English ones where a similar dispute arose on private land. It also cites some seventeenth-century European natural-law treatise writers much in vogue at the time of the decision; it cites the Emperor Justinian whose jurists in the sixth century A.D. wrote a passage which supports but does not compel its holding; it further anglicizes these continental writers by references to Fleta and Bracton. However, all this discussion really shows that the court was free to decide for either party.

What did it decide? Its holding, read most narrowly, is that Post did not state a cause of action. This says little of value as a precedent; it is only in the court's discussion of why Post fails that it makes statements giving any precedential value to the opinion.

But how important is this case anyway? The issue presented to the court is novel and interesting, but not much seems at stake here. Much if not all law, however, follows from procedure and much law in its incipient stages closely reflects procedural rules. So it is here.

Another reason for stating the holding in procedural terms is the notion that though in some non-legal sense Post deserves the fox, he should not get it because this will encourage other people to bring such petty disputes to the courts. However, this aim probably was not uppermost in the court's mind because limiting litigation and protecting the docket was not accomplished in the cleanest possible way with this opinion. It would have been far more effective just to deny certiorari. Likewise, the objective of limiting litigation assumes that parties to future disputes will read and, even more unlikely, act on the basis of the opinion in the present case. Moreover, the facts of future cases may well be easier to decide if some substantive rule of law is laid down and used. Each of these rationales seems, finally, judicially self-serving to some degree and so might naturally be downplayed, particularly by courts in the early years of the Republic, when the role of the judiciary was not firmly established.

What more disinterested and useful statements of the holding might be gleaned from this opinion? From the facts, it is clear that Post was in pursuit of the fox; the court concludes that he acquired no rights in the creature. So the narrowest substantive holding is that pursuit alone gives rise to no rights in the fox.

Like the procedural version of the holding, this statement may be too negative. True, it helps to answer the plaintiff's question as to whether he has a cause of action but it will probably not be very interesting to the population as a whole. People are seldom interested in learning about rights which they don't have; rather, they are interested in those rights they do have. On the other hand, a court will not be too interested in explicating rights in a lawsuit which it thinks is petty, breeds unnecessary litigation, or is of first impression (when later cases in the same vein may present unforeseen issues or not reach the courts at all).

In any event, will the facts of similar future cases be easier or harder to decide if a rule based on pursuit is used? Probably harder, because disputes will likely arise where there is more than one party in pursuit. Dwelling on the fact of pursuit will either make two or more pursuers indistinguishable as litigants before the courts or force the judges to rely on distinctions as to the types of pursuit. Either result is unsatisfactory. To avoid both, the appellate court in *Pierson v. Post* went on to state that a right in a wild animal arises only (1) when a person intends to control the animal and (2) when that person gains possession of it. Pursuit is a factual component of this rule. It shows the requisite intent while possession is shown by control of the animal.

Post, by pursuing the fox, showed his intent to control it, but the very fact which showed this intent also showed that he lacked control and hence possession of the animal. Thus he failed to show a sufficient possessory right to the fox and failed to state a cause of action.

From the court's viewpoint, a rule based on intent, pursuit, capture, and control provides an easier standard to apply to future cases. Why?

Because the first appropriator or possessor of a wild animal has distinguished himself from a "mere" pursuer of game. This implies that the facts of these cases should be allowed to develop or "sort themselves out" sufficiently to provide a court with the grist to elaborate on their legal ramifications. How much development the facts of a particular case need before a court can usefully intervene in a dispute is a matter about which judges and lawyers develop a capacity for determining. This capacity is, needless to say, a high art.

An additional benefit of this rule is that with the standard clearly enunciated, it may discourage disappointed pursuers of game from bringing this type of suit to the courts. However, if this opinion is a search for a definition of possession of the fox, then it is important to recognize the premises and the logic used in conducting the search. The majority assumes that in the future hunters, after learning how and why the majority decided for Pierson, will hunt more furiously than ever in the knowledge that they must become the first possessor of the fox. The dissenting judge in *Pierson v. Post* looks at the case very differently. He wants to encourage fox hunting; horseback riding in the fresh air does not serve his purpose, unless it is done with the aim of killing those noxious beasts. In this, he assumes that foxes are bad, that hunters will hear of the court's decision and that they will be encouraged to hunt. People need to be encouraged to hunt, to start the fox, in order that they might kill it. The law should not rely on the chance interloper (such as Pierson) but upon the hunter whose intent it is to rid the countryside of foxes.

Pierson v. Post has been cited by courts, state and federal, down to the present day.

A. CONTROL

No rule of first possession (or of law) can be inflexible. If it were to be (say it required that to acquire a right in a wild animal, that animal must be dead), what of many forms of live traps for wild animals and the rights of trappers? To obtain the right to a wild animal, a hunter must assume a degree of control which deprives the animal of its natural liberty and which must inevitably result in possession. Just wounding the fox is insufficient; so is pursuit. In *Pierson v. Post,* it would not make any difference if Post had caught up with the fox, seized it manually and was about to put it in a cage, when the fox bit his hand and escaped. *Buster v. Newkirk* (1822).

In *Buster v. Newkirk,* op. cit., the plaintiff was a hunter who with his dogs wounded and was in pursuit of a deer; he gave over the pursuit as night descended, but his dogs kept on. In the morning, the plaintiff resumed pursuit and came to the door of the defendant's house, where the deer had been killed the previous night. The defendant alleged that the deer had been shot at by an unknown party just before the defendant killed it and that he had cut its throat just as the plaintiff's dog laid hold of it. (The court wisely ignores the tale about a third party and keeps its focus in this opinion on the two parties before it.)

The trial court, in an action for the monetary value of the animal, gave the plaintiff judgment for seventy five cents, judged to be the value of the skin. The slight value of the judgment is perhaps testimony to the defendant's willingness to compromise: the defendant had offered the plaintiff the venison, but not the skin, and plaintiff sued for the latter. This judgment was reversed, in favor of the defendant. Even though the plaintiff's giving up the chase for the night argues abandonment, the continuous use of the dogs negates an intent to abandon pursuit. The facts, however, highlight again the thin line between a rule against interference and a rule of capture—between a tort rule and a property rule. The *Newkirk* opinion relies exclusively on *Pierson.* Its language is replete with many of the latter case's words of art. As to the pursuit, for example, that the plaintiff did not deprive the deer of "its natural liberty" before the defendant seized it, disposes of the case for the court. Its result is further testimony to the unforgiving, winner-take-all nature of the rule of capture.

However, if a wounding is followed by active pursuit the hunter who (1) closes in on his prey and who (2) is about to administer a fatal wound, has a right to do so without interference. This infliction of the mortal wound must be inevitable in order for the hunter to be protected from the interference of interlopers. For example, if Post had placed the fox in the cage referred to earlier and if Pierson had opened the cage door and let it escape, Post would recover from Pierson on a tort theory of interfering with Post's possession. *Liesner v. Wanie* (1914).

What, however, if the hunter has no opportunity at all to inflict a mortal wound or capture the animal? Will the writ of trespass on the case still serve him? Another leading case, *Keeble v. Hickeringill* (1707) says yes. In this English case, the hunter (Keeble) was a landowner who maintained his decoy pond in a meadow. The defendant fired a gun off on his adjoining land and scared the ducks away from the plaintiff's pond. The plaintiff could not in all likelihood show what his damages were because he did not take possession of the ducks and he could not do so because of defendant's interference. This interference alone was held actionable, using the writ of trespass on the case. We will have occasion to return to the *Keeble* case to discuss the fact that in this case the hunt took place on private property.

In another context—fishing—fish in a weir which remains open may still be captured by another fisherman. A question of fact must usually be settled to decide these cases: the net or trap may be substantially closed (say with the fish being 60–70% encircled by the net), but the remaining

gap may be large enough (say, 50 feet) for another
fishing boat to enter and throw its own net. These
were the facts in *Young v. Hichens* (1844). Whether the second fisherman damaged the net of the
first, will be relevant if the tortious aspects of the
case are dispositive; they will be less so if the
possessory aspects are emphasized. In *Young,* the
first fisherman had driven the fish against his net
by beating on the water with oars and throwing
the fish into flight against the net. This served to
deprive the fish of their natural liberty, but because beating the water with his oars also meant
not closing the gap in the weir, it diminished the
inevitability of the first fisherman's taking the
catch on board his boat.

Still, with careful pleading to emphasize the
negligent interference of the interloper, the first
fisherman might prevail with a writ of trespass on
the case. Trespass, however, will not work as well
for him, since to use it he must show a willful or
forceful interference with the rights of the first
fisherman. (To establish these rights, the damage
to the first's nets or violation of local ordinances
would be crucial.) Trespass on the case, however,
requires only that the plaintiff make the easier
showing of recklessness or negligence in the conduct of the defendant. Young's attorney pleaded
in trespass. That was a bad mistake. It also
denied him the use of *Keeble* and *Pierson* as precedent.

Finally in this discussion of control, what about
the fisherman who, using another's nets which

have confined fish so that escape is not impossible, but control of them is practically inevitable, takes these confined fish for his own? Is this larceny—a statutory crime involving the carrying away of a chattel in the possession of another? In one court, when charged with larceny, such a fisherman's conviction was upheld. *State v. Shaw* (1902). Considering the presumption of innocence that attaches to criminal defendants and the policy of construing criminal statutes narrowly, this result may seem surprising. When the uncertainty in the concept of possession is taken into account, it is even more surprising that decision in a criminal case would turn as it did in this case on a finding that the first fisherman had taken possession of the fish in spite of the fact that they were in an unattended net. However, even in a criminal case, possession is a relative concept: the first fisherman has possession as against the secretive defendant who trespasses on another's nets and interferes with another's efforts. Trespass on and interference with a line of actively worked traps would yield the same result and would also sustain a criminal conviction.

One later criminal case took a balanced view of the amount of control necessary over fish in a net; talking about a two and a half foot wide opening, from which some, but not the majority of fish caught, would escape, the court said: "Very likely it would be going too far to say that escape must be rendered impossible under all circumstances .... But the avenues of escape must be closed, and the chance at least reduced to a minimum." *State v. Thomas* (1901), quoted in *People v. Burtt* (1980).

B. CUSTOM

Possessory intent and a possessory act are the two requirements for gaining rights to a wild animal. The second—the possessory act—may in some instances be modified by custom so that a person need not gain actual control over the animal.

As has been suggested, the requirement of control as applied to hunters may have to be modified for trappers. However, the leading cases arise in the whaling industry. O. W. Holmes, *The Common Law* 167–68 (1881) (M. Howe ed., 1963). Herman Melville, in *Moby Dick* (1851) (Garden City Publ. Co., 1937), at 571–80, provides one summary of the industry's customs. Where a whale is harpooned by a bomb-lance identifiable as a particular whaler's, the persons who find the whale washed ashore dead cannot take possession of it without paying the whaler the market value of the whale. The courts use the custom of whalers, that "the iron holds the whale," to decide for the first harpooner. *Ghen v. Rich* (1881). So where a live fox in a trap, a fish in a net, or a harpooned whale on the beach, are customarily regarded by other trappers, fishermen or whalers as already "reduced to possession," the courts will take the custom as controlling.

Proof of a custom requires a showing of a shared set of values between the parties to the litigation.

No such thing was present in *Pierson v. Post,* for example, and similarly, custom would not control a case between one set of whalers respecting the rights of the first harpooner to hit the whale and another set who require a fatal harpooning. Custom is confined by circumstances and is not therefore as broadly applicable as a basis for judicial decision as is a rule of first possession. In some instances, however, it remains a doctrinal substitute for actual control.

The facts of *Ghen v. Rich,* op.cit., provide a good illustration of the limitations of this doctrine. The plaintiff sought to recover the value of a fin-back whale. The custom of fishermen from Provincetown, Massachusetts, was to pursue such whales in open boats launched from shore, shooting them with bomb lances fired from guns expressly made for this hunt. Fin-backs swim too swiftly to be pursued with harpoon and line, in the usual fashion of whale hunts. Once lanced, the whales sank, and were recovered later, when floating in the sea or washed ashore. A person coming upon a lanced dead whale customarily towed it or got word of the dead whale's location to Provincetown, receiving a salvage award for his services, and the harpooner went to it and removed the valuable blubber.

The whale in question was lanced, killed immediately and sank, coming three days later to rest on a beach seventeen miles away. The defendant bought its carcass at auction from the finder. The plaintiff, however, proved that the custom among whalers in this region was that the lancer who shot and killed a whale was its owner and that the subsequent finder was obligated to send word of its carcass' location to Provincetown. "I see no reason why the usage proved in this case is not as reasonable as that sustained in the cases [involving other whaling regions]. Its application must necessarily be extremely limited, and can affect but a few persons. It has been recognized and acquiesced in for many years. It requires of the first taker the only act of appropriation that is possible in the nature of the case. Unless it is sustained, this branch of industry must necessarily cease, for no person would engage in it if the fruits of his labor could be appropriated by any chance finder." The judge, saying this, found the custom valid and the property of the whale in the plaintiff.

Ghen has some interesting aspects—the failure of more widely-used whaling techniques, and specialized, bomb-lance technology among them. However, the dispositive feature of the custom sustained here is that the custom is absolutely necessary, in the court's view, to the continuance of this type of whaling. Preservation of the whaler's economic incentives to engage in the hunt is important, but more important is the continuance and organization of the whalery itself. (This decision coming down, of course, at a time when that whalery was in decline.)

There is no mention of the finder's occupation. Was he a competitor, or not? In the cases cited by the court, the facts seem to indicate that the disputes were between whalers all bound by the customs of the ground. Was the defendant here so bound, or was he bound to know of the custom by being not far distant from the place of the kill?

The procedures involved in the custom sustained here are somewhat vague. The lance attached to the beached dead whale was not so distinctive that it could readily be identified as the plaintiff's. If this case represents more than the law applicable to the tip of Cape Cod, this lack of identifying marks might well make a difference to the outcome of the case. Any system of property rights depends in part on assigning those rights to a person readily identified as their holder—and later their vendor, so that purchasers of those rights can be secure in the knowledge that they are buying from their true owner and not some pretender. Again, we see that the writ of custom does not travel well.

C. WILD AND DOMESTIC ANIMALS

Usually the intent and actions of the parties have been the dispositive factors in hunting cases. In some instances, however, the type of animal involved may make a difference.

Animals are customarily (and the word, you can now see, isn't used lightly) classified by the law as either wild or domestic—*ferae naturae* or *domitae naturae*. A deer, moose, or elk will be wild. Wild animals which are subject to the rights of hunters are not just the noxious ones such as foxes, but food-producing ones as well. On the other hand, sheep or cattle are domestic. These classifications will hold even if an elk has been raised for food on a farm and the sheep strayed from its flock. That is, the classification of an animal as wild or domestic is by species—and not according to the wildness or tameness of a particular animal.

The owner of escaped wild animals are absolutely liable for the trespasses and damages caused by such animals. For domestic animals, the English rule was similar: an owner was absolutely liable for trespasses of domestic animals likely to escape and do damage and he was under a duty to restrain or to enclose them. The liability for failing to do this was very early rejected as contrary to the customs of many American states, but was (in many states, again) reenacted in statutory form. Ternus, "Liability for the Escape of Animals," 30 Drake L.Rev. 257 (1980). Thus an owner may be liable either in strict liability or negligence. An owner was strictly liable when he or she knew or should—with the exercise of reasonable care—have known that the animal had a propensity to cause the particular type of damage or injury suffered by a plaintiff. When unaware of a propensity of an animal to mischief, an owner is liable when failing to exercise reasonable care in preventing the plaintiff's damage or injury. See e.g., *Pahanish v. Western Trails, Inc.* (1986) (a negligence action against the owner of a riding stable for injuries sustained in fall from horse); *Hodges v. Smith* (1912) (involving the sale of a vicious horse sold as a gentle one); *Jones v. Ross* (1893) (involving the sale of a vicious horse not known to be so by the seller).

Many states have enacted "dog bite statutes." These sometimes impose liability regardless of the dog's former viciousness or the owner's knowledge of the dog's viciousness. Ariz.Rev.Stat. § 11–1025 (Michie 1991); Rev.Code Wash.Ann. § 16.08.040 (West 1991). Such statutes are aimed at repealing the popular notion that "every dog gets one bite." Other statutes impose liability in damages for owners of dogs biting a person on public or private property, including the owner's [Mich.Comp.L.Ann. § 287.351 (1991)], liability for biting without provocation a person who has a right to be where he is when bitten [Ala.Code § 3–6–1 (Michie 1991)], or who is required, like the postman, to be where bitten [Ind.Stat.Ann. § 15–5–12–1 (Burns 1991)]— or some combination of these terms. See e.g., Calif.Civ.Code § 3342 (Bancroft–Whitney 1992). Some of these statutes seem aimed at incorporating, sub rosa, a rule that trespassers may freely be bitten. See Mass.Ann.L. ch. 140, § 155 (Lawyers Coop 1992) (excepting trespassers and persons teasing, tormenting, or abusing the biting dog). Dogs running loose and injuring other domestic animals sometimes subject their owners to a statutory liability for damages. See e.g., N.H.Rev.Stat.Ann. 466:19 (Butterworth 1991).

A trespassing animal of either type may be distrained or seized by a land owner suffering damages and held until the damages are paid or the animal is sold in order to pay them. In addition, a state or local government may have statutory powers to impound a lost or stray animal and hold it, eventually offering it for adoption and transferring all rights in it from its prior owner or possessor to a new one. *Johnston v. Atlanta Humane Society* (1985).

Stray cattle or sheep will not become property of the hunter who takes possession of them. The elk, deer or moose will. Why? Because the domesticity of the sheep puts the hunter on notice that there exists a prior possessor with rights superior to any which he might acquire. This notice does not pertain to the deer, moose or elk; no one would reasonably be expected to know that they were domesticated if found in their natural environment, unless their actions and movements provide reasonable notice.

Where there is agreement in a community as to the classification of an animal as either wild or domestic, classifying an animal as one or the other helps to answer the question of whether a second captor ought to know of (and so respect) the rights of a prior possessor of the animal. If domestic, the second captor is on notice of such rights. If wild, no notice is given.

No matter which label is used, prior rights in any animal can often be deduced from the type of environment in which the animal is found. Cows in a pasture belong to the farmer who owns the pasture. Deer in an undeveloped forest (as opposed to a game preserve) are fair game.

By the same token—and to carry this line of reasoning to its final conclusion—if a wild animal was wounded by a hunter, but rose and escaped with the hunter on its back, the hunter has not reduced the animal to possession, but any interloper would certainly know of the hunter's pursuit and be bound to respect it.

Besides providing notice, the hunter's ride may also show an act of taming or hunting the animal so as to exclude others from doing the same. This is an argument to the effect that the rider has a degree of control over the animal sufficient to possess it.

A less fanciful set of cases illustrating this same reasoning involve animals formerly wild, but then domesticated, only to escape later. Here again, a common law policy of encouraging the domestication of wild animals and a concept of notice underlie judicial decisions in this area. However, some state statutes may alter this policy by prohibiting the keeping of wild animals and/or by requiring the domesticator to secure a permit before doing so. If an animal has regained its freedom, it usually has no intent to return (*animum revertendi*) to its first captor. Actions in line with an intent to return will reflect its prior training by the first captor, as in the instance of a carrier pigeon or a hunting falcon. Such animals exhibit behavior linking them to their first captor.

In another instance, a wild animal may have escaped but not yet regained its native habitat when set upon by a hunter; he nevertheless is required to recognize that the animal is not native to his hunting ground; such an animal, too, remains the property of its first captor.

By extension, it is possible that an escaped wild animal may have made it back to its native heath, but retains some identifiable features (a clipped wing, a band, etc.) which link it to its first captor who would again be able to reclaim it.

The same result may obtain when the first captor has expended considerable effort in raising the animal, but this is not compelled unless that effort would be obvious to its second captor.

In summary, if a wild animal has escaped and has no intent to return and is found in its native habitat, then it is the property of its next captor. However, if the animal has not returned to its native habitat and has identifiable features or exhibits behavior that link it with its first captor, its ownership stays with the latter.

When a formerly wild animal escapes from its domesticator, a second captor may wound or kill it in defense of his property. The farmer who kills an obviously rare and valuable fox about to enter his chicken coop may use whatever means are necessary to protect his chickens, but if killing force becomes necessary, he will have to return the fox's pelt or carcass to its first captor.

Although the law speaks of the *animum reverten-di* of a single animal, rather than of a species, this is a bit awkward as a legal concept because it is hard enough to fathom the human mind with its capacity for speech, let alone an animal's, lacking human capacity. So it is preferable to deal with the law involving once-tamed but escaped wild animals in terms of the notice of previous rights which the escaped animal in particular surroundings gives to a potential second captor. If the underlying policy is to encourage the taming of wild animals, one way to do this is to return escaped animals to their first captor.

Thus judicial attitudes toward the rights of first and subsequent captors of animals depends on an interplay between the actions of the animal and the habitat in which it is found. This interplay is illustrated—with the habitat aspect of the case replaced by a factor of land ownership—in cases involving bees.

Where bees swarm, the owner of their hive has the right to possess their honey; he has this right not because he has taken possession of every bee in the hive, but because his possession of the hive gives him as much control of the bees as he can reasonably be expected ever to have. As such, he has a qualified right to these bees even if they go onto the land of another. The qualification is that he must pursue them there or keep them in sight (if he cannot go onto another's land). So the owner of the land on which the bees swarm a second time has a right to them where they are unreclaimed. Although the original hive owner has a right in them, that right is defeasible upon his failure to pursue or keep them in sight.

At this point we can ask whether the second landowner does not have a right superior to the first after the bees have swarmed upon the second parcel of land, for then having the hive on his land would seem to give him present control. He does not have prior control, however; the concept of prior possession is one to which we will return in the next chapter. For now, it is enough to recognize that the first possessor of a previously unclaimed animal (or chattel) will be preferred; this is particularly so if, up to the time his right is disputed, he has labored to make sure that bees build their hive and give their honey on his land.

One final context in which there is authority for classifying an animal as either wild or domestic is in a condemnation case. Where private submerged land is condemned when being used as seeded or planted oyster beds, shall the owner be compensated for their loss? Oysters in their natural habitat are classified as wild. If, however, they are seeded where they do not naturally grow—on posted beds—they are domestic and subject to private control. They stay put but are not rooted in the bed; they get their food from the water and not the bed. On this basis, one court has ruled them to be personal property, not real property, and denied their owner compensation for them as part of the award given for the taking of his real property. *Coos Bay Oyster Cooperative v. State Highway Commission* (1959).

As realty or personalty, however, oysters can be carried off the bed with larcenous intent. Control of them may not be actual but, like the bee-keeper, so long as the possessor of the beds has done all reasonably expected of him to indicate an intent to possess them and control them, interference with his beds can lead to a charge of larceny.

1. Estray Statutes

In the instance of an escaped, domesticated animal, some states have statutes which permit another landowner to take the escapee into his possession and work him as it is wont. Usually he must register his find with a public official and sometimes criminal penalties are provided for failing to register the estray. The original owner has the right to reclaim it within a certain period of time. When reclaimed, the finder can collect the cost of the animal's keep from the original owner, set off by the value (if any) of working the animal as his own while it was in his possession. If unclaimed after a time, the animal can be sold at public auction. See e.g., Mich.Comp.Laws Ann. §§ 433.-15–433.18 (1991). The finder of the estray generally is given a lien on the animal for the cost of his keeping it until the owner reclaims it. This is satisfied from the proceeds of the sale of an unclaimed animal or else must be paid by the owner when reclaiming it.

Such statutes have two legal consequences. First, the finder of the unclaimed estray obtains title to it after a report of the find and the passage of the required amount of time, whereas the common law would provide him only with a right to possession. Second, these statutes provide a rule of liability for the owner or the keeper of estrays by either (1) making any owner of estrays strictly liable for property damages done by the animal, and in the case of an escaped wild animal, for personal injury as well, or (2) making the negligent owner liable for "reasonably foreseeable injury" by the estray if the estray was fenced, but imposing strict liability on the owner when the estray was unfenced. The person with a claim for damage done by an estray is also generally given a lien on the animal for payment of the claim.

D. LANDOWNERS AS FIRST POSSESSORS

The rules gleaned from cases involving bees can be stated from two perspectives—that of the owner of the land on which the bees had their first hive, and of the owner of the land to which the bees go. Both have a defeasible or qualified right to take the bees into their possession. They do not have possession itself, and their right to take possession exists generally only so long as the bees remain on their land; more specifically it exists until the bees fly away, unpursued or until they are reclaimed by pursuit or identified by sight on the land to which the bees go.

More generally, a qualified right of possession, which arises out of the ownership of the land on which a wild animal is found, is called the *rationi soli*. It is an English doctrine, never very popular in the United States because it smacks of the hunting rights of the English landowning families who used it to make meatless meals for and poachers out of England's yeoman. American courts have made grudging use of it. The doctrine legitimizes the use of one's lands to hunt and take possession of the wild animals found there. However, only a right to pursue wild animals arises from landownership *per se*. Ownership of the wild animals themselves does not arise as an incidental right of landownership. Rather it arises only by pursuit (possessory intent) and capture or control (a possessory act). If the animal in question were not likely to flee, as are wild animals, ownership of the land could more easily be equated with possession, as in the case of minerals on the land.

A hunter must, however, have a chance to commence hunting before he can reap its rewards. If H is a trespasser, starts an animal on O–1's land and kills it there, H acquires no rights to the animal and it is O–1's property. This result obtains even though a court could hold that H owns the animal but is liable to O for the trespass; a principle of judicial economy to avoid rights which are not reduced to judgment or perfected and the avoidance of multiple suits dictates this result. O–1 has "constructive possession." See Chapter V, section III *infra*.

In another instance, if H starts a wild animal on O–1's land but pursues it onto the land of O–2, the logical extension of the first rule is to deny H any rights in this situation too. However, with two landowners involved, both have claims based on *rationi soli*. O–1 will argue that the animal was naturally on his land and his right to pursue it was cut off by H; O–2 will argue that, though this is so, O–1 had no intent to capture it and anyway his right to capture it was terminated when the animal left his land. O–2 further argues that because possession of the animal was not achieved when the animal crossed the boundaries of his parcel and death occurred on his land, only there was possession of the animal achieved.

If the litigation over the animal only involved H and O–1, H might be tempted to argue that O–2 has a better right than O–1 to the animal. This argument is the defense of *jus tertii*. Few courts would permit this, on the theory that one must argue the strength of one's own claim, rather than the weakness of an opponent's.

If both O–1 and O–2 were present, H would argue that O–1 lacks a possessory intent and that O–2 has no control and so did not completely take possession whereas he (H) has both. However, to permit H to put these two weaknesses in O–1 and

O–2's claims together to establish a claim of his own, is to allow a two-time trespasser to gain property by crossing a boundary and committing a second trespass. Thus a court, without deciding which owner has constructive possession of the animal, would reject the trespasser's claim to it in both instances just discussed.

Now consider a slightly different situation—a variation on *Pierson v. Post*. What would be the result if O–1 had been hunting on his own land when H (Pierson), observing the hunt in progress from adjoining wild lands, shot the fox as O–1, like Post, pursued it? Under these facts, H was not trespassing on O–1's real property when he shot the fox (although perhaps he will have to do so to recover its dead body). Peering over the boundary into O–1's land at the ongoing hunt, however, H started on a course of action which no less than before interfered with a legitimate use which O–1 was making of his land. O–1 was in the course of exercising his right to hunt (*ratione soli*) in a setting in which he would not reasonably expect such interference. Thus the facts now emphasize the maliciousness of H's acts and one need be less concerned with O–1's rights to the wild animal. If H is liable for a trespass in these circumstances, O–1's and Post's attorney would have been well advised to argue from this position, rather than attempting to prove his client's right to possession of the fox. *Keeble v. Hickeringill* (1707).

The *Keeble* case was even easier to decide for persons like Post. In that case, Keeble, like our O–

1, improved a duck pond, maintaining it with de-
coys and taking the ducks with nets "and other
machines". He was, the court concluded, "in the
trade of seducing ducks to come there in order to
be taken" and when O-2 (which stands for Hickeringill here) fired a gun from his neighboring land
and scared off the ducks before O-1 could capture
them, O-2 was liable for hindering the trade of the
plaintiff. Whether the benefit claimed by the
plaintiff is premised on his ownership of the pond
or his rights as a hunter, is a question to which we
should now turn.

O-1's ownership is not the basis for the decision.
It is, however, a precondition. If O-1 was hunting
on his land profitably while O-2 passed up a similar opportunity, this difference makes the protection of O-1's decoy pond as a man-made improvement on his land all the easier for a court. The
facts that both parties are landowners with similar
opportunities highlights the industriousness of O-1
and makes the interference of O-2 seem more
malicious. The fact that the two are neighbors
puts the interloper among them on notice of O-1's
intent to capture the ducks decoyed to his pond.
This reenforces the idea that malice underlies the
interference. O-1 thus becomes in the eyes of the
law a hunter whose landownership and improve-
ments give him protection from the interferences
of interlopers disturbing his hunt. Turning O-1's
freedom from interference into an affirmative
right one might say that a landowner has the right
to exclude others from his land in this situation.

After an act of possession with an intent to possess, an intent to exclude others from the benefits of property is often thought to be a third attribute of property as an institution.

E. MORE BEE–HIVE CASES

The keeping of bees has spurred several puzzling, important personal property cases. Marking a bee-tree was not sufficient to vest a right in the honey. *Eads v. Brazelton* (1861), citing *Gillet v. Mason* (1810) [hereafter *Gillet*]. This is so because the finder at least needs possession of the hive to have a right to the honey. Cutting down the tree is likewise insufficient. Id., citing *Ferguson v. Miller* (1823) [hereafter *Ferguson*].

Gillet was decided in 1810. It was an action in trespass for cutting a tree with a bee-hive and carrying away the hive and the honey. The honey was worth ten dollars. The tree was blazed by the plaintiff (Gillet), who was the son of the deceased landowner on whose land the tree was located. Plaintiff's blazing the tree was insufficient to establish a right to the hive or the honey. The court stated: "Marking the tree did not reclaim the bees, nor vest an exclusive right of property in the finder, especially in this case, against the plaintiff in error, who, as one of the children of Timothy Gillet, (who does not appear to have made a will,) must be considered as one of the heirs, as, as such, a tenant in common in the land." Thus the presence of other holders of the title to the land was important to the outcome of the case. Blazing the tree was insufficient to extinguish the claim of the co-tenants of the plaintiff and so was likewise insufficient against the defendant. Then, in dicta, the court states that seizing the hive is—according to that powerful trio of treatise writers, Justinian, Bracton, and Blackstone—the minimum that would be necessary.

Ferguson, decided thirteen years later, was also a trespass case. Plaintiff claimed a license to go on the land of another and cut down a bee-tree. Plaintiff marked the tree with his initials, but did not cut the tree. Meanwhile, the defendant paid the landowner fifty cents for the same license, removed plaintiff's mark, substituted his own, cut the tree and carried off the hive. In the court's short opinion, the rule of capture was but one ground on which the court based its decision. The other was the matter of the licenses. The plaintiff's first, oral license was without consideration. This lack of consideration rendered the license revocable. Construing the license as a right to cut the tree and reduce the hive to possession, the court reasoned that, under the terms of the license, the landowner retained the right to capture the hive himself. Reserving this right, he also must have reserved the right to assign his right of capture, which assignment he proceeded to make to the defendant. This second license, the court said, "may have been a revocation of the former license. But suppose it was not, then the two parties stood on an equal footing; and he who first reduced them (the bees) to possession became the owner". Here the rule of capture looks like a device for filling gaps in the record about the licenses. In *Ferguson*, then, the rule of prior possession is an afterthought and is clearly dicta, the conveyancing rules of the common law having already disposed of the case.

More generally, in both *Gillet* and *Ferguson*, the right of the landowner figures in crucial portions of the opinion. However, even the rights of the landowners in these two cases do not amount to a right to prevail in trespass against the possessor of the hive. In a sense, the landowner does not have "possession" (here constructive possession) of the hive merely by holding title to the land on which the hive is located. That is not possession sufficient to bring trespass successfully. Neither the land title, nor the marking or blazing of the hive tree, is sufficient for this purpose. A policy of actual possession or use of the hive is thus encouraged and its user preferred over the holder of the passive asset—the title. Here neither landowner shows that he is holding the land as a repository for the hives on it; or that he has, for example, some special way of processing the honey and needs all the honey from his hives to sustain this process. Absent such a showing of a honey farm, mere title is insufficient grounds for obtaining a trespass judgment.

F. RATIONI SOLI IN THE UNITED STATES

The rights of landowners to exclude hunters was well-settled in England, where the land tenure pattern was one of large estates. In this country, on the other hand, the tenure pattern involved many smaller land-holdings. If H starts a fox on O–1's land, the fox is before long being pursued on O–2's land. O–2 would not have the benefit of rationi soli—the fox not being naturally on his land, and O–1's right is lost, so H is free of both landowners' claims if he is not trespassing.

In England, though Blackstone argued against this hunting monopoly, English statute extended the privilege of hunting only to those of "substantial means". This meant landowners in an age when most wealth was land-related. In the United States, these rights of landowners were suspect from the start. They smacked of royal prerogative so recently overthrown.

The law of trespass, as we have seen in two instances just discussed, still had the potential for excluding hunters from private lands. Early in our history, however, this threat was countered by state legislatures' enactment of statutes allowing entry by hunters on undeveloped lands. This put the burden on the landowner to enclose his lands, post a "no hunting" notice, or otherwise put them to use. *State v. Outlaw* (1986).

Judicial emasculation of the law of trespass also occurred. The courts made an owner show a property right in the animal claimed—possessory intent and a possessory act are not usually shown by the observation of game on one's land. Even if they are, the trespass may be found to be without injury.

For policy reasons, the courts may wish to steer clear of silly, petty suits over game. Even if Post were to be found to have a claim to his fox, the court in *Pierson v. Post* may want to give judgment for the Piersons of the world as a way of discouraging petty suits such as this was.

From the early days of the Republic, hunters were regarded as foragers controlling "noxious" beasts. Foragers could wander freely, unless they were warned off undeveloped land by means of a posted notice. Early statutes required them to respect the boundaries of agricultural land or land otherwise enclosed or developed (what the common law called a "close"). These statutes gave rise to the presumption that they could go elsewhere without fear of being charged with trespass. Other statutes permitted hunters to retrieve wild, wounded game animals from agricultural lands. See e.g., *State v. Corbin* (1984). Custom also fostered a presumption that land owners welcomed hunters on their unposted, unenclosed, and undeveloped lands. *McKee v. Gratz* (1922) (Holmes, J.). Such a rule rather than a strict adherence to the English law of trespass was more suited to the American wilderness, over which "... it is customary to wander, shoot and fish at will until the owners see fit to prohibit it ...." Id.

In the context of the criminal law, all of this legal lore may be encapsulated in one word— "poaching"—made a crime in a state's criminal code—and referring either to hunting in violation of a landowner's posted notice not to hunt or to hunting out of the state's hunting season. There is authority for the proposition that such a word is not constitutionally void for vagueness when applied to a hunter (1) trespassing upon another's land (2) in violation of a landowner's posted "sporting rights." *Cabot v. Thomas* (1986); *State of Florida v. Little* (1981).

Posting land both protects the landowner from intrusion and permits hunting on unposted lands. See e.g., Neb.Rev.Stat. § 37–213.02 (1991) (recognizing both purposes). Although some states still only require a "conspicuous posting" [N.J. Stat.Ann. 23:7–1 (1991)], recently some states have enacted statutes requiring that permission to hunt on posted land be express or in writing. See Official Code Ga.Ann. § 27–3–1(a)–(b) (1991) (providing that permission be obtained or, when land is posted, in writing if a law enforcement agency is first informed of the posting); N.D.Cent.Code 20.1–01–18 (1991).

With the advent of the environmental movement, hunting has become more controversial and hunters in pursuit of game have been interdicted by persons opposed to hunting in general. Game particularly subject to such confrontations include endangered species, such as bighorn sheep, wolves, moose, or wildlife with symbolic meaning, such as American eagles. *Michigan Humane Society v. Natural Resources Commission* (1987) (litigation over having a hunting season for mourning doves, characterized as birds of peace). Some state legislatures have responded to this activity with hunter harassment statutes. They protect hunters from intentional interference and so indirectly protect the right to hunt. Such statutes prohibit, for example, driving or disturbing animals in the path of a hunter, or interjecting oneself into the hunter's sight line. See e.g., Mich.Comp.L.Ann. § 300.262a (1991). In response to such controversies, other legislatures have, as previously noted, heightened the permission requirements needed in order to hunt on the land of another.

Not only have recent years found hunters and their detractors at odds—there have also been controversies between state licensed hunters and Native Americans asserting tribal hunting rights. Such tribal rights are held by the entirety, that is, collectively by the whole tribe, and not as a collection of individual rights held by members of a tribe. Thus a Native American holds a use right to hunt derived from the tribal right. See e.g., *United States v. Felter* (1982).

II. GOVERNMENT AS FIRST POSSESSOR

The opening section of this chapter recited the maxim from Roman law that a wild animal is no one's personal property and hence the property of everyone living in the commonwealth. This statement must now be qualified to some degree—at least, its implications must be discussed. Wild animals are everyone's property, as we have seen, only in the sense that everyone has an equal opportunity to reduce them to his or her possession. Alaska Const. Art. VIII, § 3 ("Wherever occurring in their natural state, fish, wildlife ... are reserved to the people for common use."). As one Chesapeake Bay waterman reportedly said, echoing John Locke and looking over one of the Bay's oyster beds: "The Bible says the Lord's a cheerful giver, and He put those oysters there for me to take." But wildlife is everyone's property in another, second sense as well: that is, every citizen (and so the government) has a collective interest in seeing that wild animals are conserved and protected so that they can continue to be reduced to private possession. As a trustee for the rights of its citizens, the government acquires an authority to protect every citizen's hunting rights. See e.g., Ohio Rev. Code § 1531.02 (Baldwin 1991) (codifying the trust). At minimum, this means that there is a regulatory power in the government that extends to wild animals. This is called a power of the sovereign, so labelled in an age when the sovereign was someone who might actually want to do some hunting!

Perhaps the government has proprietary or ownership rights as well. Consider a chemical spill by a private corporation into public waterways. If a large fish kill results, can the state bring a suit in trespass, trespass on the case, or trover for compensation for the damages wrought on local fisheries? If the state has to show that it had the fish in its possession, its suit will fail; instead, the state will have to argue that its suit is necessary to protect the fishing rights of its citizens and that such suits are a precondition for the fisherman's initiative and the functioning of the private law governing this resource. One court has rejected this argument. See *Commonwealth v. Agway, Inc.* (1967), which held that the state did not have possession of the fish and so could not maintain a suit in trespass.

What effect will such a suit have? If the state sends its agents out to clean up the dead fish, and so takes possession of them, would it have sufficient possession then to maintain a suit? Any possession it has lacks the utility of a fisherman's (the dead fish cannot be used for food) and so the government is not standing in the same position that its citizens would wish to be. On the other hand, if the company got to the fish first, it might preclude the state's suit by becoming their first possessor. In this situation, the company still would not have the possession of a hunter. If we asked whether the company in cleaning up had acquired such possession of the fish that would give title to the animal, the answer would be "no": the state can regulate the taking of wild animals and the company "took" them by poisoning them. Any method of taking possession which spoils their utility to a fisherman is presumably a method not authorized by regulation. More particularly, the company will normally not even have a fishing license. In any event, it acquired no title. On the other hand, if the company's "possession" were found sufficient to award it the status of a first possessor, the system of private law surrounding wild animals would have at least encouraged the cleaning up of the waterway.

There is, moreover, a conflict between the public regulation and the private acquisition of wild animals. That is, the two schemes of laws have very different ends: the state's public law seeks to conserve animals so that its citizens may acquire them, but there are no comparable incentives in the private law to spur conservation: acquisition of possession as quickly as possible is the effect of a rule requiring first possession.

If the state is to gain rights to preserve fisheries and wild animals, its right must be premised on an encompassing right to preserve them in trust for its citizens, not as an extension of private law governing the hunting of wild animals. The terms possession and ownership must be understood to have shifting connotations. A government may have enough ownership to regulate the taking of wild animals, but would surely not be strictly liable for their trespasses onto private lands and the damage they might do there. A government's ownership is no more than a legal conclusion pending its showing a strong interest in preserving and protecting an important resource and subjecting it to "skillful capture" by its citizens. *Douglas v. Seacoast Products, Inc.* (1977); cf. *Metier v. Cooper Transport Co.* (1985) (state's ownership interest does not impose liability on it for deer colliding with motor vehicle on highway).

Thus the trust theory of state ownership should be sufficient to sustain a state's trespass action against a person polluting an environment and so destroying fish or wildlife. The weight of the case law supports this proposition in the case of either a negligent destruction of fish or wildlife or illegal hunting or fishing. *Attorney General for the State of Michigan v. Hermes* (1983). See also, Idaho Code § 36–1404 (1991) (providing for damages against a person for illegal waste of animals, birds, or fish).

In twenty-five states, statutes permit public officials to sue to recover damages for the loss or destruction of fish and wildlife. F. Halter and J. Thomas, "Recovery of Damages for Fish and Wildlife Losses Caused by Pollution," 10 Ecol.L.Q. 5, 9 (1982). Federal and state endangered species acts provide further authority for such actions.

In the absence of such legislation or a possessory interest in fish or wildlife, state officials have predicated such damage suits on a claim to act as a trustee for the public or as the guardian or *parens patriae* of the fish or wildlife. Nineteenth century jurisprudence showed a willingness to accept the proposition that the state had a property interest in wildlife that by definition no individual citizen can own before capturing. *Geer v. Connecticut* (1896). More recently, however, courts have emphasized the importance of the state's role in regulating the capture of wild animals. *Hughes v. Oklahoma* (1979). Today one implication of this regulatory power is that, when one plans to raise for profit a fish or animal labelled "wildlife" by statute, the permission of the state should first be procured. *Maddox v. State* (1984) (holding that the sale of ten pounds of crappie, a fish designated wildlife by statute, was a misdemeanor even though the fish was raised in private waters on a fish farm).

Regulation over the time, place, and methods of hunting are routinely sustained in the courts. Cf. *State v. Stewart* (1979) (invalidating as overbroad a regulation prohibiting the use of automobile headlights to immobilize wildlife at night). However, regulation of the number of hunters has often become a subject of controversy. *Terk v. Ruch* (1987) (bighorn sheep permits). And one attempt to assign exclusive territories to hunting guides was invalidated under a state constitutional provision intended to insure broad public access to hunting. *Owsichek v. State, Guide Licensing and Control Board* (1988) (involving a unique state constitutional provision for common use of wildlife, incorporating common law principles).

With the precise nature of the state's interest in fish and wildlife unclear, state officials must phrase their interests in the alternative and appear as owners, as well as trustees and guardians, of the state's wild animal resources. While courts scrutinize the interests asserted by the states, most of them have upheld the state's right to bring an action for damages as an assertion of its *parens patriae* guardianship. See, e.g., *Maine v. M/V Tamano* (1973). There are cases to the contrary (e.g. *Agway*), but they constitute a distinct minority among all courts considering this issue. Bean, The Evolution of National Wildlife Law 13–20, 34–45 (1977).

Where no statutory authority exists for damage suits and the common law of a state is unfavorable, the Comprehensive Environment Response, Compensation, and Liability Act of 1980 provides a federal statutory basis for a damage suit. This Act is popularly known as the Super-Fund Act. It provides for liability of individuals who release a hazardous substance which causes injury to or destruction of natural resources. This Statute sets a dollar limitation on the amount recoverable and the only plaintiffs authorized to sue under it are state officials acting as trustees for the damaged natural resource or the President of the United States. The coverage of this Act is also somewhat limited; it does not cover oil spills and it does not permit the recovery of damages resulting (1) from the release of a substance under a federal permit or (2) from an application of a registered pesticide. Furthermore, the election of a plaintiff to sue under this federal statute precludes any further litigation by him under any other state or federal law. See 42 U.S.C.A. §§ 9601–9675 (1992).

CHAPTER II

POSSESSION OF ABANDONED PERSONAL PROPERTY

I. A LEADING CASE: *EADS v. BRAZELTON*

Eads v. Brazelton (1861), is a Mid–South variation on the themes of *Pierson v. Post,* but the suit is less silly and the facts more appealing—a cargo of lead looks like something of value, other than a hunter's wounded pride, is at stake. One of the litigants in this case was a famous man in his day.

A. JAMES BUCHANAN EADS

Eads was an engineer and inventor. He was born in 1820 in Indiana and named after a rising, second cousin of a politician from Pennsylvania, James Buchanan—later to become the fifteenth President of the United States. With his family, he arrived in St. Louis in 1833, where he would become both prosperous and famous. 5 Dict.Am. Biography 587–588. Over the next several years, he was a clerk in a dry-goods store, but in his spare time he worked on his mechanical inventions and built model steamboats and educated himself in engineering, using his employer's library. In 1838, he signed on as a purser on a river steamboat, beginning what was to be a nearly twenty year career on the Mississippi River and its tributaries.

1. Ead's Salvage Technology and Business

Once on the river, Eads quickly realized that the river was awash in wrecks, so for the next several years, he tinkered with the machinery and apparatus needed for a diving bell to recover them. At the age of twenty-two, he obtained a patent on a diving bell and in 1842 brashly offered local boat-builders a partnership in a salvage venture if they would build a boat of his own design.

Eads called the boat a submarine. It was a modified "snag" boat, of the type which had for years been used to free the River channel of under-water snags and logs, so dangerous to wooden-hulled steamboats. It was a double-hulled, wooden catamaran, with a deck bridging the hulls, and above the deck masts and rigging for hoists and tackles. In the deck was an opening through which Ead's diving bell could be raised and lowered.

Ead's first job was to raise a cargo of lead in the upper Mississippi River. During this first salvage job, his diver failed to reach the wreck in fifteen feet of swiftly moving water. Eads purchased a forty-gallon whiskey hogshead, slung a seat within it and lead weights around it, put it on a derrick and rigged it with air-pumps, got in and was lowered into the current. After experimenting with the handling of this rig, he and his crew raised all of the cargo. At depths of thirty feet or so, the pressure of the water became dangerous to the workers within the bell. Many divers of the day were afraid to go too deep into the murky currents, laden with silt. So Eads made numerous dives himself, sometimes at depths of sixty feet, sometimes at full flood.

Eads' business depended on good contacts with river pilots and crewmen for information about wrecks. Often insurance companies, having paid the claims of the owners of lost boats and cargoes, engaged him in exchange for half of the cargo raised. When working for himself, his salvage [1] fees ranged from 20–70 percent of the cargo raised. The states abutting the River helped him through enacting short statutes of limitations on the assertion of owners' rights in wrecks and cargoes, making river salvage a risky but profitable business.

Ead's method was to attach the submarine to a line strung from one shore to another and move the submarine along the line, with the bell under the boat and diver walking the bottom under the boat. Once the opposite shore was reached, then the line was moved downstream and the walk repeated in the opposite direction. Doing this repeatedly—Eads himself made over 500 dives, and his firm many more—Eads eventually prospered

1. The law of salvage, a traditional body of maritime law, permits a person voluntarily to save a vessel or its cargo, once in peril, and recover a fee for his successful service. The presence of a maritime peril, the voluntary nature of the service, and its success, are the three elements entitling a salvor to a fee award. Of the law of salvage, more in Chapter V.

sufficiently to retire from the business in 1857. He
was then only thirty seven years old. Thus it was
in the years of his retirement that the case of *Eads
v. Brazelton* was proceeding through the Arkansas
courts.

Eads went on to build Civil War ironclad gun-
boats for the Union, to develop and build new
technology for steel bridge-building, and to plan a
railway to carry steamboats over an isthmus in
Central America.

2. The Lead Ingots and the Steamboat

The lead Eads raised from the river's bed in his
first job came from the upper Mississippi River
valley, around the river town of Galena, Illinois.
This is also probably the source of the lead which
was the source of the controversy in *Eads v. Brazelton*. Extensive lead mining operations were undertaken there in the 1820s. At first the ore
deposits of lead and zinc lay near the surface and
the easy accessibility of the lead in particular
brought a rush of squatters and miners to the
region, so that by 1829, there were fifty diggings in
the region; that year the first steamboat docked at
the townsite in the Galena River, one of the many
tributaries of the Mississippi in the region. These
small rivers made lead shipments by steamboat
feasible.

By 1829, thirteen million pounds of lead were
mined and shipped from Galena and by the 1840s,
there were twenty some lead smelters operating in

the region, with the largest having a capacity to produce 15,000 pounds daily. The diggings, meanwhile had become underground mines. Their lead production waxed and waned with the economy, from the 1829 high of thirteen million pounds. In most years of the 1830s and 1840s, between five and ten million pounds were produced. Peak production for the region was in 1845, with over fifty-four million pounds, and waned thereafter, particularly in the 1850s.

As to the steamboat. In the year 1827, the side-wheel steamboat America was navigating downriver off Plum Point, Tennessee. The boat was a new one, built and completed that year and weighing 263 tons, a moderate-sized boat in its time. Plum Point is about one hundred miles below the confluence of the Ohio and Mississippi at Cairo. It is the first turning in the river around the Tennessee shore. Near it, the America was snagged in the channel and sank near the opposite Arkansas shore on November 12th of that year. No lives were lost. After several shifts in the channel, the America was, by the mid–1850s, in forty feet of water.

B. THE CONTROVERSY

The America was lost "within the limits of Mississippi county". That county is the northernmost county in Arkansas abutting the Mississippi River (which forms the state's eastern boundary at that point. Today Memphis, Tennessee, is the nearest large city.

The plaintiff, Brazelton, having been informed of the site of the wreck, proceeded to the site and blazed trees on the shore to help him locate the spot. He also fastened a buoy to a weight which rested upon the wreck, to mark the spot, but a combination of bad weather (it was January, 1855), the need to repair his equipment, and the press of other salvage business, forced him to cease salvage operations over the America. Brazelton left his buoy and blazed trees to mark his effort and help him relocate the wreck.

One month later—in February, 1855—first come the defendants, who finally, on September 28, 1855, with "Submarine No. 4", raised the cargo. So far as the court's record shows, they located the America independently of the plaintiff's earlier effort, including the blazed trees. Eads was shown to have known the wreck's location as early as 1843 and persons who lived along the River both at the time of the sinking and also while the defendants were locating the wreck, directed their efforts. Pilots along the River also had provided information on the location. The court stated: "Neither the sinking of the America nor its locality seems to have so obscurely remembered as the bill [of the plaintiff] supposes." That the defendants had independent grounds for knowing of the location is important in characterizing their efforts as not building upon or taking advantage of the labor of the plaintiffs. The defendants were thus able to place Submarine No. 4 over the wreck and began to raise the remaining cargo—lead worth $4,507.96—and even the boilers from the wreck.

Plaintiffs sued for an injunction against further work by the defendants. As the remedy indicates, this suit was in equity. It was brought in this manner because of the uncertainty of the plaintiffs about their legal (as opposed to their equitable) right to possession of the cargo and the wreck. Plaintiffs brought the suit this way to protect their work in progress.

1. The Judicial Opinions

The trial court granted the injunction, restraining the defendants, who at first pulled their boat away from the site of the wreck, permitting the plaintiff to restart his salvage operation, but the defendants then put their boat so close to the plaintiff's operation as to endanger and hinder it.

How close was that? Close enough so that the plaintiff again sought to enforce the restraining order of the court. Defendants were held in contempt of court and were fined one thousand dollars. The fine was a fairly heavy one, considering that the value of the cargo was between four and five thousand dollars. It was compensatory and civil in nature and so was paid to the complainant/plaintiff. The defendants appealed.

The Supreme Court of Arkansas stated that "the principal ground of controversy ... is Brazelton's

right of occupancy of the wreck by finding, and ...
that may depend upon its possession". This statement of the issue emphasizes the difference between finding a thing and assuming possession of
it. The act of finding does not by itself confer any
legal right to a thing. What is important is what
happens after that. This latter focus is necessary
because possession requires an intent to reduce a
thing to possession, plus an act amounting to possession. Brazelton had shown the intent, but not
the act. Judgment reversed, for defendants, on the
issue of possession.[2]

The contempt of court issue, this court thought,
was a severable issue and the fine against the
defendant, if it had been considered separately by
the court, might be permitted to stand. As it was,
the defendants also recovered the amount paid to
the plaintiffs as a fine, even though they are examples of a person who, having a substantive legal
right, proceeds to disobey a court order in the
course of asserting his right before its eventual
vindication, flaunting the judicial process in the
meanwhile. Then the protection of the judicial
process might be an issue separated from all others
involved in the litigation. Of this, more later.

Assuming that the plaintiff Brazelton marked
the wreck's location with buoys and blazed trees,
the court found such actions insufficient to estab-

2. As another court, citing *Eads*, stated the rule of the case:
"Abandoned property is owned by him who takes it into his
ownership." *Foulke v. New York Consol. R. Co.* (1920).

lish possession of the wreck. These actions were at most only one component of a salvage operation that could lead to possession. In effect, they show that Brazelton's complaint pleads facts insufficient to show possession and that he was in the process of taking possession, but that process remained incomplete when he pulled his boat off the site. Because the plaintiff had not acquired possession of the wreck, it was available for capture by the defendants.

Neither does that court require Brazelton to capture the cargo or the wreck before his right of possession is complete, for the opinion recognizes that according to the custom of the River, putting one's boat over a wreck gave the salvor the right to complete the operation without interference.[3]

Severing the issue of the fine for contempt of court in disobeying the lower court's injunction could have been a recognition in the trial court that, even if the plaintiff had not completed the operation so as to gain a right of possession in the cargo or the wreck, he still had a right to pursue his operation free of interference. This is an interesting point because at the time of the opinion, a civil fine as a remedy for contempt of court was just being recognized by our courts when the complainant suffers a loss.

3. By way of analogy, one can compare the *Eads* opinion on this point with the dissent by Judge Livingston in *Pierson v. Post,* op. cit., or to the custom of the fisherman in the *Bay of St. Ives* in *Young v. Hichens* (1844). See Chapter I supra.

There are two types of contempt (criminal and civil) and two types of civil contempt (coercive and compensatory). *Columbus–America Deep Search, Inc. v. The Unidentified, Wrecked and Abandoned Sailing Vessel, Her Engines, etc.* (1988) The compensatory contempt was involved in *Eads.* A compensatory civil fine in the amount of one thousand dollars must indeed have been a stiff one, considering that the raised cargo was stated in the pleadings to be worth $4,507.96. Without considering how the amount of the fine was determined and whether the defendants intended to cause the complainant's loss of the possession, it is difficult to tell exactly what the fine was intended to compensate. Once the court decides that Brazelton has no right of possession in the cargo, however, such questions become moot because there can be no interference if there is no right on which the interference can be bottomed; there is in effect no intent to interfere with anything the defendants can protect, and no loss of any right either.

The court said, however, that a decree should be entered for the recovery of the thousand dollars, with interest, that were assigned to Brazelton as "his damages for being obstructed by the defendants in his work upon the wreck after the service of the injunction upon the defendants...." The opinion expresses a willingness to let the fine stand if it was intended to punish Eads' employees' disobedience to the process of the court. Then, the opinion states, "a different decree would have been called for upon this branch of the case."

These were the days of common law pleading, so this may be a correct result for that day and age. However, today, is this right? Why couldn't the portion of Brazelton's petition requesting the fine be styled as one for damages for interference with Brazelton's right to conduct operations, rather than a right of possession in the wreck or its cargo? So styled, the fine could provide what the petition requested; severance of the issue raised by the fine would not have been necessary; and Ead's possessory right would then not stand in the way of plaintiff's keeping the fine.

Perhaps the attorneys for the plaintiff mispled this aspect of the case. The right to conduct the salvage business lawfully could indeed have been protected by the court, if not with a contempt of court order, then by a suit in trespass or in trespass on the case, if the plaintiff feels strongly enough to bring such an action. [Recall that trespass on the case deals with the consequences of a trespass, rather than the trespass itself.] Eads and Brazelton, the two salvors litigating here, were both based in St. Louis and were competitors, both for the information on wrecks as well as for work at the site of wrecks. In the end, the court only states that a fine is appropriate as a means of protecting the integrity of the judicial process, even when that process enforces an incorrect version of the law. What the trial court probably meant to do with the fine is take some of the sting out of the competition with which the defendants meet the plaintiff's efforts.

Brazelton eventually did choose to remove his boat. His reasons for doing so were several. One reason is that he had difficulty with his rig and had to make repairs in it. Brazelton looks like the possessor of old technology for raising cargoes, while the defendant seems to have the latest gear. In fact, the firm of Eads and Nelson were running a fleet of salvage boats, consecutively numbered and each one more up to date than the last. They were steam powered and could hold a position in the swiftly moving main channel of the River. (Eads later developed an abiding interest in the River's hydraulics.) This meant that the operation did not completely depend on lines slung from shore to keep the boat over the wreck. The court said: "If Brazelton's boat had been accompanied with steam-power as was the Submarine No. 4, the rise of the water in June, or the season of floating boats and rafts, would not have been uncontrollable obstructions to his desire to save the lead of the America...."

So in part, when Eads is given judgment, the appellate court is protecting the most efficient salvor and the trial court is reversed because it attempted to protect the least efficient one. This is just the sort of efficiency which the rule of *Pierson v. Post* was meant to promote.

Yet efficiency is not dispositive in this opinion. Another reason Brazelton chose to remove his boat from the site of the wreck was that he had to attend to other business. Reasons of efficiency aside, the court might also have chosen with its decision to protect the first salvor to complete the salvage operations, regardless of the efficiency of the successful operation.

Why protect the first salvor to complete the job? Because the speedy removal of the wrecks from the main channel of so large a waterway as the Mississippi serves an important public interest in safe navigation. Recall the River was indeed awash in wrecks. The court might as well have put the question before it this way: do we want to encourage people to start to search for wrecks, or do we want to encourage them to take possession and remove them? The latter best serves the interests of commerce.

2. Third–Party Rights

Defendants had made one other unsuccessful argument in the course of gaining the reversal of the trail court's decree. This was the argument that the title to the wreck and the cargo was not held by the plaintiff. The court rejected this argument with the citation and discussion of admiralty cases in which the wreck or the cargo was found to have been abandoned by their former owners. The evidence showed that in the first two years after the sinking, the owners removed the specie, furs, and a small amount of lead from the wreck and "contented themselves therewith". The last phrase seems not much more than a conclusion, for it is hard to tell what a person intends by what he doesn't do, or doesn't do next. In addition, however, one hundred sixteen ingots of lead were removed by local residents. The owners' standing by in the face of this looting is better evidence of the original owners' abandonment and allows the court to jump to its next conclusion of law, that the right to such abandoned property belongs to its next possessor. Moreover, the decline of the lead mines in the Upper Mississippi by the mid–1950s makes the assumption that the miners and smelters there were no longer interested in reclaiming the cargo seem reasonable. The court might reasonably assume that they have abandoned their claim.

Abandonment by the owners—actual abandonment, plus an intent to abandon the wreck and its cargo—ends their rights. This is the most cited rule of *Eads*. Fascinating questions, however, can be asked about what the situation would be if the owners had not abandoned and if further the ingots Eads recovered identified them. If the true owners of the cargo were known, Eads might then have had the obligation to search for them and, if and when he found them, return the chattel, accepting a reward for his efforts at least sufficient to recover his expenses in taking possession. Information about the true owners might, arguably, have made a significant difference to the outcome of this case.

In any event, the defendants should not be permitted to show that the title to the property lies with third parties not before the court. The court's concern is the relative rights of the litigants before it. Any other, more wide-ranging inquiry into "title" is, in the context of litigation between two alleged possessors, beyond its jurisdiction and probably its competence as well. Regardless of the question of abandonment, the defendants' argument was rightly rejected if third-party rights were not to influence the decree. Of the question of third party rights, more in Chapter IV, Section V(2).

3. The Court's Research

Many civil law authorities are reviewed. Such reviews were common in the nineteenth century when a court was presented with novel issues, previously undecided in the jurisdiction. Civil law authorities traveled in portable treatises, and in the developing states of the 1850s and 1860s like Arkansas, were thus more readily available than common law case reports.

More particularly, Roman law is cited: "Found means not merely discovered, but taken up", an annotator of Justinian's Code stated. "Without the intention there is no possession. . . . Without the detention, the intention is useless, and does not make the possession", stated a civil law treatise writer. So was Roman, civil, admiralty, and Louisiana law reviewed for statements of the general rule that possession requires both an intent to possess and possession itself. The reason for basing some of the civil law authorities in Louisiana

law makes sense for another reason: New Orleans
was the home port of the America and using its
law removes the temptation to the losing litigant
to apply a conflicts of law rule to reverse the
decision here.

Another reason for citing treatises and law from
another jurisdiction riparian to the Mississippi River is the need for uniformity among such jurisdictions when matters arose pertaining to commerce
on the River. This need was probably particularly
felt by the riparian state courts in the age when
admiralty jurisdiction on the River was not as yet
definitively established. G. Gilmore & C. Black,
"Admiralty" 31–32, note 99 (2d ed. 1975) (reporting
the slow assertion of such jurisdiction between the
1820s and the 1860s).

4. The Court's Use of Case Authority

It is tentative. "The following adjudged cases
may have a bearing upon this case....", stated the
court. With this statement, the opinion proceeds
to a review of, inter alia, *Pierson v. Post* and
another hunting case, *Buster v. Newkirk* (1822).
Since you are already familiar with both *Pierson*
and to a lesser degree *Newkirk,* some discussion of
their use as precedent here is warranted.

Pierson v. Post. The locale of *Pierson v. Post*
makes it seem applicable. It occurred on "wild
and uninhabited lands", really a beach or state
land, although the state asserted no interest in the

wildlife on it. Similarly, *Eads* took place within the main channel of a navigable waterway. This is an important public space if there ever was one. The state has an interest in clearing the channel of wrecks, so that the controversy in *Pierson* between two private hunters is less affected with a public interest than is the controversy in *Eads,* where there is a public interest in commerce on the waterway.

While this characterization of *Eads* makes the search for authorities more urgent, it also obscures the fact that the litigants were two competitors. The hunters in *Pierson* were competing—although they may have had different motives for hunting, those motives converged on the same fox—but they were not regular competitors. Their convergence was on a one-shot basis. In *Eads,* however, the parties were more clearly competing for a livelihood on a regular basis, attempting to harvest the same, limited resource—the wrecks in the River.

Perhaps too, commercial motives were more clearly separated from personal ones by the time of *Eads* than was possible in the time of *Pierson.* Perhaps this is why the *Eads* court is more tolerant of the bullying use of Ead's more efficient boat than some interpretations of the facts warrant. All this being so, underlying the question of whether the *Pierson* cite is rightly used, is the issue in the law of whether the legal rules applied to private litigants should also be applied to commercial ones. When the courts are confronted with disputes between commercial parties, should they apply law made for private (meaning non-commercial) parties? One answer is that the relative expertise and investment of the parties, as well as the regularity of their competition, should make a difference.

Why does the law make a distinction between commercial and non-commercial parties? To take account of expertise, to protect investment, labor, and effort, and to regulate competition—all are possible rationales for the distinction. In addition, there are judicial process rationales of inducing flexibility and fact specificity into the law.

Thus the case illustrates the rule of capture formulated in *Pierson*, but used here to resolve a commercial dispute. Several points can be made. First, the citation of *Pierson* is perhaps an illustration of the judicial urge to have one rule for all types of litigants. Whether a case involves two hunters or two commercial salvors should not make a difference, because relatively, the parties in each dispute have the same status inter se. Judicial psychology aside, a second point is that the facts of the case show one result of the rule of capture. After the decision in *Pierson*, one might expect that each of the hunters would hunt more furiously. This might mean one of two things; either they modify their hunting practices—honing their marksmanship, shooting at random, more wildly, or more frequently, in the hope of hitting the game—or they will invest in better hunting equipment—a better gun, a faster horse, etc. In the commercial case, the litigants will already have modified their practices—i.e., honed their skills until they are of professional quality. Thus, if the rule of capture is still to control their actions, they will have to invest more heavily in the technology of their trade. The heavy investor captures the prize! This is surely one lesson of *Eads*.

A corollary lesson is that old technology and less investment loses. However, the talk of technology blurs the human facts of *Eads*. The defendants' boat was able to hold its position in the current, close to the wreck, but also close to the plaintiffs' boat, which, being the more technologically backward, had to have more room to maneuver and eventually, had to back off. The newer technology interfered with the old, in the sense that it perhaps lets the defendants bully the plaintiffs into backing off from the wreck, ostensibly to pursue other salvage work.

Buster v. Newkirk. The *Newkirk* opinion presents an unpleasantly close hunting case and on that account, less useful for the *Eads* court than *Pierson*, which has already (in this discussion) been found of limited usefulness. *Newkirk* as a precedent helps the *Eads* court turn away from any sympathy its members might have felt for the outmaneuvered (on the river and in court) plaintiffs before it. The result in *Newkirk* is a reward for the honesty and willingness to settle of the defendant there.

This point is brought home in the *Eads* opinion in a different way. When explaining why the plaintiff did not resume work on the wreck, the court states that "the sinking of the steamboat Eliza offered the opportunity of other work". After that, the plaintiff "would have applied himself to the America", but high water prevented him "and when he was nearly ready, with his boat the machinery in order for effective labor, with favorable water for work, safe from rafts and flat and coal boats, the Submarine No. 4, belonging the defendants, passed him ... and, within two days, was placed over the wreck." [4] Submarine No. 4, in other words, won the race to the wreck. The faster boat, like the hunter with the faster horse or the better gun, gets the judgment.

The trial court had slapped a compensatory, civil, contempt fine of $1,000 on the defendants for the plaintiff "being obstructed in his work by the defendants". The Arkansas Supreme Court or-

---

4. These statements are made after the main summary of the facts and is often missed. Indeed, only one case subsequently citing and relying upon *Eads* makes much of this "race to the wreck." See *Treasure Salvors, Inc. v. Unidentified Wrecked and Abandoned Sailing Vessel* (1981) ("Brazelton was, however, first, distracted from this task by another salvage operation and then, disabled from the undertaking by a rise in the river which made it impossible for his salvage vessel to pursue the project. In the fall of 1855, Brazelton again headed toward the site of the sunken barge (sic). On the way, however, he was passed up by a swifter vessel belonging to Eads.") *Treasure Salvors* was a suit in which the petitioner sought an injunction against rival salvors operating on the site of the wreck of a Spanish galleon in an area 2,500 yards on either side of the petitioners' description of the wreck site.

dered this money repaid to the defendants. This result might amount to no more than the reward for relatively heavy investment, but it also might be seen as a tacit endorsement of sharp practice as well. Ferreting out sharp practice is not a job for which an appellate court will be well-suited and is better left to the trial judge. But the trial judge was not clear as to what he in fact was trying to accomplish with the fine, so its imposition was quashed.

The line between a malicious interference with a competitor and the use of a technological advantage over him will be a thin one. [An easier case would involve the interference of one neighbor with another. *Keeble v. Hickeringill* (1707).] Nothing shows that more clearly than the payments of the fine below, followed by its subsequent repayment here on appeal.

Eads thus plays out the consequences of the rule of capture designed in *Pierson*. In so doing, it raises a question about the extent to which courts should interfere in commercial endeavors. Favoring old technology is not this court's way and the opinion is in its result supportive of legal rules that keep up investment in new inventions and the accumulation of capital, rather than individual initiative unsupported by capital investments. We do not know much about the investments and capital of Eads' competitors, so the contrast between these competitors is not conclusively shown here; however, from the biographical materials we have, it is apparent that James Eads was interested in putting his own and others' capital to work on his inventions. At least, it can be said that the person taking the judgment of the court presented himself in this light.

The rule of capture, formulated in *Pierson,* was there applied to settle a dispute between two hunters equally equipped; in *Eads,* the opinion of the court gives us good reason to think that the court did not believe that both parties were equally equipped in this case. Thus the question arises: why does the court apply a rule, meant to settle a question of use, occupancy and possession, in such a way as to favor and reward the accumulation of investment capital in Ead's inventions? The probable answer to this question is that the opinion writer didn't recognize the change as such. The protection of capital was too new a thing; the shift from protecting use to protecting capital was too gradual to notice. Anyway, whose capital was being protected? That of Ead's employers, if he had any, or Ead's own property in his inventions. The shift from protecting the hard-working inventor, to protecting his financial handlers and backers, is present, but only in a shadowy way.

However, if the court could hold two, somewhat conflicting purposes for the rule of capture in their mind at once, why can't we today do the same thing? Our capacity for doing just that is what is at stake when we try to understand this opinion. It marks a shift, using a rule of capture formulated

for possessors, toward a rule protecting capital
investments. This is certainly a significant shift in
the use of a rule.

C.   ACTUAL POSSESSION

However, "Brazelton's act of possession need not
have been manual." What does this mean? The
court explains that "[p]lacing his boat over the
wreck, with the means to raise its valuables and
with persistent efforts directed to raising the lead
... would have been such acts of possession as the
law would notice and protect." The court does not
explain this statement, but such acts might have
sufficed on two grounds. First, they would have
provided notice to interlopers like the defendants.
Second, they would have been (from a statement
elsewhere in the opinion) in accord with the custom of salvors, a signal to other salvors and thus
provided freedom from interference. Because two
competitors on the same stretch of the river were
litigating here, unlike *Pierson v. Post,* the custom
of the salvor provided a rule which the court would
enforce. Further notice was probably unnecessary,
unless to protect the cargo from other types of
interlopers. Would a court be justified, however,
in fashioning a rule of law out of the "custom of
salvors"? After all, such customs can change with
time—and faster than the law might want to
change. Today, such a case might be (if the parties
agreed) given to a panel, composed of other salvors,
for arbitration. A principle of judicial economy

might encourage this practice, but it was unavailable at the time of this litigation.

The value of the lead in *Eads* takes on added importance when the date of the case is considered. The opinion was handed down during January Term, 1861. The Civil War was imminent. Between December 20, 1860, and January 26, 1861, the tier of states between South Carolina and Louisiana, plus Florida, seceded. Arkansas would follow the Deep South out of the Union on May 8, 1861, along with the Confederacy's border states. Lead for shot would soon be rising in value. So in a state which would soon secede from the Union, awarding judgment to James Eads, a strong Unionist from a state that would not secede, is an act of judicial statesmanship.

D. CITATIONS TO *EADS*

Since the *Eads* case was decided, it has been most frequently cited, not for its rule on establishing possession, but for its rule on the abandonment of personal property by a former owner. The abandonment of property has two elements—an intention to abandon, and action (or inaction). The inaction of a former owner, over a long period of time, gives rise to an inference that an owner intends to abandon. See e.g., *E.H. Wiggins v. 1100 Tons, More or Less of Italian Marble* (1960) (sunken cargo untouched for sixty-six years presumed abandoned, and stating: "In *Eads v. Brazelton,* 22 Ark 499, it is intimated that the lapse of years will enable a salvor in possession to be characterized as a finder acquiring good title against the owner.") Thus the true owner's inaction has satisfied both elements. In *Eads*, however, the more precise characterization of the true owners' actions would be—initial action (or salvage), followed by long inactivity.

The abandonment holding is the title-clearing portion of the opinion. It might even be said that it rids the rule of capture of its immoral tone and justifies its amoral tone, because it defeats the possibility that the true owner of the property is losing his right or title as a result of the later capture.

A good example of this use of *Eads* is *J.A. Bel Lumber Co. v. Stout* (1914). This Louisiana opinion was decided in 1914 and involved the recovery, from the depths of the bayous of the lower Mississippi River, of logs lost while floating from the logging site to the saw-mill. The lost logs, known as "sinkers", sank during a log drive. Ten percent of the logs starting out in a typical drive were lost in this manner. They were often marked with a brand by either the loggers or the mill-owner, who might have bought them in mid-drive. Branded, they rested on the bottom of the bayou until raised. However, their wood remained sound for an indefinite period. This fact also made it difficult to distinguish a sinker lost ten years ago from one lost fifty years in the past.

Sinkers were not raised in great numbers until the loggers ran out of prime timber and began harvesting smaller and inferior logs. Of the smaller, inferior logs, a greater number (approximately twenty to thirty percent) became sinkers and never made it to the mill. Thus did the value of the sinkers rise as the loggers shifted more and more into secondary operations. Loggers engaged in such operations have the look of scavengers—perhaps not the savoriest of their number—because they are not engaging in the traditional work of the forest. However, such work was probably getting hard to find.

Eventually, then, salvage operators began to raise the sinkers. The plaintiff's mill began to buy them, and to employ others to raise them, but the plaintiff's mill was not as well situated as others for this work, so that eventually, the plaintiff and nine other mill-owners published a notice warning third parties to respect the brands on sinkers. The brands, however, were often used by more than one logger, while some logs were sold in mid-drive after branding. The court states: "... the mere fact that a 'sinker' raised from the bottom of a stream, bears the brand of a logger falls considerably short of proving that it belongs to him, or belonged to him when it sank." Such confusions rendered the brands of little use in sorting out the conflicting rights of loggers and millers and no concept of constructive possession could be justified by the registry of a brand. Moreover, the plaintiff continued to buy sinkers with many brands on them after the newspaper publication of the notice—and this activity might make the plaintiff into a bad actor.

By "common understanding", the court found that the sinkers were abandoned. This is not as clear a use of custom as in *Eads*. Thus the court vindicated the rights of secondary recovery in the spoils of the logging industry. Clearly this is a useful holding, since it kept the industry in business for a longer period than would otherwise have been possible. A similar value might be assigned to the lead cargo involved in *Eads,* raised ten years after the year of peak production of lead from the mines in the Galena region, and probably more valuable on that account.

Other citations to *Eads* have involved its constructive possession language. Here the conflicting rights of treasure hunters (or salvors—see infra, Chapter V) on the high seas have been litigated. In one case, a court refused to grant exclusive salvage rights to a Spanish galleon (or perhaps two galleons) driven over a mile-long shoal during a hurricane in 1733. *MDM Salvage v. Unidentified, Wrecked & Abandoned Sailing Vessel* (1986). The shoal had dismembered the galleon as the boat scraped across it, leaving objects strewn along a long swath of the sea bed. One can easily imagine a different result in *Eads* if the lead had been similarly strewn along a stretch of riverbed. Neither of the galleon's salvors had (the court found) spent sufficient time, invested sufficient capital, or formulated an archeological plan for the site. Even though the case of the galleon is factually distinguishable from *Eads*, this court cites *Eads* for its principal rule none-the-less. It states: "The law of finds ... dictates that the finder of abandoned property must continuously possess or be in the process of reducing to possession the property which he has found." (citing *Eads*).

This citation is off-the-mark for another reason as well. Given the close competition for the cargo in *Eads*, it presents a version of the rule of capture that would have been equally useful to either side in the *Eads*. Further, as the rule of capture is a result-oriented rule, its reference to the time spent is off-the-mark. The result, possession, not the effort or the time spent achieving it, is the relevant factor.

The last two references of the opinion in the galleon case are more interesting, but in other ways. Its reference to "sufficient capital investment" suggests that the rule of capture can protect that, as an extension of protecting the salvor's inventiveness in *Eads*. Protecting accumulated capital is thus a step removed from the rule's function in *Eads*. Its function there was protect an inventor's investment in his invention. This function was in its turn an extension of protecting the individual effort of the successful hunter in *Pierson*. In the background material available on the Florida keys salvage cases, there is some evidence that the backers of the various salvors are drawn from other occupations, "drawn" however in the way the owner of a successful business is drawn to owning a professional sports team. A capital-intensive hobby business gets the sportsman's version of the *Pierson* rule applied to it.

The last reference, to an "archeological plan", may either be a reference to a possessor's intent to possess or it may refer to a precondition imposed by state or federal statutes to raising the treasure found in public waters.

Over the years since *Eads* was decided, citation to it has been spare, but frequent enough so that two types of citations are discernable. The first is as an authority for clearing title. Here its use as authority meant a reference to its rules of abandonment.[5] The economic utility of such authority is most evident in cases authorizing secondary or scavenger recovery of a resource, such as sunken timber or "sinkers," and functioning to place goods

5. The rule that personal property may be abandoned provides the section of the opinion most often cited in later cases. See e.g. *Wilmore Coal Company v. Brown* (1906), construing a coal deed, the court stated that abandonment "... is the voluntary throwing away or forsaking of property, leaving it open to be appropriated by the first comer"; *McCabe v. Baltimore Trust Company* (1935); *Collins v. Lewis,* 149 A. 668, 669 (Conn.Sup.Ct. 1930) (abandonment requires an intent to abandon as well as physical abandonment); *Coulombe v. Gross* (1930); *Foukle v. New York Consol. R. Co.* (1920) (a finder's case, in which the court found that personal property found in a railroad car cannot be presumed to have been abandoned). In the context of admiralty law, the rule of abandonment was cited in *State v. Flying "W" Enterprizes, Inc.* (1968) ("It is well-settled law that the owner of sunken or derelict vessels or their contents may abandon them so effectively as to divest title and ownership.")

back in circulation that were previously not valued sufficiently to be marketable.

A second use is the more recent. As salvage operations became more sophisticated (and expensive), the rule of capture came back into vogue. It has been particularly useful in the salvage cases involving wrecks and cargoes off the coast of Florida and in deeper seas. Much is at stake in these cases, but much investment is required both to stake the claim, establish a field of operations by constructively taking possession of the stake area, and then seize the stake. The rule of capture in *Eads* has again proven adequate to the task. It brings both the need for inventions and investment, as well as the need to use them actively, to a court's attention. In the treasure salvage cases, in which it is cited today, it is used, not just to protect individual effort, but effort backed by considerable capital investment. In *Eads,* the rewards for individual effort and one man's invention are close to simultaneous, whereas, in the modern salvage cases, the investors appear more passive, energizing with capital the effort of others. In the latter opinions, the function of the rule of capture seems to shift again, this time reenforcing the role of accumulated capital.

II. A RECENT CASE: *THE CENTRAL AMERICA*

Recent citations to *Eads v. Brazelton* have involved situations similar to the original case, for

recent advances in the technology available to salvors have made their work feasible in deep-sea
locations which previously would have defeated
their efforts. In particular, the location and recovery of wrecks of archeological, cultural, and monetary value has become possible through the use of
new sonar and remote television cameras mounted
in unmanned, radio-controlled submarines. An example is the opinion in *Columbus–America Discovery Group, Inc. v. The Unidentified, Wrecked, and
Abandoned Sailing Vessel* (believed to be the S.S.
Central America) (1990), [hereafter *Central America*] (an admiralty action involving the contents of
a wooden-hulled, side-wheel, luxury steamboat,
awarded by the District Court to its finders, the
plaintiffs in this action).

In 1857, the Central America was plying a
course between Panama and New York City when
it sank, one hundred sixty miles east of Charleston,
South Carolina, in the Atlantic Ocean. The cargo,
and most passengers, had first taken ship to Panama, thence across its isthmus, and then on board
the Central America, this being the fastest way to
the East Coast at the time. The ship had encoun-
tered the fringe of a September hurricane but had
sailed on, into the center of the storm, until a leak
disabled its boilers. Adrift, passengers and crew
together attempted to bail the ship, but they failed
to keep her afloat. When the boat sank, many
lives were lost. Many of the passengers were pros-
pectors returning from the California gold-fields.
Their lost possessions included several hundreds of

thousands of dollars in gold. Lost as well was a
large, insured cargo of gold; it was worth $1.6
million in 1857 and shipped from California mer-
chants, banks, and express companies to New
York.

Many passengers survived, however, and reached
shore with harrowing tales. Their tales made the
sinking famous at the time. Many survivors also
reported the loss of their gold, giving the wreck a
fabled notoriety all its own.

Plaintiff's efforts to locate the wreck spanned ten
years and expended over ten million dollars—
"[u]tilizing numerous written accounts, oceano-
graphic, meteorological and other data, modern
search theory mathematics, advanced technology
and equipment, along with the services of numerous experts ..." The technology employed in the
search was described as "side-scan sonar, satellite
navigation, tele-operated deep-sea equipment (submersible with stereo camera and robotic arms) and
computer modelling software", all on a specially-
outfitted ship. In this case, the deep-sea equipment operated at ocean depths a mile and a half
beneath the surface.

Plaintiffs in the *Central American* litigation
learned one of the lessons taught by the *Eads*
litigation: that is, they filed to protect their search
efforts from the interference of rival search parties. They sought the protection of the admiralty
jurisdiction of the federal courts in doing so. That
jurisdiction is in rem, against the cargo of the

Central America, as well as in personam against potential rivals. In their original complaint, they asked for a temporary restraining order against their rivals and, once the order was granted and in successive complaints, they enlarged the search area to which the order applied. Enlarging the area in which their rivals were enjoined from working had two consequences: it both baffled the rivals as to the particular location of the wreck and freed the plaintiffs from further interference and surveillance.

The basis for the injunction was the remote television pictures taken of the wreck by a submersible robot. These pictures were sufficient for the issuance of the injunction, for the enlargement of the area covered by it, and the finding of civil contempt made by the court against parties violating the injunction. The right to work the site of the wreck, free of competitors, was thus granted on the basis of what the court had, in an earlier opinion, dubbed "tele-presence" [6]—that is, the presence of the remote, unmanned vehicle. Not quite a new legal basis for establishing possession, it is

6. *Columbus–America Discovery Group, Inc. v. The Unidentified, Wreaked and Abandoned Sailing Vessel,* S.S. Central America, in Rem (1989) ("Effective possession of an object is attained in this unique environment by: (1) locating the object searched; (2) real time imaging of the object; (3) placement or capability to place teleoperated or robotic manipulators on or near the object, capable of manipulating it as directed by human beings exercising control from the surface; and (4) present intent to control including deliberately not disturbing the location of the object (so-called 'telepresence' or 'telepossession'.").

as close as the court can come to one and, moreover, is a doctrine that should probably be sparing-
ly used only when a manned presence is impossible.

Here the use of the temporary restraining order,
available under the law of salvage, aids the salvor
in the early establishment of a right to pursue
possession of the sunken cargo under the law of
finders. Salvage law, as administered by federal
courts asserting admiralty jurisdiction, combined
both the law of salvage and of finders. Admiralty
jurisdiction first has the saving of the cargo or
wreck uppermost in mind, but if the true owner of
the cargo does not appear, can later order the title
of the cargo transferred to the finder. 28 U.S.C.A.
§ 1333 (1991). Thus skillful pleading by the person whose initial rights are those of a salvor,
seeking a reward for the salvage from the owner,
can turn control of the wreck site gained through a
restraining order, into possession, and then into
title to the cargo or wreck. The exclusive right to
continue working the wreck site modifies the unforgiving nature of the law of finds. The investment, the effort, and the continuous work, all take
an equitable right to an injunction and ripen it
into a possessory right. Thus the doctrines of
salvage and finds merge. The commercial character of the investment seems dispositive in this
loosening or expansive interpretation of the possession requirement.

Before concluding that the requirement of actual
possession serves only the aims of development and

capitalists, consider the opinion in *The Indian River Recovery Company v. The China* (1986). Here the court denied the claim of a professional treasure hunter and instead awarded concurrent possession to a group of local charter boat captains and divers, conducting amateur diving trips over a wreck of an eighteenth century ship loaded with ironware, and recovering the cargo slowly in the course of operating their local charter and diving businesses.

This said, however, the *Central American* opinion is none-the-less reminiscent of the case of *Keeble v. Hickeringill* (1707) (protecting the owner of a decoy pond from a neighbor's firing a musket frightening away waterfowl from the pond in an action in trespass on the case). "[E]veryman that hath a property may employ it for his pleasure and profit." Id. The *Keeble* opinion however emphasizes the control of competition. The neighbor with the gun could set up a competing decoy pond and fire a musket in order to reduce the fowl to possession by killing them, but could not fire the musket to scare away the fowl from the neighboring pond. A similar control of competition is evident in the law of salvage when considering the issuance of a temporary restraining order.

The order does not traditionally come without penalty: a bond must be posted, to provide damages if the order injures other parties to the litigation when and if the injunction is lifted, the judgment on the merits running against the party moving for the order. "The 'finder' or salvor is entitled to protection of the Court to continue working a wreck as long as he exercises such complete and continuous possession as the circumstances dictate and demonstrates reasonable success in saving the valuables from their peril." *Cobb Coin Company, Inc. v. Unidentified, Wrecked, and Abandoned Sailing Vessel* (1982).

In the *Central American* opinion, the opinion provides a right to take possession, not by physically seizing the cargo, but by remote location of it, with television and robotics. Seizure by robot would be, however, an unduly narrow reading of the type of possession authorized by this opinion. Location and continuous working of the site, by remote control, becomes the basis for a right to possess the cargo. Indeed, while the temporary restraining order was binding on the plaintiff's competitors, the plaintiff's crew was locating, and then having the robot relocate, some of the cargo to a central location near the wreck, but still on the ocean's bottom. This comes as close to physical, manual seizure of the cargo as is possible if technology, seen as an extension of the human arm, is the means employed in the seizure. The interesting point about the opinion at this point is that the court is willing to envision the plaintiff's technology as just this sort of extension.

That, however, is not the end of the story of the Central American's gold. In *Eads*, the true owners of the lead ingots never stepped forward to claim

their own; indeed, the court found that they had
abandoned their claim.   Lapse of time, during
which the owners asserted no right; the removal of
the boilers and other valuable objects, followed by
further neglect, caused the court to infer abandonment. This is one advantage of the law of finders,
as opposed to the law of salvage. The salvor is
presumed to be working for the owner, but the
finder works in the absence of an owner. Thus
American courts have applied the law of finders to
long-wrecked ships when no owner is likely to
appear.

In the *Central American* case, things turned out
differently: several types of putative true owners
appeared. There were, for example, the alleged
insurers of the wreck, who claimed to have paid
the claims of some owners and now further
claimed, in their own right, to be subrogated to
those owners' rights. The District Court dismissed
their claims. There was no dispute that the wreck
was long lost and that only the plaintiff could now
produce a map of its location.

Shortly after the sinking, the insurance companies entered into a salvage contract, agreeing to
give the salvor seventy-five percent of whatever he
recovered. However, nothing ever came of this
salvor's efforts. The next effort at recovery on the
insurers' part was more than a century later when,
in 1979, another salvage contract was executed.
Meanwhile, the insurers had thrown all of their
claims records away: their payments were estab-

lished by newspaper accounts of the claims at the
time they were made and paid. They were able to
produce no invoices, bills of lading for the cargo,
packing lists, or insurance policies. Destruction of
the claims and payment-related documents would
seem, by the same token, to destroy the subrogation of the insurers. If they ever intended to
assert a subrogation right, why destroy those documents? In response, the District Court states:
"Why? Their actions speak clearly. They had no
hope or idea that they could locate the Central
America, and even if they located it, they had no
hope they could recover anything from it. They
destroyed the documents and intended thereby to
abandon any claim they might have."

So much for the District Court opinion on this
issue. If it sounds convincing, realize too that,
besides newspaper accounts, the insurers did produce the following: (1) minutes of meetings of some
of their Boards of Directors discussing the claims,
as well as (2) Board resolutions to pay them; (3) an
insurance industry study on the sinking; and (4)
the 1858 salvage contract. As to the destruction of
claims records, the circuit court noted that there
was no evidence of their intentional destruction:
"documents that may have once existed can no
longer be located," the court said carefully.

Moreover, the insurers made no effort to use
technology akin to the plaintiff's once it was available. When offered a chance to participate in a
search in the early 1980s, they made no invest-

ment. For the District Court, their inaction again
speaks louder than the fact that they never waived
their rights expressly. For the Court of Appeals,
however, a lack of recovery activities by the insurers and of investment in various salvage operations
presented to them, is inconclusive on the issue of
an abandonment. Before finding an abandonment,
two elements must appear: first, taking no action
to recover the cargo and, second, a relinquishment
of the right to recover it. The court found that
there was indeed a century of inaction, but refused
to find that the right of recovery had been relinquished. The insurers took no action when they
had no technological hope of recovery, but once
their hopes returned, they exhibited a care never
to deny or relinquish their right in more than a
decade of correspondence with various salvors, including the plaintiffs. *Eads* was distinguished as a
case in which the true owners had in fact performed whatever salvage operations were of benefit to them. Also distinguished was *Wyman v.
Hurburt* (1843).

The Court of Appeals found that the vessel, the
uninsured cargo, and the passengers' possessions,
including the gold in possession of the passengers,
had been abandoned, but that the insured cargo of
gold had not been. It remanded the case for a
determination of the insurers' rights in the insured
gold, noting that the salvage award should none-
the-less be "by far the largest share of the treasure"—including perhaps an award in specie.
That dicta echoes the fact that Eads was himself

usually able by contract to procure a large percent of the value of goods he salved from the Mississippi River.

The Court of Appeals concludes that the law of salvage, where the title to the cargo remains with the true owner, should be applied unless an abandonment is found; finder's law should be applied thereafter. Only for an ancient and long-lost shipwreck should abandonment be inferred by lapse of time; commercial record-keeping can thus preserve a claim never formerly relinquished, even though all the while there is no practical hope of recovery. True owners of personal property have durable and long-lasting rights; perhaps the wonder of the circuit court opinion in the *Central American* case is that the insurers were able to wrap themselves in the mantle of the true owners.

CHAPTER III

OTHER FIRST POSSESSORS AND THE FORMS OF ACTION

The rules discussed in the first chapter, having to do with wild animals, present a particular instance of the law's sanctioning a person's acquisition of a property right in a chattel (meaning any piece of goods or personal property). Hunting being one of man's oldest and most essential pastimes, acquiring a property right in wild animals strikes deep into man's history on earth and perhaps deep into his personality as well. However, a wild animal is not the only type of personal property which can be acquired by a person who becomes its first possessor. Any chattel, even one as insignificant as a seashell, a nut, or fruit, is equally subject to capture and control when found on lands open to public access (the foreshore of the beach or a public highway) and not previously claimed as the property of another.

This rule can be modified by legislation. For example, in the state of Georgia, pecans are big business. When grown on private property in a tree overhanging a public highway, any pecans falling on the road are still the property of the

owner of the pecan tree until the end of the harvest season. Thereafter anyone may remove them
from the roadway. Official Code Ga.Ann. § 44–12–
241 to 44–12–243 (1992).

Much like Georgia pecans are standing timber
and growing crops of various types. They have not
been previously possessed but because they are
normally grown on private lands, any claim to
them must take into account the ownership of the
land on which they are found.

The right to reap the profits from a growing crop
is called an emblement. It is not a right to the
crop itself, but is a right to harvest it where, for
example, a lease to agricultural lands expires during the growing season and the tenant has already
sown the leased ground.

Chattel which are attached to real property and
intended to be permanently attached or annexed to
it are called fixtures. They are personal property
before attachment and real property thereafter,
being then considered part of the realty on which
they are located. Immature crops are often classified as fixtures to prevent their being levied on by
a farmer's creditors while not yet ready for harvest. However, marijuana plants growing between
rows of corn in a field may be personal property in
the possession of a grower who is not in possession
of the field, for purposes of enforcing the criminal
laws' prohibition against the possession of marijuana. When crops are severed from the land—cut or
harvested—they again become personal property.

Their classification as real or personal property thus depends on circumstances to a high degree.

As the basis for legal action, the crop or timber is probably more valuable as personal property and so whatever cause of action is brought to protect them after a wrongful severance, its objective will be to assert rights in what is now personalty. Even if an original or prior possessor has treated a chattel as real property, his seeking to assert his rights to it in their present form allows him to bring an action that relates only to personal property. And, in any event, the defendant will have treated it as personal property and is in no position to assert that, as to any rights which he might claim to it, it is not personal property.

The first objective in this chapter is to review the choices which must be made when deciding what type of lawsuit should be brought to enforce claims relating to personal property.

I. THE FORMS OF ACTION

In our discussion of wild animals, we considered that oldest form of action—*trespass*—which pertains to personalty. An unauthorized and intentional interference with the possession of a chattel of another is a trespass to that personal property. The trespass can be under a mistake of fact or law and still be intentional. The intent necessary for the action does not require wrongful motive.

The trespass must result in more than nominal damages. Although there is some conflict in the authorities on this point, courts gloss over the point by regarding the loss of possession as being of sufficient value to satisfy the requirement of actual damages.

As discussed with regard to *Pierson v. Post*, the objective of an action for trespass has always been to protect the possession of the disputed chattel as it was at the time of the trespass. This requirement of a present right to possession has been expanded somewhat over the years by allowing the action for a plaintiff not in possession at the time but having a present right to possession. (Indeed, this is but another way of restating the issue of the *Pierson* case.) A still further modification in this line of reasoning extends the action to one with a present right to future possession—as with a bailor of chattel presently in a bailee's hands. Finally, because it is possession (and not title) to the chattel which lies at the heart of the action, the defendant cannot set up the rights of a third party as superior to the plaintiff's—i.e., the defense of *jus tertii* is unavailing.

Conversion has today largely replaced trespass as the basis for most causes of action involving personal property. It is the wrongful exercise of dominion or control over personalty rather than (as with trespass) the interference with another's rights in personalty. *Chiappetta v. LeBlond* (1986) (conversion action for the return of a TV from a repair shop). It is completed by any distinct act of control, whether by way of assumption, use, detention of or interference with personalty. It does not involve the wrongful taking of a chattel (as would trespass) but looks instead, later in time, at a wrongful exercise of control over the chattel. That exercise must be a denial or repudiation of another's right to the property. Originally this writ was intended to lie when a finder of lost chattel did not return it to the true owner or prior possessor but instead uses it as his own or, worse yet, sells or disposes of it to another. If the personal property allegedly converted is afterwards incorporated into real property, an action for conversion based upon its use thereafter will not lie.

Thus a conversion occurs when a person, without authority, assumes, uses, and exercises possession, or the right to possess personal property, to the exclusion of the rights of another. Notice here that it is easier to say that a conversion occurs, than to state what it is; the courts have found it virtually impossible to agree on a definition. Although conversion can involve a tortious taking, in that the possession is initially wrongful, how personal property came to be where a plaintiff locates it, is often not susceptible of proof. Because of this evidentiary problem, conversion is the usual presumption. It is the use or exercise of another's right when the possession, initially authorized, becomes wrongful by reason of the property's detention, persisted in even in the face of a demand for its return. In a first class of cases, there need be no allegation that the defendant refused upon demand to return it when the initial taking can be proven. (That taking becomes the conversion of the property to the use of the defendant.) In a second class of cases, a demand and refusal is a necessary allegation of the complaint because it shows that, notwithstanding the manner of acquisition, or more precisely, the plaintiff's failure to allege a wrongful acquisition, the defendant wrongfully withholds its possession from the plaintiff. *Epstein v. Automatic Enterprises* (1986).

An act of control is the basis for the last, but the most important, allegation in a complaint in a cause of action called *trover* (or trover and conversion), to wit, that the defendant "converted the thing for his own." It is preceded by an allegation that the plaintiff was in possession of a chattel, that he lost it, and that the defendant found it and refused to return it upon request, and that he "converted it to his own use". This last allegation long ago became the only one that the plaintiff had to prove—the rest were either surplusage (following as they did from the conversion) or fictions (the original possession, the subsequent loss and the defendant's finding) which the defendant was not permitted for historical reasons to deny. [This history, in case you are interested, is briefly reviewed in *Federal Insur. Company, I.C. v. Banco De Ponce* (1984).] The focus of trover was the conversion and as the other allegations fell away, trover and conversion loom larger in the mass of litigation over personal property until they drove trespass from the field in all cases in which there was no forceful taking of the chattel by the defendant.

It being easy to be stealthy in the acquisition of personalty, proof of how the defendant acquired the chattel was often unavailable to the plaintiff and so much litigation centers quite naturally around its conversion.

The theory of trover is different from that in trespass actions. In trespass, the title is assumed to stay with the plaintiff, but in trover, the defendant is assumed to have acquired the title from the plaintiff. (At least the plaintiff does not contest the acquisition of title.) The plaintiff's bringing an action in trover is like an offer to sell the chattel and a judgment for the plaintiff in trover confirms this sale and transfers the title to the chattel to the defendant. Thus trover is in effect a "forced sale" of a chattel. With this theory in place, plaintiffs had an economic incentive to use trover instead of trespass. They can recover a larger measure of damages in so doing. Trespass gives them a recovery for any damages done to the chattel and the value of their lost possession for the time during which the defendant has the chattel, but trover allows them to treat the chattel as already sold to the defendant, and so the measure of damages is the value with which the plaintiff parted—the full fair market value of the chattel.

More generally today trover and conversion are described as so serious an interference with the rights of another in personalty that the defendant may justly be required to pay its full fair market value. *Dressel v. Weeks* (1989).

Courts will then impose this measure of damages when the exercise of control over another's chattel is a serious interference with the plaintiff's rights. One young attorney, Abraham Lincoln, convinced an Illinois court that taking someone else's horse for a fifteen mile ride was not so serious as to warrant liability for a conversion. *Johnson v. Weedman* (1843). The seriousness of the interference is a matter of degree, involving many factors including the extent of the damages done to the chattel, the loss or inconvenience caused the plaintiff, and the extent and duration of the defendant's exercise of control.

In evaluating seriousness, the bad motive or the intent to interfere will be taken into account as one of the many factors considered. *People v. Sergey* (1985) (involving a criminal conversion of an automobile and comparing the facts—no intent to interfere with another's rights, no damage, and the owner's recovery of the auto—to Lincoln's case in *Johnson v. Weedman,* op. cit.). If good faith is present, the measure of damages may be reduced by any amounts expended by the defendant to protect, maintain or improve the chattel. On the other hand, when personal property in which another has an interest is sold without authority, the full measure is imposed, particularly if the authority should have been discovered by resorting to official records. *Bank of Landisburg v. Burruss* (1987) (a trover and conversion suit for selling a farmer's cattle and giving the $24,000 proceeds of sale to the farmer, instead of the bank with a recorded security interest for $46,000 in the cattle).

As in trespass, a defendant can lack a motivation to interfere with plaintiff's rights and still have the requisite intent to convert another's chattel.

While the carrying away of a chattel may not constitute a conversion when it is done without serious consequences, even a verbal assertion of ownership can be sufficient for a conversion when serious consequences are present. In this type of lawsuit, most important as a matter of proof is the defendant's refusal to return the chattel upon demand. This refusal is prima facie evidence of conversion. No wonder the demand and refusal counts of the original action in trover became surplusage with time! When a plaintiff attempts self-help, these counts are absorbed into proof of the conversion itself which takes place at that time if no wrongful taking or earlier act of dominion is provable.

Often, then, the time of the demand and refusal is the time of the conversion. The place of the conversion provides the law applying to the incident.

Finally, using the cause of action in *replevin,* a plaintiff can physically recover a lost chattel. This action is designed to recover the possession of a chattel wrongfully detained by another. It is not necessary that the plaintiff know how the chattel came to be lost, or into the hands of the person having present possession of it. *Ganter v. Kapiloff*

(1986) (involving postage stamps thought to be in the plaintiffs' possession until they were found in the defendant's). It does not lie against a person in possession in custodia legis—that is, in possession of a chattel subject to a judicial proceeding, as say the police might hold a chattel pending prosecution of a person accused of stealing it.

The property sought must be personal property. Fixtures permanently attached to real property do not qualify, although items such as a tenant might remove at the end of a leasehold do. Conversely, a landlord seeking replevin of property removed from premises while a tenant was in possession, would have to allege and prove that the tenant had abandoned his or her right to it. *State v. Green* (1984). Crops and timber severed from the land are also proper subjects for replevin.

Replevin is an ancient writ. Its original use in feudal England was to permit a tenant to recover a chattel distrained by the lord of the manor for nonpayment of rent or one of the feudal incidents. The writ was never widened much beyond this original use in England, so that Blackstone could correctly say, when he wrote his commentaries on English law in the 1770s, that the writ was limited to cases of distraint. American judges quickly rejected this limitation and extended it to any unlawful conversion of a chattel. *Pangburn v. Patridge* (1810). Thus the trespasser and convertor, as well as the distrainor, could be defendants in suits involving this writ. It became the most widespread form of action for the specific or in-kind recovery of personal property wrongfully taken by a defendant.

Our law also extended the writ to cover instances in which specific recovery was sought for a chattel not necessarily wrongfully taken but wrongfully detained. The common law writ in such a situation was called detinue, but although at first some courts refused to simplify the writ system this way (*Harwood v. Smethurst* (1861)), legislatures stepped in to do the job and the writ of detinue was subsumed in our writ of replevin. Then a new controversy sprang up, for if replevin was available when there had only been a wrongful detention of the chattel, some argued that the taking could be constructive or ignored altogether while others said that both a wrongful taking and detention were required. Legislatures stepped in again to solve this second problem and provided that a wrongful detention shall be deemed an unlawful taking. So replevin lay for a taking and/or a detention of a chattel. One example of the end-product of this process is N.J.Stat.Ann. § 2A:59–1 (West 1991).

> If the goods or chattels of any person be wrongfully taken and detained, or wrongfully detained, the sheriff, or other officer authorized by law, of the county where the goods or chattels may be, shall cause such goods and chattels to be replevied and delivered.

The theory of replevin is that, through all the facts alleged in the complaint, the title to the chattel remained with the plaintiff. This has one very important procedural consequence: unlike a suit in conversion or detinue, the plaintiff, after posting a bond and a preliminary hearing, becomes entitled to possession of the chattel and the sheriff takes possession of it for him shortly after the cause of action is filed. The bond is usually for double the value of the chattel. Until recently in many jurisdictions, posting the bond was the only requirement plaintiff had to meet before the sheriff took possession of the chattel and delivered it to him. E.g. Mass.G.L.A. ch. 247, §§ 2, 8 (Michie/Law.Co-op 1992); Ohio Rev.Code § 2737.10 (1992). The bond was intended to indemnify the defendant in case the chattel was damaged or destroyed while in the hands of the plaintiff and it turned out that the defendant was entitled to its possession back.

Recently, however, a second requirement, that of a preliminary hearing to determine whether the plaintiff should get immediate possession of the chattel, has been imposed by the courts. This change is an attempt to provide due process before transferring possession of the chattel between the parties. The mandate for it is a constitutional one. *Fuentes v. Shevin* (1972); *White Birch Farms v. Garritano* (1987) (holding a procedure for a private sale of a horse under a stableman's lien statute unconstitutional when there is no notice and hearing with regard to the sale). Many state legislatures have responded to these and other cases by incorporating a preliminary hearing on the right to possession into replevin procedures in state codes. Some state codes permit the defendant to post a bond for the value of the chattel in lieu of delivering it over to the sheriff. Mich. MCR § 3.105 (1992); McKinney's—N.Y.Civ.Prac.Law § 7102(e) (1992).

So the imposition of a bond or a preliminary hearing, conducted by a judge or magistrate, has been one response to the constitutional problems involved in replevin statutes. Another has been a statutory limitation on the instances calling for the initial seizure of the chattel by the sheriff. In some states, this initial seizure is now only possible when the goods have been the subject of a felonious taking, are in danger of destruction, or are property of a particular type—e.g., a credit card. West's Ann.Cal.Code Civ.Pro. § 512.020(b)(1)–(2) (1992).

Still another response has been to abolish replevin altogether. Virginia has adopted this course of action Va.Code § 8.01–218 (1992). However, because this course of action may leave detinue in place (Virginia had codified the action) and because detinue requires only a wrongful detention of a chattel, care must be taken that the statute of limitations and other procedures which attached to replevin, but are also necessary to detinue, are not repealed as well. If for example, the statute of limitations for detinue were inadvertently repealed, that would force defendants in detinue

actions to plead and prove adverse possession of
the chattel in order to avoid reaching the merits of
even a stale case.

At the hearing and trial in an action for replevin, the plaintiff seeks to justify his taking of possession through the sheriff. At trial he also seeks any
damages due him for the wrongful taking or detention. The damages component of this cause of
action may explain in part why American courts
have no qualms about expanding replevin to cover
trespasses and conversions of a chattel—for in trespass, damages were the normal remedy.

For the defendant's part, he seeks to show that
he had been rightfully in possession of the chattel.
He cannot show (and this lack of defense may
again partly account for the widespread use of
replevin in the United States) that the title to the
chattel lay in another, not a party to the action.
Our courts rejected the defense of *jus tertii* (right
of a third party) during the course of the nineteenth century. Finkelstein, "The Plea of Property in a Stranger in Replevin," 23 Colum.L.Rev. 652
(1923). Prior possession alone will support the
cause of action. (At a later stage of the proceedings, when the court considers the matter of measuring damages, the *jus tertii* defense may be considered by the court. In the context of the awarding of damages, a lesser award may indeed be
appropriate (1) if a plaintiff has a right to possession without having title or (2) if he sues and wins

in trover but the defendant still faces the possibility of a later lawsuit by the true owner.)

Replevin lies so long as the chattel can be identified and until the doctrine of accession (dealt with in chapter XI) cuts it off. Thus if the identity of the chattel is substantially altered or its value has become an insignificant portion of the value of another chattel, the doctrine of accession cuts short the right to a specific recovery of the original chattel.

A. A LEADING CASE

An example of the uses of replevin is the case of *Goodard v. Winchell* (1892). Imagine that a meteorite drops to earth, embedding itself in the soil. It contains valuable minerals. The land on which it fell was rented prairie, the grazing rights of which were leased; the lessee allowed H to enter the premises and dig the meteorite up. H sold it to B, against whom the owner of the land brings suit to recover (or replevy) it.

In an action for replevin, the complaint must allege (1) some immediate right to possession of or title to the chattel; (2) a wrongful taking or detention of the chattel by the defendant; (3) defendant's retention of it at the time of the suit and after the plaintiff demands it back and the defendant refused to return it; and (4) damages. When the complaint is filed or after a preliminary hearing, the chattel is transferred to the plaintiff pending the outcome of the suit or else the defendant must post the bond in the amount of the value of the chattel for which recovery is sought.

B is the present possessor of the chattel. His rights in this litigation will depend on H's right to the meteorite. No possessor's right can rise any higher than those of his transferor and when H dug up the meteorite, the issue becomes whether the labor he expended on another's land gives him any rights superior to the owner of the land on which he is digging.

Let us first consider H's status on the land while he dug up the meteorite. Is H like the trespassing hunter pursuing a wild animal onto the private lands of another? No, not technically, because the tenant of the owner invited him onto the land where the meteorite fell. Because H did not trespass, a court is free to decide that his rights in the meteorite are superior to the landowner, O, unless there is some difference between the meteorite and a wild animal which the law should recognize. And there is an obvious distinction: the animal is not part of the ground, while the meteorite is found in the ground.

Next let's consider the expenditure of effort and labor involved in the digging. Does that avail H? When compared to O's non-existent efforts, it might, but its legal effect still depends on (1) whether a court will treat the meteorite as it would a wild animal, subject to a rule of capture and control, and also (2) whether H's labor was expended at a time before the rights of others arose; in other words, on whether H is the first possessor.

The court concluded that H was not the first possessor of the meteorite. Remember that replevin lies only for the recovery of personal property. So the landowner's suit is initially judged by the type of property sought at the time that the lawsuit is brought. The meteorite was clearly personalty when the complaint was filed, so bringing an action of replevin is proper. However, this classification of the meteorite as personalty is for the sole purpose of judging the adequacy of the complaint. On the merits of the case, the issue of whether H is the first possessor turns again on the classification of the property. If it is part of the land in which it is found, it is real property and so possessed by the owner of the realty. If it is not part of the land, no one can claim to have "possessed" it before H dug it up and he becomes its first possessor. The status of the meteorite at the time H dug it up, is therefore important to the outcome of the case on the merits. Because the meteorite was embedded three feet into the soil and because its components were no different from other elements found in the earth in nature, the court in *Goodard* has a basis for concluding (and did conclude) that it was a part of the real property when the defendant first interfered with the landowner's rights.

So the meteorite is realty when in the ground, but this status is not immutable. After it was dug up it was personalty, and so when it was sold to B, it remained personalty. Why is this close attention to the time-warp of the facts important? Because the sale to B will be governed by different rules of law depending upon whether the thing sold is realty or personalty. For example, in a sale of personalty, there may be an implied warranty of title. B might reasonably expect that H owned the object which he offered to sell and by offering an object for sale, H implicitly represented that he had title to what he offered. Such a warranty is absent in sales of real property—*caveat emptor* being the rule there. When B is forced to give up the meteorite to O, once the court decides that it is real property, he (B) will certainly want to explore the possibility of suing H. What he (B) knew about H's title (or lack of title) will be important to the outcome of this second suit, but as a preliminary matter, he will surely have to show that, at the time H sold the meteorite to B, it was personalty and so sold with a warranty of title.

Because it was real property before H dug it up, and only upon its severance from the soil did it become personal property recoverable thereafter in replevin, the landowner O became its first possessor. He had, not only the right to dig it up and so reduce it to possession, but also an ownership right in the thing itself. This is *rationi soli* (discussed in Chapter I) in the rawest and broadest form. These initial rights, conferred by the meteorite's status as real property, is what H interfered with. Answering the definitional question of which type of property it was when H thwarted these rights, permits the court to award possession of the meteorite to O.

How did the court justify this result? By asking questions about the consequences of deciding otherwise. Were the law otherwise, wouldn't the industrious H's of the world be able to mine the sand, stones, and gravel on another's land with impunity. The rubble made by glaciers eons ago broadly speaking arrived on a particular parcel of land by the same forces of nature sending the meteorite to earth. Unless a court could say that the owner of the parcel is less likely to make good use of the minerals in the meteorite than he would of this glacial debris, the owner becomes the first possessor of it recognized by the law and occupies a special place in the law. If he can show that he had first possession, his title to the meteorite remains intact regardless of the number of persons into whose hands the thing later passes. Absent an intentional transfer of his title, the title of the first possessor also remains intact regardless of the good faith of subsequent possessors.

Thus where objects are found embedded in the soil, their possession is to be awarded to the owner of the soil on the basis that his possession of the soil carries with it possession of whatever is found therein. The land owner's possession is thus said to be constructive. To deny him this meteorite would call into question his right to other components of his land and eventually his title to the land itself. This is a path down which the law should be hesitant to move. Thus there is a heavy burden of persuasion on one asking the courts to move away from upholding the right of the first possessor. This burden is considerable because to have it otherwise also calls into question the titles of those who purchase or improve the property of a first possessor.

However, in *Goodard,* the court chooses to protect the first possessor without a detailed discussion of the problems of doing so. There is some question as to the good faith of the purchaser raised by the facts of the case, but the opinion makes nothing of this. Why? Because O never intended to transfer the meteorite to either his lessee, H, or B. Apparently the good faith or bad faith of the subsequent possessor of a piece of property makes little difference to the court. It isn't nearly as important as possession of the meteorite. This is a judgment rooted in an overly-broad conclusion. Society as a whole has a stake in firmly grounding the title to a chattel in the first possessor in order to protect subsequent ones, but it also and equally has a stake in overseeing a smoothly-running economy, which requires that trade be maintained and titles to things remain fungible and negotiable. Perhaps protecting the first possessor's title is at the same time to protect society's interest in later trade and to foster that trade but whether this is so is a question that would seem to merit some extended discussion by the court. In some instances, the rights of a first possessor underlie, not just a chain of transactions, but institutions vital to society. In this case, land-ownership seems to be such an institution. Epstein, "Possession as the Root of Title", 13 Ga. L.Rev. 1221, 1238–43 (1979). First possession and as we shall see its second-best alternative, prior possession, protects the institution that has grown up in its wake. The rights of a first possessor has both a transactional and an institutional justification. This has proven an unbeatable combination in Anglo-American courts, no matter what cause of action—trespass, conversion, trover, detinue, or replevin—he brings to protect himself against convertors.

The legal path followed by the meteorite in *Goddard* from real property to personal property, is not a one-way street: property classified as personal property, can again become real property. For example, consider the tailings of a gold or coal mine, once thought not to contain enough minerals to justify further processing, but, with the rise in mineral prices, justifying a reconsideration of this matter. When the holder of the realty is not the holder of the personalty around the mine—as when it is owned by one and operated by another—the title to the tailings may become unclear. *Hayes v. Alaska Juneau Forest Industries, Inc.* (1988). This issue must be settled before further processing is likely to start up.

Finally, more on meteorites. Less complicated than the dispute between private parties over the meteorite in *Goddard*, is the tale of the largest meteorite ever to crash into what is now the United States and be discovered (in Lake Oswego, Oregon, in 1902)—the so-called Willamette Meteorite. This bell-shaped rock weighs fifteen and a half tons and is in the possession of the Natural History Museum in New York City. It was initially found by a miner who, with the aid of his family and a horse, dragged it from the land of the Oregon Iron and Steel Company, to his own. There he exhibited it, charging a quarter for admission. His exhibition came to the attention of the Company, who filed a replevin suit against the miner and won. The Company exhibited the meteorite at a World's Fair, where it was bought for $26,000 by a wealthy patron of the Museum and donated to the Museum's collection. Recently school children in Oregon have asked for the meteorites' return to their state as a bit of its natural history. T. Egan, No Stone Unturned in a Battle for a Rock, N.Y. Times (June 2, 1991), at 26, col. 1.

B.   PROPERTY IN ONE'S BODY: MOORE v. BOARD OF REGENTS

Time was, casebooks and courses on property often began with a discussion of cases dealing with rights in a person's dead body or cadaver, from the Latin *caro data veribus,* or "flesh given to the worms." While the courts generally recognized no property rights in a cadaver, a quasi-property right to possession for purposes of burial or cremation was recognized. *Floyd v. Atlantic Coast Line Rail-*

way Company (1914) (negligent mishandling of a dead body not actionable), and following *Williams v. Williams* (1882) (right of burial actionable); *O'Donnell v. Slack* (1899) (decedent's body not the property of his estate, but testamentary disposition of body permitted). The hunting cases often dealt with today are the remnant of such a beginning. This choice of subject was not just a macabre interest of my professorial predecessors, for cadavers were an important source of medical knowledge.

Biotechnology merged with medicine has today made the living bodies of a physician's patients into an even more vital source of knowledge—and litigation. See *Moore v. The Regents of the University of California* (1988), 51 Ohio St.L.J. 499 (1990), 25 Ind.L.Rev. 559 (1991). In 1976, John Moore was first diagnosed as having leukemia. A month later, he sought a second opinion, which confirmed the first, from a specialist at the University's medical center. The cancer affected Moore's bone marrow, spleen, liver, and peripheral blood. The cancerous cells in Moore's blood has a rare type of white blood cell that produces a protein regulating the immune system. Moreover, this protein can sometimes be reproduced in large quantities through recombinant DNA techniques.

The physician attending Moore at the University hospital recommended a splenectomy to slow the cancer's progress and in preparation for this surgery Moore signed a consent form. The form au-

thorized the surgery and provided for the disposal
of severed tissue by cremation. The attending
physician, however, obtained tissue from Moore's
spleen from the pathologist. With it, he and a
colleague established a Mo cell line—Mo referring
to Moore—capable of reproduction indefinitely and
producing proteins with considerable commercial
value.

Some five years after taking the tissue from
Moore's spleen, in 1981, the physicians patented
the Mo cell line, along with the method for producing the proteins as well as isolating and cloning the
DNA genetic information contained in them. The
patent was granted in 1984 and was assigned to
the University. Agreements for the commercial
development of the cells were then executed with
pharmaceutical firms. The physicians were paid
stock rights and over $400,000 for the exclusive
rights to the cells and research performed on them.
The value of the products that could be developed
from the line has been estimated at three billion
dollars.

Moore returned to the University hospital several times during the years 1976–1983. In April,
1983, he executed another consent form, this one
authorizing the use of his blood in research and
granting the University all rights he or his heirs
may have in any cell line or any other potential
product made from it. He was told that the form
was a standard one and was necessary for continued treatment. Several months later, in Septem-

ber, he was presented with an identical form, but refused to sign it after inquiring about the commercial value of his blood, which was not disclosed to him. He was told instead that the form was a formality. A month later, his physicians published their findings concerning his cell line in a well-known scientific journal.

He sought legal counsel and in 1984 brought suit alleging thirteen causes of action and seeking a share of the profits derived from the use of his cells in research. The cause of action of primary interest is conversion because it formed the basis of most of the other causes of action, although others based on lack of consent and breach of fiduciary duty are of interest as well. No matter what the basis of each action, the defendants (the two physicians, the University, and the pharmaceutical firms) demurred to all of them.

The trial court upheld the demurrers, the intermediate Court of Appeals reversed, and the California Supreme Court affirmed in part and reversed in part, overruling the demurrers as to the breach of fiduciary duty and lack of informed consent brought against the physicians, holding that the complaint states no cause of action for conversion, and stating that "the use of excised cells in research does not amount to a conversion."

Conversion is generally any wrongful act of dominion over another's personal property that is inconsistent with the other's rights therein. It is often thought of as a form of strict liability in tort and requires that the plaintiff (1) have a right to possess personal property, (2) that he loose it, (3) that the defendant find it and (4) convert it to his own use by either refusing to return it or disposing of it to a third party. Here Moore alleged an interest in the cells after their removal from his body: "He theorizes," the court states, "that he continued to own his cells following their removal from his body, at least for the purpose of directing their use...." The court states that finding such a retained interest required a balancing of a patient's interest in personal autonomy against the right of a physician to engage in socially useful research free of the duty to search the pedigree of the cells used. Balancing these interests, the court thought that the utility of permitting a conversion was outweighed by the chill on future research. See E. Paul, Natural Rights and Property Rights, 13 Harv.J.L. & Pub.Policy 10, 14 (1991) ("Utilitarians live to balance competing interests...."). Further, the court reasoned that, if such a continuing interest is to be found, it was better that the California legislature do it. No precedent supported the claim of such an interest and the court found that privacy and consent requirements were sufficient to protect Moore.

Were they? The choice between tort and property protection is a basic one and we will return to it later in this section.

Moore's allegation of a conversion raises another basic and interesting issue involving the pleadings:

when does the conversion occur? There are two possibilities: it occurs either after the cells' removal when the research takes place, or at the very moment of their removal. If the latter is chosen, that is a time when it is difficult to deny that Moore has possession of the cells. Moore's attorney may have mistaken the nature of the conversion and mispled this cause of action as a result.

A second issue of pleading is the nature of the property claimed. Moore alleged, the majority concluded, an interest in the genetic code for chemicals regulating the function of the immune system—a code which does not vary from individual to individual—and thus pleaded too broadly. (This is an interesting point, but one suspects that such a conclusion, made by a lawyer about a medical matter, is on a par with a physician's conclusion on an arcane legal point.) On this point, the court wisely left the matter open, stating that it "refused to hold that excised cells can never be property for any purpose whatsoever." Narrower pleading may well in the future come within the bounds of some court's willingness to find a property right in human cells.

As to the temporal aspect of Moore's right to possession of the cells, his counsel probably pled as he did because of several statutory restrictions: first on a person's right to possess tissue removed from one's body and requiring sanitary disposal of such tissue; second declaring that the procurement of blood is a service, not a sale; and third regulating the gift of all or part of a body or its organs for specified purposes. "It is the specialized statutes, not the law of conversion, to which courts ordinarily should and do look for guidance on the disposition of human biological materials." Moore's property interest was rejected because these and other statutes drastically limited what may be done with bodily materials.

Moreover, the court found, the patent issued to the physicians and assigned to the University was a determination that the Mo cell line was the product of invention, distinct from the tissue taken from Moore, and not occurring naturally. Thus, the lack of precedent, statutory limitations on the use of bodily materials, the patentability of the cell line, and policy considerations, made the court reject Moore's claim of a property interest in the cells sufficient to sustain his action for conversion.

This rejection may be unwise. First, just because the plaintiff asks the court for an unprecedented extension of the law to the facts of his case, is per se no reason not to oblige him; the common law has long adapted itself to new circumstances. That adaptation is one of its virtues. Second, no statute prohibits Moore's claim and many of the statutes cited by the court are aimed at promoting research in which Moore is equally interested. In keeping with some of these statutes, Moore argued that he consented to research, but not to the commercial exploitation of his tissue and cells. In any event, he argued that deference to statutes is irrelevant to the scope of a common law form of action, unless the statutes are directly on point, expanding or limiting the action in some way. Third, the patentability of a thing is different from a determination of the basis for sharing the profits from it. Finally, it should be recognized that biotechnology is an industry, not a guild of researchers in which information and research results are freely shared. Contracts, trade secrets, and patents are jealously guarded; indeed, the patentability of the cell line undercuts the policy arguments for rejecting Moore's claim of a property interest in the cells; it instead recognizes a form of property in them.

Moreover, stating that the legislature is competent to act on this subject and enact statutes on it, is also to say that the legislature can act either before or after the courts decide Moore's claim, however they decide. Legislative competence is the same, no matter what the court decided. Deferring to it or anticipating it, is really also a judgment, by judges, about their own capabilities, not those of the legislature.

The result in *Moore* is bolstered none-the-less by a fear that the sale of tissue is subject to abuse. Such abuse is typically represented by the nineteenth-century trade in cadavers. See R. Scott, The Body as Property 5, 7–8 (1981). A spectre of a poor person forced to sell his body's organs is haunting; market features, such as the highest bidder, the introductions of middlemen and brokers, tinge that spectre with exploitation, rather than economic opportunity. So some abuse is possible, but abuse can be separately regulated, either by the courts or the legislature. See e.g., *Brotherton v. Cleveland* (1991) (holding that the removal of corneas from body of widow's decedent requires pre-deprivation due process). For example, it is difficult to contend that the sale of fetal tissue by a mother, imperilling the fetus, would be countenanced by a contrary result in *Moore*, albeit the holding in *Roe v. Wade* (1973), implies a right of disposition (however regulated by more recent cases) in the fetus until the end of the first trimester of a pregnancy. Surely any "used body parts" shops that did open for business would quickly come under strict regulation. Indeed, the Congress has legislated on organ transplants. See 42 U.S.C.A. § 274 et seq. (1984) (banning the sale of organs in interstate commerce). More than a dozen states ban the sale of fetal tissue and organs. See e.g., 18 Pa.Cons.Stat.Ann. § 3216 (Purdon 1983). Blood and sperm banks are also regulated and the ability to contract for surrogate mother services are proscribed as well.

Many of the regulated activities involving bodily material involve healthy individuals, but Moore was far from healthy and was undergoing very expensive treatment. Indeed, his ill-health was the source of the uniqueness of his cells. This raises again the issue of whether Moore's cells fit the definition of personal property. (It also recalls the caveat about lawyers' and physicians' distinct expertise.) Should the uniqueness of the cells fa-

vor the recognition of Moore's conversion action, or
more narrowly favor a recognition of the value of
his cells as an offset to his medical expenses?
Immunizing the physician's profit from Moore's
conversion action may be to ignore the patient's
financial needs. Health costs are a national concern today. Shouldn't those in the health care
system for treatment be able to pay for that treatment through their bodily contributions to it, rather than spreading those costs around, ultimately to
the public at large?

The majority's final point in *Moore* is that an
adequate alternative remedy exists. The dissent is
quick to point out, however, that it sounds in
negligence and normally will provide no crisp rule
as to when it applies. Physicians will not know
when they transgress it, but will instead be subject
to litigation, with attendant costs and uncertainties. A physician certainly has a duty to disclose
to a patient that the former will profit if a patient
accepts treatment by purchasing a particular drug,
but if a physician's research is on-going at the time
the tissue is extracted from the patient's body, who
is to say what profit there might be? Moreover,
the patient as a negligence plaintiff will often have
to show that, had full disclosure been made, consent would not have followed. For a cancer patient, consent to the surgery would typically be
given, but the extent of that consent will likely
become an issue thereafter; few triers of fact are
likely to believe that a patient would refuse treatment because the tissue extracted during the

course of it, might later be used in profitable research. The cost-benefit equation weighed by the patient whose health is at stake declares treatment worth the cost—particularly when "a reasonably prudent person," not an individual patient, is making the decision. Finally, the class of plaintiffs in this type of negligence action is limited to those to whom the physician owes a duty of disclosure—namely, to the formally-declared physician's patients as a group. Other parties need not bother to file!

Finding property rights is to declare settled expectations for which all parties can plan. Negligence actions are meant for situations in which expectations are unsettled, and they can be stopped dead at any of several stages. No certain rules there. Planning to win a negligence action is almost a contradiction in terms. Giving a patient the right to refuse consent, as the *Moore* opinion does, doesn't give him the right to consent on the condition that he share the profits of future research. A veto power is not a right to participate. It is just the reverse. A property interest, on the other hand, provides greater assurance of a right to participate and share in future profits.

The judicial choice in *Moore* was between tort and property causes of action. The court regarded that matter as the product of sufficiently unsettled expectations that a tort or negligence claim best suited, but in so doing, it also decided to leave expectations unsettled for a time. In another section of this book (Chapter VI, Bailments) you might consider whether another, traditional way of treating personal property, isn't adaptable to the problems Mr. Moore might have faced if a full disclosure of his physicians' interest in his spleen had been made to him.

II. THE PLAINTIFF'S ELECTION

No matter which of the previously discussed causes of action are brought, a plaintiff who proceeds to judgment in one of them is barred from bringing any of the others. The rationale is that a defendant should not be doubly vexed, or brought to trial twice, for a single trespass or conversion. A judgment in either trespass, conversion, trover, detinue, or replevin is a bar to bringing any other of these actions against a defendant who at the time the judgment issues, is still in possession of the chattel.

This immunity from further suit gives the defendant, even though now a proven trespasser or converter, a kind of property right in the chattel. He is freed from suit, in much the same way he would be if the statute of limitations or an adverse possession period tolled on the other unused causes of action. Thereafter, creditors of the defendant convertor who retains the chattel can levy on it, and a purchaser from such a defendant, after judgment is given, should take a perfect title to it.

If the defendant, before judgment, sells the chattel to a third party, the plaintiff's right to recover it is undiminished; indeed, the change of possession enlarges the number of the plaintiff's remedies, in the sense that his new right to sue the third party purchaser (or third convertor or whomever) does not bar his rights against the defendant. The plaintiff can thus sue the third party using the same or any other available cause of action which he used against the defendant. He cannot, however, have both judgments satisfied on the theory that he should not receive double compensation for the same trespass or conversion.

Where the plaintiff has a cause of action against more than one defendant, all of whom together deprived him of his possession or rights in a chattel, he may sue them jointly or severally. If he proceeds against each separately, he can pursue the others as well in the same or another available cause of action. He can, however, satisfy only one of the judgments received.

CHAPTER IV

PRIOR POSSESSION

In this fourth chapter we will broaden our treatment of the subject of possession with a discussion of the rights of prior possessors as well as first possessors. The term prior possessor includes any possessor of a chattel whose rights arise earlier than another's in the chain of possession or title to that chattel. The first possessor who was the focus of the last three chapters becomes one example of a prior possessor who holds the initial link in the chain.

Where the chain is a particularly long one, there will be many prior possessors having rights against those subsequent in the chain. To sort out their rights, the law needs a flexible rule because it would not do to decide any first case as if the state of the title were thereby definitively established. What if two other possessors litigated the same question separately? What if the winner was then sued by a possessor prior to him? The law would be a muddle of absolutist statements about who has title.

This sort of confusion is avoided by a more flexible rule regarding the title: not a rule that makes statements awarding absolute title, but a

rule saying that, as between the persons now before the court, the judgment holder has the superi-
or right to the chattel. This is the doctrine of the
relativity of title.

This doctrine entered Anglo-American law at an
early date. In 1722, a chimney sweep found a
jewel in a setting. He took it to a goldsmith to
have it appraised. The smith's assistant returned
the setting, but, saying that the sweep was not the
true owner of the jewel, refused to return it. In a
case styled *Armory v. Delamirie* (1722), the sweep
sued the goldsmith for damages and won.

I. CHOOSING REPLEVIN OR TROVER

We dealt in the third chapter with the action of
replevin. It was originally a common law writ, but
is today a statutory action at law. Being an action
for the recovery of possession, the defendant must
be in possession of the disputed chattel at the time
the action is commenced.

If a plaintiff like the chimney-sweep does not
wish to recover possession, the law offers him another option. He can bring a writ in trover. Trover is an action for the recovery of damages for a
wrongful taking of a chattel. The wrongful taking
results in an exercise of dominion over the chattel
and as previously discussed, is referred to as a
conversion of it. If the plaintiff wins, he obtains a
monetary judgment, but not the chattel itself; if
the defendant has it, he can keep it.

The possibility of the defendant keeping the chattel is all well and good when he has it. What, however, if he does not possess it? What then does he receive in return for paying the judgment? In the first place, he keeps the sheriff from his door, but with time, the courts came to regard the payment of this judgment as the completion of a sale of the chattel commenced at the time of its conversion. This sale has an element of fiction to it. Because the purchaser was first sued and then compelled to pay the judgment against him, the sale must be regarded as a forced one.

Trover is an instance of the rights in or title to the chattel trying to catch up with its possession. What plaintiff has is his prior right to the chattel. So payment of the judgment transfers the plaintiff's right to it. The plaintiff who pursues a trover action to a judgment has in legal effect elected to give up, or be disseized of, his right to the chattel.

If an action in trover, pursued to a judgment for the plaintiff, is a forced sale, the question arises as to when the sale is effective. There are two possible dates to consider—the date on which the wrongful taking took place (when the sale supposedly commenced) and the date on which the judgment is paid (when it was completed).

The former, or date on which the wrongful taking took place, is the one selected by the courts. Why? There are at least two reasons. First, an action in trover is one for damages, and the damage was done upon the taking of the chattel; on that date, the plaintiff/vendor had done everything he could do to effect the sale and the convertor had an unfulfilled obligation to pay for it. This was an obligation which the courts would enforce, so the sale can be regarded as complete, as far as the plaintiff is concerned, on that date. Second, because the defendant/purchaser through this forced sale acquires the vendor's right or title to the chattel and will be entitled to replevy it as against any subsequent possessor of it, he must acquire his rights before the plaintiff chose trover over replevin and so limited himself by his own election to that one particular type of recovery.

If, in an action in trover, the plaintiff elects to recover damages, these damages will generally be measured by the fair market value of the chattel taken. This value is computed as of the time it was taken.

When will this choice of dates matter? It will matter when the value of the chattel is not constant. If the chattel has after its conversion decreased in value, it is more advantageous to the plaintiff to sue in trover rather than in replevin. If, on the other hand, there has been an increase in value, replevin would be the preferred remedy for the plaintiff, provided that the party in current possession of the chattel can be located and brought within the jurisdiction of the court.

Not to put too fine a point on it, but replevin may still yield an equivalent benefit to the plaintiff when there has been a decrease in value caused by the defendant's wrongful taking. In that event, the successful plaintiff is entitled to (1) an additional monetary damage award for the decrease in value caused by the defendant and (2) still another award for the mesne or interim damages which he incurred because of his lost possession. The possibility of the second award will be useful where the decreased value was not caused by the defendant, but by the depreciating value of the chattel itself, in which instance the plaintiff would have sold the chattel and prevented further loss to himself. This second award is then measured by the value to the plaintiff of a lost opportunity to sell just after the wrongful taking.

Finally, where the chattel is still appreciating at the time of the lawsuit, a plaintiff is clearly going to prefer an action in replevin to one in trover. Getting the thing back will then be worth more than getting its value at the time of the conversion.

A. THE CONSEQUENCES OF CHOOSING TROVER

Originally the common law writ of trover lay in cases where the defendant found the goods of the plaintiff, refused to return them and converted them to his own use. After the allegations of a loss and a finding became matters of fiction and then dropped away entirely, the action of trover was one of remedying any interference with or detention of the chattel of another. The plaintiff has to have a right to possession at the time of the alleged conversion, the chattel claimed must be specific enough to be identifiable, and the conversion must be wrongful.

As mentioned previously in the more general context of the doctrine of relativity of title, *Armory v. Delamirie* is the leading case in Anglo-American jurisprudence concerning trover actions. The facts have been simply stated, but they can be distilled still further: a finder gives an object to another for a limited purpose and the latter refuses to give it back. Giving possession of a chattel to another without giving up whatever right or title one has in it is called a bailment (a subject which we will treat extensively in Chapter VI). A bailment is thus a transfer of possession of a chattel for a limited purpose. In *Armory*, it was for appraising the value of the chattel.

In *Armory*, the finder—the chimney sweep—won. Is this a fair result? It seems so until one stops to think that the finder had no title to the jewel, did not earn it, and gets a windfall if allowed to keep it. But should we be thinking of these things in the context of a trover action between a finder and bailee? The true owner of the jewel, wherever he is, is not before the court. In a legal system such as ours, where the due process of law is constitutionally guaranteed, his rights are not affected by the present litigation. So the answer to the last question is no, the true owner's rights are irrelevant to the trover action before the court.

In awarding the finder damages, the *Armory* court was careful to make this point, "(t)hat the finder of a jewel, though he does not by such finding acquire an absolute property or ownership, yet he has such a property as will enable him to keep it against all but the rightful owner, and consequently may maintain trover."

As to the rights of finders, this principle of law is perhaps too broad. The court could have used tort rules to decide the case, because the goldsmith and his assistant had interfered with whatever rights the sweep had and committed a conversion of the jewel. It could also have used the contract of bailment (and if there was no actual contract, then an implied one), one term of which is implied by the law to the effect that the chattel be returned in the same condition in which it is tendered. Both of these tort and contract characterizations of the lawsuit would have allowed the court to decide a narrower legal question—because both exclude consideration of the status of the sweep as the finder of the chattel—and thus the case could have been decided with a narrower principle of law.

However, and apparently ignoring these opportunities, the court used instead the rule that the finder of a chattel has the right to possess it against all but the true owner.

By referring to the finder's "property" in the jewel, the court uses a phrase that encompasses the range of interests it means to consider—a range of persons wider than were involved in just the bailment contract or the tort of conversion but, instead, broadened to include the interests of the "true owner" as well.

This means that if and when the true owner of the jewel sues the finder, he will have the right to recover what the finder has already recovered from the bailee. If, as happened in *Armory,* the finder's recovery lay in trover, then the true owner could recover the amount which the finder had already recovered (if the true owner was willing to accept the forced sale and loss of his rights to the chattel itself). When the finder took the jewel for appraisal, he was behaving as if he owned it; when he sold it through the forced sale involved in a trover action, he again acted like its owner and so converted the chattel, thus giving the true owner a basis for a suit in trover against him. The finder has transformed his legal status by suing for damages and so rendered himself liable to the true owner in trover.

While it might seem unfair to stigmatize the innocent finder as a convertor, it should also be remembered that at the same time the finder acts as if he owns the chattel he is also starting to run the period of time necessary to acquire title by adverse possession.

If the finder's lawsuit against the bailee had been in replevin and the finder was successful and able to recover the chattel, then of course the true owner would have the option of bringing either replevin or trover against the finder. If the owner

seeks replevin, then his complaint must be somewhat longer than it would be in trover. In addition to the finder's conversion of the chattel, must
then be added the allegation that his retention of
the chattel at the time of the suit, was wrongful as
against the true owner.

The forced sale which resulted from the trover
action in *Armory,* gives the bailee the finder's right
in it. Lawyers speak of this substitution of one
person for another as a subrogation. The person
who is substituted receives or "is subrogated to"
the rights of the person who is replaced; they say,
"the bailee is subrogated to the finder's right."
This right however, does not amount to unqualified
title to the chattel; it is only as good an interest as
the finder himself had to transfer. That right was
subject to the rights of the true owner, should he
appear. When he does, and chooses to sue the
smith in trover, he alleges that the bailee has now
converted his chattel by wrongfully withholding it.

If the true owner is allowed to prevail in this
suit, the bailee will be forced to pay twice for the
chattel. Double liability seems a harsh result but,
on the other hand, the bailee who holds himself out
as an appraiser but does not supervise his assistant
is not the natural object of our sympathy.

Actually, the smith is first paying to acquire the
finder's right in the chattel and when later sued in
trover by the true owner, he will acquire the latter's interest as well. Strictly speaking, the two
plaintiffs in these suits have different interests and

are recovering for separate conversions arising out of the same incident involving the jewel. It is a case of one incident provoking two injuries.

There is no case law precisely on point, but the possibility of his paying twice exists because the rights which the bailee acquired from the finder will not protect him from a suit by the true owner. The court's rule on finder's rights allows it to gloss over this double liability problem: better to emphasize the status of this plaintiff as a finder than to sort out the goldsmith's duties as a bailee and to try to resolve all possible law suits which might spring from this situation in advance of their actually being brought to court.

II. THE REACH OF THE ARMORY RULE

Beyond this analysis of the *Armory* rule, it is necessary also to discuss its scope. In this regard, consider a situation in which there are multiple finders of a chattel. For example, O, a gardener, is hauling home a bag of mulch in his pick-up. The mulch falls off his truck and A finds it. A is hauling it home when it again falls into the street and B finds it there. B hauls it off, loses it again, and C finds it.

What are the rights of each party in trover? Under the *Armory* rule, both A and B are protected as finders against B and C respectively. Why? Because each is a "finder" as to a person subsequent in the chain of possession of the chattel.

What is presented then by the *Armory* rule are a series of relative rights, arising in turn in possessors immediately prior in the chain of possession. *Armory*'s is a rule of relative prior possession. (As we shall soon see, that same sort of relativism applies when defining the "rightful owner" or as referred to here, the true owner.) When the *Armory* court refers to finders and words its rule in terms of finders' rights, one might just as well, and logically read "prior possessor" for finder.

One further reason for reading the rule this way lies in the *Armory* rule's potential for holding the bailee liable twice, once to the finder and again to the true owner should he turn up. The rule's reference to finders is perhaps one way the court has of saying that it is unlikely that the true owner would ever trace the chain of possession through the finder to the bailee. The reference makes clear that double liability for the bailee was only a remote problem in *Armory;* when it is not so remote, then, presumably the rule of the case can be reformulated or the question of the defendant's possible double liability squarely faced.

III. JUSTIFICATIONS FOR PROTECTING THE PRIOR POSSESSOR

With the substitution of "prior possessor" for "finder," the rule of the *Armory* case becomes that the prior possessor of a chattel has a right to it as good or superior to all but the rightful or true owner. The first advantage of such a rule is that it acts to discourage or prevent an endless series of conversions of the chattel once it comes into the hands of one who cannot prove title to it.

This first advantage, however, is not helpful in judging the issue of the *Armory* case (whether or not the bailee can be compelled to pay damages to the prior possessor for not returning the chattel). On this issue, however, the rule has a second advantage. It aids the enforcement of bailment contracts, particularly the promise of the bailee to return the chattel, and so encourages a business practice useful to the development of trade and commerce.

A third, related advantage is similarly utilitarian. There may also be, in the broadly-stated version of the *Armory* rule, a preference for keeping chattels in circulation. The finder was in the process of removing the chattel from the netherworld of lost objects and restoring it to a position in which it can once more be used and useful.

A fourth, and perhaps the most general, advantage of protecting the prior possessor is that, in so doing, ownership and title will be protected as well. The prior possessor will be in the best position, often, to locate or be located by the true owner— protecting the one protects the other.

IV. THE MEASURE OF DAMAGES

The *Armory* court awarded the full value of the chattel to the finder. Is this justified? When it is remembered that the finder did not prove full title to it, the award of full-value damages seems too much. Some reduction in the award might have been made in recognition of the fact that the finder does not have full title and that the true owner might someday show up and make the subsequent possessor or bailee pay twice. The latter parties' risk of double liability can be hedged somewhat by discounting the value of the chattel to the finder. On the other hand, if there is no liability to the true owner, then the full measure of damages—the total fair market value of the bailed chattel— might more equitably be given to the finder or prior possessor. *The Winkfield* 42 (1901). There is no problem of the bailee's paying twice for his conversion, and the judgment will still hopefully deter wrongdoing. For example, the postal service can recover for a conversion of the mails, even though it has by statute no liability to persons who post letters. There is a strong policy to deter wrongdoing where the mail is concerned. Where deterring the conversion is an overriding goal of the law, a bailee can recover the full value of the chattel even though the bailee has no liability even to his bailor. A bailment in which the public has an interest gets special protection.

V. THE *ARMORY* RULE IN REPLEVIN ACTIONS

1. Who Is the "True Owner"?

What if the prior possessor has found the party with possession of the chattel which he claims? A suit in replevin is likely to follow if the chattel has increased in value or when the prior possessor for whatever reason wants it back.

The *Armory* case was a trover action in which the plaintiff merely had to show his prior possession of the chattel to receive damages. If his suit had been in replevin, would he have had to make more than a showing of prior possession? In replevin, after all, he is asking to get possession of the chattel itself. To obtain possession, would he have to show title to the chattel?

To answer this question, one must resolve an ambiguity in the *Armory* rule to the effect that the prior possessor has a right to retain a chattel against all "but the rightful owner." What does the last, quoted phrase mean?

When the cause of action is in replevin, at least three meanings, two substantive and one procedural, are possible. (The two substantive ones are discussed in this section, the procedural one in the next.) First, that when two possessors or convertors of a chattel are litigating their rights, the prior possessor among them, although he recovers in the present litigation, would have to yield the recovered possession only to the person who can show title to the chattel. Such a result makes the phrase "true owner" the equivalent of any person who proves title to the chattel. Given the doctrine of relativity of right worked out for the phrase "prior possessor", however, it is inconsistent to make one part of the *Armory* rule a relative matter of prior right, referring to and protecting every prior possessor, and now give the phrase "true owner" an absolutist cast by saying that it refers to the one person who has a deed or bill of sale for the chattel.

Instead, it is wiser to keep these two parts of the *Armory* rule consistent, by assigning a second meaning to the phrase "true owner". That is, any person who has a right of possession arising prior in time to the two possessors or converters litigating their own rights; anyone in the chain of possession prior to them is a true owner as to them.

Not only is the second meaning in keeping with the doctrine of relativity of title or right, it also avoids one further difficulty, for, although there is some authority for the first meaning, its acceptance would mean that any later litigation in replevin—and even any second litigation between possessors of a chattel—might require a showing of good title, as opposed to a right of possession. This heightened standard of proof would not only be inconsistent with the relativity in the *Armory* rule, it would also make righting the converter's wrong that much harder. For that reason, the authority to support it is slight. Any possessor, whether a finder, bailee, or even a tort feasor, has a better right to the possession of a chattel than a person who converts or seizes it from him. If the law is to discourage an endless series of such seizures, it must respect the right of the prior possessor and validate those rights even when the latter cannot show good title. *Anderson v. Gouldberg* (1892).

These different meanings can however be fused into one rule, using the mechanisms of modern pleading and a legal presumption. It is generally presumed that the prior possessor prevails over subsequent possessors because he holds the title of a true owner, but in a replevin action in which the defendant, although he is a person further along on the chain of possession than the plaintiff, can produce proof that he stands in the shoes of the true owner, or can interplead the true owner, the plaintiff's claim in replevin is defeated. Compare *Anderson v. Gouldberg* (1892) with *Russell v. Hill* (1900), to which this discussion will soon turn.

2. The Defense of Jus Tertii

The *Armory* court could thirdly have had a more procedural meaning in mind for the phrase "all but the rightful owner". It could have meant that its rule applies "except when the title to the chattel is at issue". This of course admits of the possibility that, if the state of the title is injected into litigation between possessors, such evidence is admissible.

What if the defendant can easily identify the true owner, and in fact produces a deed showing that the title to the chattel is in this true owner, who is none-the-less not before the court? In this instance, where the deed shows that the title is in another, but does not convey the chattel to the defendant, the deed should be inadmissible because it is not relevant to the relative merits of the claims of two (or however many are litigating) possessors. To permit the latter type of deed to influence the outcome of a replevin action would be to allow a party to litigation to plead the weaknesses in his opposite number's claim, instead of doing what he is presumably best able to do: plead the strengths and merits of his own claim.

This inadmissible claim is known as a defense of *jus tertii*, a Latin phrase for "the right of a third party." It is the claim that neither party to the litigation, but rather an absent third party, is the true owner. However, the defense can only be considered when the true owner has a right to bring the same lawsuit which the plaintiff filed. Ruling the defense inadmissible is based on a rule of judicial prudence not to determine the rights of parties not before the court. Moreover in our legal system, this prudence is constitutionally grounded in the due process clauses of Federal and state constitutions.

Rejecting this third meaning saves the proof of title for litigation in which the person with title is actually before the court. Moreover, questions of title to personal property typically present difficulties of proof. No title records are maintained (automobile titles excepted) and proof depends on bills of sale, cancelled checks, and the testimony of witnesses. Thus plaintiffs should be relieved, it is argued, of the burden of proving title in personal property cases.

Another, historical reason for denying a defense of *jus tertii* has to do with theories of trover and conversion previously discussed. The necessary allegations included one to the effect that the plaintiff, possessing a chattel, lost it. A person cannot lose a thing without first being in possession of it and so trover and conversion came to be called possessory actions—a remedy for an interference with possession, rather than title.

As previously noted, it is often said, when rejecting a *jus tertii* defense, that possession is presumptive of title. What is meant is that prior possession is presumptive of title, and this in turn, typically means that the prior possessor is in the best position to settle or litigate title issues with the true owner should he appear. Perhaps also the prior possessor is better positioned than a later possessor to know of the initial conversion which took the chattel out of the true owner's hands.

Whatever the justification—and whether it is intended to protect the true owner, protect the courts from difficult choices, or simply to protect prior possession and keep the peace—a majority of American jurisdictions consistently reject the *jus tertii* defense: thus the defendant in replevin, trover, or conversion may not introduce evidence of a third party's title to converted chattels, unless that defendant is claiming that his or her own rights are derived from that third party. The weight of precedent for this rejection is overwhelming.

A famous 1856 English case has provided an illustration. *Jefferies v. Great Western Railway* (1856). It involves an action of trover "for trucks" or the frame with two pairs of wheels used to support one end of a railroad car. The plaintiff purchased the trucks from a bankrupt who, while still in possession of them, made a second assignment of his right to them to the defendant. The latter took them out of the plaintiff's possession and when sued attempted to argue that the creditors of the bankrupt were the true owners. The court rejected the defense: the defense of *jus tertii* is impermissible unless the defendant had evidence showing that his right derived from the creditors. See also *New England Box Company v. C & R Construction Co.* (1943), for a more recent illustration of the same ruling.

A consistent rejection of the defense of *jus tertii* permits the standard for measuring the sufficiency of the complaint in both trover and replevin actions to remain constant. This also makes a virtue out of the problem in the two cases discussed in the next section.

3. Two Leading Cases

When the *Armory* rule is stated more broadly, it is sometimes said that "possession gives rise to a presumption of title". North Carolina had such a proposition in its case law, derived from the case of *Barwick v. Barwick* (1850) (a trover action for two slaves which the plaintiff had purchased from a remainderman while the life tenant was still alive; the defendants claimed the slaves under a later purchase from the same remainderman; held, a jury instruction that prior possession in the plaintiff was sufficient to maintain the action was found in error).

Having this broader statement of *Armory* in the case law, the later North Carolina case of *Russell v. Hill* (1900) concluded that when the title to the chattel in dispute was shown to be in another, the plaintiff's action in trover could not be maintained. *Russell* concerned timber cut on land which had been sold twice, that is, granted to two adverse parties by the state land office. The parties' land grants, as shown on their respective deeds, overlapped. The plaintiff was a logger who had the misfortune to be logging with the permission of the second grantee. The first grantee was not a party to this litigation which the logger brought after the defendants not only took possession of the logs but also sold them to a lumber company which was insolvent at the time of the litigation. The defendants were thus convertors of the logs and lacked any title or right, from the first grantee or anyone else, to do what they did.

In *Russell,* the second grantee with whose permission the plaintiff logged the land, was not in possession of the land. (And no question of constructive possession was argued so far as the court opinion reflects—such an argument would have been a weak one in any event because the second grantee lacked priority of title under the state's recording act.)

At trial, "the defendant showed no title in himself, but proved the plaintiff's lack of title". There is no discussion of the *jus tertii* defense in this case, so that one can only assume it was not raised. Instead, the court defines the action in trover in terms of an analogy to the action of ejectment for real property. Both, it said, require title. Why? Because trover is a forced sale and the plaintiff has to have the title to sell when the judgment is paid.

There is much wrong with this analysis. First, the rule that "possession is presumptive of title" is not so much a rule as a rationale for a rule of prior possession which makes the proof of who holds title irrelevant. Second, if trover is indeed a forced sale, it is the legal fiction and a slim reed on which to base a decision. Third, the analogy between ejectment and trover is questionable. Real property titles are more carefully researched, guarded, and are matters of public record than titles to many types of personalty. It is more reasonable to expect litigants to be conversant with the state of title to real property with which they are concerned than they would be with personalty.

But the final and dispositive argument for the *Russell* court is the possibility of double liability for the convertor who pays a trover judgment, receives the plaintiff's rights in the timber, but is still forced to pay the timber's value a second time to the true owner who later sues. Protection against multiple liability is perhaps the most cited rationale for accepting a *jus tertii* defense.

A close reading of the *Armory* opinion provides another justification for this acceptance. There, the defendant produced no evidence identifying the true owner, so that accepting the defense is not prohibited by the opinion.

Under the facts of *Russell v. Hill*, the result there may be justified, because the true owner is known. He is an adjoining landowner. He is nearby and his proximity makes the concern of the *Armory* court a real one.

Yet even if the court had a good reason for holding as it did, it did too much. Its holding (that trover requires proof of title) is overbroad. It need not have redefined the cause of action brought to accommodate its law to the problem of the defendant's possible double liability. All it need have done was to hold that where the true owner is reasonably certain to learn of the defendant's conversion (in this instance, through proximity or court records), the defense of *jus tertii* is permissible and proof of the state of the title admissible.

This is a more functional rule, perhaps it is even more efficient, in terms of judicial resources, and when combined with a procedural rule permitting interpleader of the true owner by the defendant, will more completely adjudicate issues concerning the disputed chattel. If the defendant can have interpleader and fails to utilize it against a known true owner, a court might reasonably conclude that he has assumed the risk of double liability.

A final rationale for accepting a *jus tertii* defense may be found in a situation in which the police raid and search a plaintiff's residence, finding stolen personal property in the process. When the police refuse to return it to its prior possessor, should they be permitted to prove that they know the true owner before retaining possession or being forced to respond to the plaintiff in damages for trover and conversion? (The latter action is unlikely to succeed when the police act under a proper search warrant and are otherwise immune, as agents of the state, from such judgments; so the replevin action is more likely.) One Indiana intermediate appellate court thought that the answer was yes and accepted a *jus tertii* defense from the police. *Noble v. Moistner* (1979) (finding that no criminal charges had been filed in connection with the chattel that the police alleged to be stolen property). Perhaps, when possible under applicable procedure rules, a compulsory joinder of the third party the police allege to be the true owner, should also be considered at the time a court accepts the defense. Note, *Jus Tertii* As A Defense

to Conversion Suits in Indiana—Towards A More
Rational Approach, 18 Val.U.L.Rev. 415 (1984).

In a replevin action in which logs were again at
issue, but in which the land from which the logs
came was in dispute, another court applied the
Armory rule. *Anderson v. Gouldberg* (1892). This
was litigation between two converters of ninety-
three logs of branded timber. The plaintiffs cut
the timber. They never showed that they did so
with permission. The defendants took possession
of the logs at a mill site in the name of (they
claimed) their true owners. The court instructed
the jury that even if the plaintiffs were trespassers
when cutting the logs, they were entitled to recover them from later possessors, the true owner or
one acting for him excepted. The court left it to
the jury whether the logs were cut and claimed as
defendants said. The jury found for the plaintiffs.
The trial court denied a defense motion for a new
trial.

The defendants appealed, but the Minnesota Supreme Court affirmed. It held that the plaintiff's
bare possession, "though wrongfully obtained," was
sufficient to maintain replevin against a mere
stranger who takes it from him.

The Minnesota court's version of the *Armory*
rule is a slight rewording of the original. The
Armory court never said anything about "wrongfully" obtaining the chattel. And its rule was used in
a trover action, not (as here) replevin. But the
second objection is a minor matter because if the

Minnesota court is willing to grant judgment in replevin on proof of bare possession and one of its sister states is *not* willing to grant trover on similar proof, then something is wrong: it takes less to get the thing back than it does to sell it. This is a strange and inconsistent result.

One explanation is that in *Anderson* the true owner seemed remote and unlikely to sue while in *Russell* he was known and likely to find out about who damaged his land. The jury in *Anderson* found that the logs were not cut on the land the defendants claimed, but that jury never did say where the logs were cut. Their ultimate ownership remained undetermined.

Perhaps one can see the benefits of deciding as the *Anderson* court did if one assumes the worst. Let's do that. It is often said that the rule in *Armory* protects the "prior peaceful possession" of a chattel. What does peaceful mean? Would this reformulation deny the benefit of the *Armory* rule to a thief or other willful convertor of a chattel? Probably not. One must ask, "peaceful" as to whom? If the litigation is concerned with a dispute between two possessors, the first's possession is peaceful in relation to the second's conversion of the disputed matter. There the "peaceful" repose of the chattel is relative and the word is superfluous in any restatement of the rule of prior possession or the doctrine of the relativity of title.

But why should not even a thief have the benefit of the *Armory* rule if he can show himself as a prior possessor? On the equities, it is easier for a court to formulate a "prior possessor wins" rule for a prior possessor who is a finder—as in _Armory_— than it is to reach the same result when he is just as much a convertor of the chattel as is the defendant—as in _Anderson._ If O's chattel is converted by A, who is then subjected to its seizure by B, the two conversions present just the sort of successive seizures or uses of force that the _Armory_ rule— read as protecting prior possessors and not just finders—was intended to prevent. _Anderson_'s reformulation of the rule makes this plain. In the hypothetical, A should have judgment against B. Better to deter the last conversion than to encourage both of the conversions involved. Even if A and B are thieves, O is not likely to benefit from one or another of the two of them having possession (if the suit is in replevin); nor is O likely to be injured by a sale of A's rights in a forced sale (in trover, fenced or "as is" goods seldom bring full market value, so the possible double liability is less injurious, and if B is a willful convertor or thief, who cares whether a thief pays twice anyway?) Moreover, if A and B's conversions are criminal in nature, their thievery is the concern of the criminal law and so long as a rule of the civil law does not encourage crime, it should be enforced.

So even if a bad guy wants replevin, he should obtain it upon a showing of prior possession. _Russell_ is aberrational, and is in fact a minority rule. _Anderson_ seems the best use of the _Armory_ rule and best result: a plaintiff can maintain both

trover and replevin with a showing of prior possession peacefully maintained as against his defendant.

Anderson, however, has its limiting facts. It was
a case between two converters—that is, between
two persons equally in the wrong. That has
turned out to be a rare situation in the annals of
reported cases. R.H. Helmholz, Wrongful Possession of Chattels: Hornbook Law and Case Law, 80
Nw.U.L.Rev. 1221, 1225–1226 (1986) (discussing the
cases and arguing that the true rule is: "What a
man has acquired illegally he cannot replevy.").

A final, more general question arises as to
whether the law should endorse a rule that appears amoral. A pawn broker should have a sufficient property interest to bring a replevin action
and in it might use the *Anderson* rule to recover
chattels, even though they have been reported stolen. *Wolfenbarger v. Williams* (1987). A gambler,
however, probably can't replevy illegal winnings
seized by the police, nor a thief the property stolen.
Helmholz, op. cit., at 1125. Likewise, the winner
and the loser in an illegal gaming operation could
not use the *Anderson* rule to settle their dispute
over the winnings. They might indeed each have a
property interest in the winnings, but only for the
purpose of showing their participation in the illegal game and then their interest would become the
basis of their conviction for violation of an anti-
gambling statute, not a ground for the recovery of
the property.

VI. THE PROBLEM OF SUCCESSIVE FINDERS

The earliest, leading American case reciting and applying the rule of *Armory* occurred in litigation between two finders of property. *Clark v. Maloney* (1840). There, the plaintiff found ten white pine logs floating in the Delaware Bay. This was like finding the logs on a public highway—no trespass would be involved in taking possession of the logs by the plaintiffs. Plaintiff made this find after a freshet—a sudden rise in the level of the Bay due to a flood, the melting of snow or ice, or heavy rains, often in the eighteenth and nineteenth centuries made worse by the deforestation of the land in the watershed. The plaintiff moored the logs with ropes at the mouth of Mispillion creek. The defendants later found the same logs adrift floating up that same creek.

With no explanation as to how the defendants came to take possession of the logs, the plaintiff sued the defendants in trover, premised on the defendants' conversion of the logs, rather than trespass, which would require that the plaintiff allege facts showing how the defendant came to take possession. So the plaintiff's choice of trover and conversion over trespass as his cause of action for the present facts seems right.

If the case is viewed in this light, and it is remembered that two finders are litigating their relative rights here, *Clark* is a better case for the application of the rule of prior possession than was *Armory*. The latter case, after all, involved a finder/bailor and his bailee and so the court could have fallen back on a contract of bailment as dispositive of the case before it. Here, where two finders are litigating and no proven facts link their possession of the disputed chattel, the rule of prior possession is necessary to dispose of the case. As between successive finders, the rule here is that the first prevails where the first has not abandoned the chattel in dispute. If there were an abandonment by the first finder or his transferee, the second finder would prevail.

The plaintiff, as the prior possessor of the logs, won the case. Why? Because "possession is *prima facie* evidence of property". The court means that possession creates a presumption that the possessor has the title to the chattel possessed. This presumption is a mandatory one when the only evidence introduced at trial establishes prior possession, but it is also a rebuttable one, and "may be rebutted by evidence of better title, but in the absence of better title it is as effective a support of title as the most conclusive evidence could be." Why so? Because of the *Armory* rule, which the court goes on to recite. In other words, this court's statement of the doctrine of relativity of title is phrased in terms of a legal presumption which in the context of this litigation, cannot really be rebutted and is justified by a substantive statement of the same doctrine. All this rephrasing amounts to a non-sequitur, not a justification. Or, to put this analytical process in its best light, it shows the close relationship between legal rules and legal presumptions. (This closeness we will discuss again in our discussion of commercial bailments in Chapter VI.) Unlike the *Russell* court, this court does not require a title to the disputed chattel in order to file a cause of action in trover. Its talk of "better title" can, as before, be recast into "relatively better title" terms and the doctrine of relativity of title.

Why does the court talk of a "property" in the logs? First of all, this word reflects the *Armory* rule, but the *Clark* court needs a word which encompasses both its talk of a "better title" and a "presumption of title" as well as a right of prior possession in the logs. This ambiguity may once more be evidence of a concern that the last finder may have a double liability: once as the defendant in this litigation and again when and if the true owner or possessor with rights prior to the plaintiff's finds out about his conversion and sues him for it. The word "property" avoids a clear reference to title but may mean more than a right of possession. When it is remembered that this court restates the *Armory* rule in terms of a legal presumption of title, one reason for this rephrasing becomes clear. If a judgment in trover is a forced sale of the plaintiff's presumed title to the logs and if it turns out that the plaintiff does not have title and the true owner shows up to sue the defendant again, he can use the plaintiff's warranty of title made or implied in the course of the forced sale as a basis for a suit against the first finder.

Maybe this double liability problem for the defendant did not in fact worry the court. There may be some feature of the legal arrangements involved in the logging industry around the Delaware Bay at the time of the case, that would solve this problem. If the true owner of the logs followed an industry practice of himself floating the logs to the sawmill, then the problem remains. But if the practice was otherwise and the true owner had given possession of the logs to a river-driving company, or they floated away from the sawmill's holding pond, a quite different situation arises. In each of the latter instances, the owner has created a bailment with the river-driver or the mill operator and can hold that party responsible for the loss of the logs. Each of these bailees will be responsible for the conversion involved in his failing to deliver the logs back to the bailor and because bailor and bailee are by definition known to each other, the true owner will in all probability be compensated for his loss by a suit against his bailee and be barred from any further recovery from the defendant.

Defendants' counsel was evidently working on a parallel argument and thinking in general terms about the finder (any finder) as a bailee for the true owner. He argued that, in the case of a "special property, it must be accompanied by possession to support trover." What was the plaintiff's "special property?" That term was often used in the 19th century and is still used today to denote the interest of a bailee in the chattel entrusted to him by the bailor, as opposed to the "general" property of the bailor. So special property was usually a reference to a bailee's limited rights in a chattel, while general property is the bailor's title as well as his right to future possession.

If the first finder is the equivalent of a nonconsensual bailee of the true owner, however, his trover suit against a second finder may be a violation of the terms of the bailment, and the forced sale resulting from it is a conversion of the true owner's general property in the chattel, on the basis of which conversion the true owner can later sue. Moreover, even if the first finder were viewed as a bailee, he cannot transfer any more than his "special property" to the second finder as the result of a trover suit. No such transfer of rights in trover will render the second finder immune later from the true owner's suit. The reference to a "special property" is a way of safeguarding the true owner's "general property" and his continuing right to sue both finders.

The second finder might also argue that he is as good a bailee as the first finder and as capable as the latter of holding the chattel for the true owner. The rule of prior possession will, however, lead a court to reject this argument since the first finder evidently crossed the track of the true owner at the location of the loss. This intersection might mean that the true owner was more likely to locate the first finder than he would any successor. But the "intersection" theory does not work well here where the logs are floating in a large tidal body of water. At this point the second finder might want to interject a factual note to the effect that few true owners, in fact, repossess their lost or misplaced chattel and that letting the chattel stay with the last finder gives the true owner, if and when he ever does show up, a clear option of suing the last finder in either trover or replevin. This choice will be denied him if the plaintiff wins, unless the double liability of the last finder is still possible. With this, the defendants may have argued too much, having in the course of his argument justified his possible double liability as a means to protect the true owner.

After all, this double liability of the second finder is a method of protecting the true owner's title. The *Clark* opinion acknowledges as much: " ... it is a well-settled rule of law that the loss of a chattel does not change the right of property; and for the same reason that the original loss of these logs by the rightful owner, did not change his absolute property in them, but he might have maintained trover against the plaintiff upon refusal to deliver them, so the subsequent loss did not divest the special property of the plaintiff." This recognition that the true owner's title is not defeated by subsequent possessors—even when they possess in good faith—again leaves open the possibility that the defendant may be liable to the owner again, and be forced to give up the logs in a replevin action or pay for them twice if the owner brings trover.

In the end the court probably means to leave this question of double liability open, as it was not before the court and then as now no reported cases resolved the problem for finders. It also leaves open the status of a finder as a bailee, but one should not necessarily assume that the law limits bailment to consensual arrangements—as we will discuss in the next two chapters. In the context of the *Clark* case, assuming that a bailment arises is one way of protecting the true owner's rights because a bailment relationship between the owner and a finder would impose a duty of reasonable care of the found object on the finder. If (say) a boat, rather than logs were adrift in the Delaware Bay, the boat owner might well be presumed to be willing to pay for a finder's reasonable expenses in preserving the boat and the finder could presumably be given a duty to take reasonable steps to preserve the boat for its owner. So too with the logs.

One reason for keeping the possibility of double liability open for a future court is that different types of defendants might be accorded different treatment. In the case of finders, the finder who earnestly searches for the true owner might escape double liability, while the more secretive finder who conducts no search would not.

The defendants might still argue that one of the policies underlying a rule of prior possession is inapplicable as between two finders. That is, finders are seldom visible as such, particularly to other "finders" and would-be convertors, except at the time and place of the find. Because finders do not stand out in a crowd, justifying a rule of prior possession as a way of avoiding an endless series of forceful conversions makes little sense. Indeed, the development of the forms of action from trespass to conversion underlines this point. In cases in which a crowd does not gather around the finder and threatens him or the public peace, and specifically in *Clark* where the logs are floating around the Bay and up an adjacent creek and are seemingly picked up at isolated locations, this justification for a rule of prior possession seems inapplicable. Applying the rule here will not prevent an endless series of muggings, and some less extreme justification must be sought. This search in *Clark* produced the idea that protecting the prior possessor protects a true owner's title and right.

1. The Measure of Damages in *Clark*

Another question which the court might have asked itself is whether it would be reasonable for the true owner, in the process of floating logs to the sawmill, to sue the last known convertor of the logs. The measure of damages for trover will be the value of the logs at the nearest convenient market, less the cost of transportation to that market. The logs are, in other words, more valuable at the sawmill site or other marketplace, so that the amount of a judgment for which the convertor is liable to the true owner, decreases the further the place of a find or the place at which the conversion takes place, is from the sawmill. This would mean that, in the usual case, the true owner would have a stronger incentive to sue either the log-driving company or the mill operator, the two bailees named previously, than he would to sue either of the two finders. This is economically rational because the bailees have a duty to deliver the logs from the bailment at the sawmill, a site at which the logs have a value higher than they do at a point of conversion more removed from the mill.

A second measure of damages issue is raised when one considers that the chattels involved are only identified as "ten white pine logs"—not an unusual type of wood and probably not so special as to identify them as the property of any particular logger. If identification of the owner was possible from the type of log or from any distinctive marking on them, as in *Anderson*, the defendants' conversion of them would seem less innocent. Pointing to the lack of evidence of a fraudulent conversion of the logs and the fact that innocent defendants often are permitted a reduced measure of damages in some areas of law, the defendants might argue for a reduced measure of damages, using the value of the logs as standing timber. This argument would be rejected. Why? Because standing timber are part of the real property on which they are located and there can be no conversion of real property because by definition this cause of action applies only to personalty. Moreover, both finders treated the logs as personalty. So the measure of damages for a conversion would have to reflect the value of labor that converted this portion of the real property into personalty. Their value as personalty, then, provides the measure of damages for the defendant's conversion. This value is measured by the value of the logs at the nearest convenient market for such logs, less the cost of transporting the logs to that market from the site of the defendant's conversion of them. This is not the site at which the plaintiffs moored the logs, but the place at which the defendants took possession of them. It was at that point that they committed their conversion against the plaintiff.

2. Salvage Rights

If the creek up which the logs floated into the defendants' possession were navigable, then the defendants may assert a right of salvage. The salvor's status has been awarded to persons clearing logs out of a navigable waterway or harbor; it can here be used to reduce the damages payable by the defendants to the plaintiff by way of a set-off against the amount of the plaintiff's judgment. The rights of salvors are discussed in somewhat more detail in Chapter V.

VII. CONCLUSION

In *Armory, Russell, Anderson,* and *Clark,* the holdings seem formulated in recognition of the fact that the true owner is not deprived of his right or title no matter how many converters subsequently possess the chattel. All these courts have gone to subtle lengths to anticipate the problem of double liability. One method of solving the problem and still maintaining the rule of prior possession is to recognize the trespass or tort aspect of the action in trover and measure the damages which the plaintiff incurred rather than permitting him to sue for the value of the chattel. The greater the likelihood that the true owner would turn up in a litigious mood, the deeper the discount when otherwise the plaintiff in trover would obtain a judgment for the full market value of the converted chattel.

All of these cases have been analyzed in this chapter in such a way as to protect the true owner's rights because he is the ultimate beneficiary of a rule of prior possession and the doctrine of relativity of title. There is, however, another reason for forcing your mind not to dwell on the chattel involved in each case but to ponder instead the range of persons who might have rights in the thing. Not to explore the diverse individual interests involved is to deny the law its full scope. Property law first and foremost serves people, not things.

CHAPTER V

FINDERS

I. WHO IS A FINDER?

The popular maxim, "finders keepers, losers weepers," overstates what we learned in the last chapter. The nineteenth century version—"losers seekers, finders keepers"—perhaps comes closer to the legal truth of the matter, and a much, much older Latin version of the maxim states, *habeus ut nanctus*—translated as, he keeps that finds—has an even more matter-of-fact ring.

By finding a chattel, a person acquires, as we saw in the last chapter, a qualified right of possession to it. As an early English opinion states: "he which findes goods, is bound to answer him for them who hath the property." *Isaack v. Clark* (1615). To acquire this right, the person must, as a threshold matter, qualify as a finder. The rules of law which qualify him may be paraphrased from our discussion of wild animals in the first chapter: there must be an intent to control the chattel on the part of the finder, and there must also be an act of control over it as well.

Recall the *Eads* case: plaintiff marked the location of a wreck of a Mississippi steamboat, sunk some thirty years previously, by attaching buoys to it. He intended to return the next day to raise the cargo, but was detained on business so that when he returned defendant was in the process of raising the cargo for himself. Plaintiff sought and received a trial court injunction restraining defendant from interfering further with the plaintiff and was awarded damages as well, but on appeal this injunction and award were reversed. *Eads v. Brazelton* (1861).

Attaching a buoy to the wreck gives no notice to others that the plaintiff intended to appropriate the cargo and its attachment to the wreck similarly is not the equivalent of actual control over that cargo. The court suggests that if the plaintiff had kept his boat over the wreck, he might have been able to show an intent to control the cargo; although he would still lack actual control in that instance, his "act of possession need not have been manual".

The situation of the wrecked steamboat is but one instance of the judicial requirement that to qualify as a finder, a person must be very close to actual possession of the chattel at issue. A chattel located inside another object—such as a stocking, a safe, or a bureau—is not found until an actual discovery of the valuable item is made. The discoverer then becomes the finder. Moreover, a discovery can be made by more than one person. Where one of several boys picks up an old stocking and the boys play catch with it until it breaks open in the hands of one of them, revealing $800 in currency, the money belongs not to the boy who first treated the stocking as a plaything, but to all the boys scrambling as a group for the money in it. *Keron v. Cashman* (1896). Similarly, a person buying a safe or bureau and later leaving it with another for resale, without discovering, as the sales agent does, that it has a hidden drawer containing money, is not entitled to the money. *Durfee v. Jones* (1877). There must be an actual discovery by the person or persons who claim the chattel as a finder. No constructive finding of a chattel is possible.

Similarly, there must be an intent to control the discovered chattel in order to qualify as a finder. If the boys who used the stocking as a plaything had sought parental advice, it could be argued that they *and* their families "found" the money because their intent to appropriate it was incomplete before their parents recognized their rights in it. *Edmonds v. Ronella* (1973).

Thus the act of possession must at minimum be sufficient to warn off subsequent possessors and put them on notice of the prior find. With a small, portable, chattel, only actual possession is likely to accomplish this. *Lawrence v. Buck* (1874). The first finder with an intent to control and who actually seizes control, has the right of possession prior to all others in the process of finding the same chattel.

II. BARRING THE TRUE OWNER'S RIGHT

The taking of possession by the finder must be done openly. Were the law otherwise, finders would never be able to run the applicable Statute of Limitations for personal property against the right of the true owner to bring a replevin or trover action and no finders would acquire title by adverse possession. To run the Statute the finder must possess the found chattel as openly as its normal use would permit. Its later sale, or use as collateral for a loan, may be evidence that it was so used and is certainly evidence of a conversion of the chattel as against the true owner. The finder's becoming a convertor at the time of the find or later clearly starts to run the Statute.

III. THE FINDER'S RIGHT

We have seen that, as a prior possessor, the finder of a chattel has rights in the chattel superior to all subsequent finders or possessors but inferior to possessors prior to him and the rightful or true owner. So his rights are, for example, superior to someone with whom he leaves the goods for safekeeping, e.g., a bailee. These are the facts, you'll remember, of *Armory,* discussed in the last chapter. His rights are also superior to those of a second finder and a subsequent converter of the chattel. *Anderson v. Gouldberg* (1892) (trespassing loggers had a better right to possession of logs than defendants who took possession at sawmill), whose rule was discussed in the last chapter as well.

When a claimant has not been in actual control of the chattel but asserts the same rights in it that would follow or be inferred from its actual control, those rights involve the concept of constructive possession on which may be based prior rights— prior, that is, to the finder's. The prime example of such a claimant might be the owner of the *locus in quo*—the Latin phrase for the land on which the chattel is found.

Defining who is the owner of the *locus in quo*, is sometimes difficult. Where for example a landlord claims personal property from a finder who has found it on leased premises, the landlord must typically show that the tenant has abandoned or otherwise relinquished his or her right to it. *State v. Green* (1984). Thus the owner of the *locus in quo* is a person in possession or entitled to the present possession of the property on which the find is made. A landlord is only entitled to future possession of the property—after the tenant's lease expires—and so only qualifies in the absence of the tenant's right.

For the owner of the place of the finding to claim to be in constructive possession of a chattel of which, in most cases, he was unaware at the time of finding, is oft-times presumptuous and would probably strike most courts as just that. In this connection, it is all too easy to slip the adjective "lost" into a restatement of the *Armory* rule, so that it becomes, "a finder has a right in a lost chattel superior to all the world except the true owner." Lost? By whom? If the answer is the true owner and if thereafter the owner of the *locus in quo* claims that awarding him possession of the chattel will best serve the true owner's recovery of it, he has outfitted his claim with a rationale that sounds less presumptuous and at the same time introduces an element of public policy into the court's consideration of the relative rights of the finder as against those of the owner of the *locus in quo*. (For our purposes the finder will be designated as F and such owner will be O).

O's claim, viewed as a matter of the law of "possession", is that he had prior, constructive possession at the time the finder claims his (the finder's) rights arose. But if this were acceptable to the courts, O would always win under a rule of prior possession. However, in *Armory,* the finder of the jewel won. So the facts of that case must, so far as O is concerned, be distinguished. There is no discussion of the place of the find in the opinion in *Armory*. Therefore, argues O, the court must have found it unimportant. So it was, when one considers that the litigation in *Armory* involved a finder and a subsequent convertor of the chattel. Here O is no such bad actor. Rather, O is a person who only wants to serve the interests of the true owner.

In some instances, and depending on the place of the finding, he is also a person who has expectations of his own and asks the law to protect them. A home owner may quite naturally expect that anything found in his house is his, regardless of whether he knows that the chattel is there beforehand. But see *Hurley v. City of Niagara Falls* (1967). This expectation follows from his idea that his home is a private place from which he has the right to exclude whomever he chooses. The owner of a garden or cropland may have some similar expectations. The owner of unimproved woodland would not.

The person asserting the rights of an owner of the *locus in quo* need not be in present possession. A former owner of the real property may be in as good a position as the present owner to know who the true owner of the found chattel is. However, a purchaser of the real property with an equitable title to the land under a contract of sale would not just by executing that contract acquire constructive possession of the find. *Willsmore v. Oceola Township* (1981).

A. PUBLIC/PRIVATE PLACE OF THE FIND

When a chattel is found in a place which is public (e.g., a department store aisle), F has a right prior to O, for in this situation O would have no expectation of constructive possession and would not have any duty to safeguard the chattel for its true owner. Further, as the true owner is unlikely to leave the chattel in a public place, he is presumed to have lost it there. *Pyle v. Springfield Marine Bank* (1946); Paset v. Old Orchard Bank and Trust Co. (1978).

If, however, the place of finding is private, O will have the prior right. This decision fulfills his expectations about private places and avoids rewarding a trespassing finder. Second, it recognizes the possibility that the true owner's leaving the chattel there established an implied bailment. Third, it rests on the assumption that if the true owner placed the chattel on private property, he did so intentionally, will be able to remember its location, and will return to reclaim it. In this instance, the goods are not merely lost but instead are mislaid.

B. LOST/ABANDONED/MISLAID CHATTEL

The distinction between lost and mislaid goods was early culled from F v. O cases and elaborated on, until it became an all or nothing proposition for both litigants. *Bridges v. Hawkesworth* (1851). If the chattel were lost, F won because there was no sense allowing O to take custody to hold it for the true owner's return. The latter would be unlikely to retrace his steps and reclaim it. On the other hand, if the chattel were mislaid, the true owner was likely to retrace and reclaim. *McAvoy v. Medina* (1866) (owner of a shop awarded property found there); *Ray v. Flower Hospital* (1981) (jewels found in eyeglass case on top of hospital information desk by receptionist F found to have been mislaid and put into the possession of hospital O).

The lapse of time after the find is not relevant to the issue of whether the chattel is either lost or mislaid. However, in other cases, the chattel may be abandoned. Here the true owner is thought to remember where it is but to have given up his claim to it. Abandonment of a chattel works the same legal consequence as losing it: F obtains a judgment. *Schley v. Couch* (1955).

Another category of presumably long-abandoned personalty consists of "treasure trove." It consists of gold, silver, or bullion, secreted in the ground, and is treated as if it too were a lost or abandoned chattel. Because of its negotiable nature, the policy is to return it to circulation and the finder, being encouraged to do this, is awarded the prior right in it. This fourth category is discussed more fully later in this chapter.

In the lost/mislaid/abandoned chattel cases, there is some discussion of giving incentive to the finder to return the chattel to circulation and the societal value of doing this. It is doubtful, however, except perhaps in the case of professional treasure hunters in search of treasure trove, that this policy can be implemented because finding is by definition a fortuitous event. The overriding distinction between cases holding for F and those for O is a determination of which of the two is in best position to return the chattel to the true owner.

Courts do this by hypothesizing the state of mind of the true owner when he lost, mislaid, or abandoned the chattel. E.R. Cohen, "The Finders Cases Revisited", 48 Tex.L.Rev. 1001 (1970), elaborates on these judicial assumptions. His article is a good one.

In most situations, of course, the person in the better position will be O. If the true owner is going to retrace and reclaim, he will find himself once more on O's property. Harking back to an earlier chapter, *ratione soli* as a generalized application of the idea of constructive possession also supports O's claim. *South Staffordshire Water Co. v. Sharman* (1896).

Why then does not O always win?

One reason might be that F, upon locating the chattel, has also made his own search for the true owner, or had given the chattel over to those in a position to do this (e.g., the police). If this search has been reasonably vigorous and has gone on for a reasonably long period of time, there is no reason to award the chattel to O, unless his expectations about constructive possession of it are strong, as in instances in which F was a trespasser on O's land and O would not expect to find him on the *locus in quo*.

Unless then F defeats his own claim to having an honest intent to locate the true owner by being a trespasser and violating O's expectations at one and the same time, there is another reason for holding for F after he had made his own reasonable search for the true owner. That is, the true owner will never be located unless F turns the object over to someone in a position to know who the true owner is or to locate him. The whole search process will not even get started unless the finder is honest in the first instance. Where F identifies himself as a finder and searches publicly for the true owner, he should be rewarded for his honesty. *Hannah v. Peel* (1945).

IV. OTHER CATEGORIES

A. CHATTEL EMBEDDED IN OR ON TOP OF THE SOIL

An O in possession of and in control of real property has a prior possessory right to every chattel found embedded in the soil of that property. The rationale is that the embedded object is considered part of the soil itself. It need not be totally buried to be considered embedded for these purposes, so long as it is firmly affixed to the land. *Chance v. Certain Artifacts Found and Salvaged from The Nashville* (1984) (steamboat embedded in river bottom). Sometimes this distinction is related to the lost/mislaid one. In a case involving buried gold coins, it was said the embedding repels the idea that the coins were lost by the true owner. *Morgan v. Wiser* (1985). See also *Ritz v. Selma United Methodist Church* (1991). Other examples are a prehistoric boat or canoe of archeological value, mineral ore of various types, or a meteorite.

A chattel unconnected to the soil is F's by prior right.

B. SMALL/BULKY CHATTEL

An O in possession and control of real property similarly has a prior possessory right in a bulky chattel found on his land. If it is bulky enough to be immovable, then even though it is on top of the soil, it has become affixed to the land. The best example is a house. In legal parlance, this chattel has become a fixture—a chattel annexed to the real property and so necessary to its present use or functioning as an economic unit. A small chattel is not so connected or necessary, and F may have the prior right in it.

C. LIMITED ENTRY CASES

Finally, there is some authority for the proposition that, although F is not a trespasser and is properly on O's real property when he finds the chattel, he will not be found to have the prior right when he entered upon the land for a limited purpose. The leading case is *South Staffordshire Water Co. v. Sharman* (1896). F might be an employee of O's and so, at the time of the finding, his agent, with a duty to deliver the chattel over to his principal. *Morrison v. United States*, (1974) (involving a soldier finding money in Vietnam). A restaurant waiter finding a patron's pocketbook, a chamber maid cleaning a room in the hotel, a railroad conductor, a bank employee—if any of these people find a chattel on the premises of their employment, their duty is to turn it over to their employer. The place of finding is usually restricted in access to the general public, arguably qualifying it as a private place. More than that, however, is the possibility of fraudulent finding if the rule were otherwise. What's to prevent an employee from relocating the chattel to the nearest public space and "finding" it there if they could improve their rights in the object? *Flax v. Monticello Realty Co.* (1946).

Employees for purposes of this rule can be distinguished from independent contractors; the latter are persons hired to produce a service or product but not told how to go about it. Because their work methods are their own, their presence on the land is not attributable to O's direction and their finding is their own. *Erickson v. Sinykin* (1947) (involving an interior decorator). R.H. Helmholz, Equitable Division and the Law of Finders, 52 Ford.L.Rev. 313, 316–321 (1983) (providing an excellent review of cases on the various distinctions, decided since 1939).

D.   A COMMENT ON THE PLACE OF FINDING, TYPE OF GOODS, AND LIMITED ENTRY CASES

Whether a chattel is lost or mislaid, abandoned or mislaid, embedded or atop the soil, or small or bulky, the courts in F v. O cases are using these

labels to protect the interests of the true owner of
the chattel. The labels should not be taken as
ends in themselves; either they are aids to analysis
or they should be discarded. For example, with
the passage of time, a lost or abandoned chattel
can become embedded in the soil. If it is lost, it
usually is F's, but if it is also embedded—O's, so
the labelling process is not going to help. *Favorite
v. Miller* (1978) (concerning a Revolutionary War
era statue of George III dumped by the colonists in
a swamp).

Because winning or losing the law suit depends
on the label attached to the chattel and because
the rationale for the court's decision is the same
(that the true owner's recovery of the chattel is
furthered), the all or nothing outcome between F
and O seems inappropriate. Letting O hold custody of the chattel for the period during which the
true owner is reasonably likely to turn up and
giving custody (and really ultimate control) to F,
thereafter, seems more logical. This outcome gives
F incentive to report his find and start the search
process. See *Paset,* op. cit.

Giving ultimate control of the chattel to the
finder endorses his good luck. Who can tell how
deep such a response goes into the American
psyche? Good luck and good fortune have always
been attributes of a finder and when title to land
or some larger question is not present (*Goodard,*
discussed in Chapter III), American courts have
made distinctions and found ways to favor him as

well. When Tom Sawyer and Huckleberry Finn discuss where next to dig for the buried gold, Tom says:

"I reckon maybe we'll tackle the old tree that's over yonder on Cardiff Hill back of the widow's."

"I reckon that'll be a good one. But won't the widow take it away from us, Tom? It's on her land."

"*She* take it away! Maybe she'd like to try it once. Whoever finds one of these hid treasures, it belongs to him. It don't make any difference whose land it's on."

S.L. Clemens, The Adventures of Tom Sawyer, Ch. 25, "Seeking the Buried Treasure" (1876). Another interesting piece, based on the treasure hunt of Tom Sawyer, is Million, "*Sawyer et al. v. Administrator of Injun Joe*", 16 Mo.L.Rev. 27 (1951), a fictitious, annotated decision based on Tom's finding the gold in the haunted house; the decision goes for Tom and Huck who get to keep the gold. Nowhere in American law is a bias in favor of the finder more evident than in matters involving treasure trove, a category of personal property to which this discussion now turns. American courts have here turned the rule inherited from the English on its head.

E. TREASURE TROVE AND BURIED TREASURE

This is another—the fourth, after lost, mislaid, and abandoned—type of found personal property.

It refers to gold or silver coin, bullion, or money which has been concealed by the owner in a private place. *Morgan v. Wiser* (1985). It must have been concealed so long ago as to indicate that its owner is unknown or in all probability dead. If found buried in the earth, the rule in England was to award ownership to the Crown. Attorney General of the *Duchy of Lancaster v. G E Overton (Farms) Ltd.* (1980) (declaring that the royal prerogative was confined to articles of gold and silver).

The early assertion of a regal prerogative in treasure trove was the impetus for the judicial development of the law of lost and mislaid personalty as a method of limiting the Crown's claim. The governments of the United States, federal and state, have never asserted this sovereign prerogative and the law relating to this type of found property has been merged with the law of finders generally. Some jurisdictions hold that there is no such merger, but what emerges in many American courts is an attitude at least as favorable toward the finder as toward the landowner of the real property on which the treasure is found. Absent a statute *contra* on the subject most American courts declare that treasure trove belongs to its finder. Thus treasure trove is treated as a lost chattel, although the circumstances of its concealment indicate that it was not lost.

Treasure trove is personal property that has been concealed by its now-unknown owner. The concealment implies an intent on his part to keep the property from the rest of the world and like Bluebeard or Captain Kidd, to return for it. Where chattel are buried in a grave as part of a religious ritual or for use by the deceased in the nether world, there is no intention on the part of those who buried them to reclaim them and whether they can be considered treasure trove is in doubt. In one case emerging in its procedural outlines in the appellate reports of Louisiana, the graves were those of an American Indian tribe, now dispersed but still an identifiable group. A large quantity of artifacts were taken secretly from the graves by their finder, who did not own the *locus in quo*. The finder sued the owner of the *locus in quo* to quiet title to the artifacts; the State bought the *locus* and intervened; meanwhile, the artifacts were sold by the finder and shipped off to a university museum under a sales contract, indefinite as to the final price, which was subject to appraisal. *Charrier v. Bell* (1979), discussed in C. Trillin, "U.S. Journal: Louisiana, The Tunica Treasure," The New Yorker (July 27, 1981) at 41–51.

1. Wreck of the Sea, Salvage, and Sunken Treasure

Property of the type referred to as treasure trove is buried in the earth. Property lost at sea, but later washed ashore, is called "wreck of the sea" and the English Crown claimed that too. This regal prerogative was codified in 1275 A.D. By the time of our American Revolution, whether this applied to sunken treasure was disputed by the likes of Blackstone. The dispute was not settled by litigation (in favor of the Crown) until after the Revolution and so its resolution was not received as part of the English Common Law inherited by the United States.

Treasure recovered from the seabed is not technically "wreck of the sea", in that it has not been washed ashore. Sunken treasure, moreover, is not treasure trove unless the ship was scuttled by the former owner of the treasure to conceal it.

Increasing amounts of sunken treasure and under-sea artifacts, thought lost forever before recent technological advances in under-sea exploration, are being brought to the surface. Surfacing also are many legal problems involved in their recovery, problems not unlike those discussed previously in this book. Jurisdictional problems come first: when the treasure has antiquarian value and the state has asserted regulatory power over a recovery within its coastal or inland waters, the state may be an indispensable party to litigation over the treasure not conducted in its courts—i.e., conducted instead in federal courts. Some federal courts have held that the litigation may not proceed without the state's participation, unless it asserts no regulatory power or has waived what power it has asserted. This result is grounded in both procedural rules and the Eleventh Amendment to the Constitution, barring non-consensual suits against a state by citizens of another state in a federal court. Other federal courts have held that the federal court may hear the case in order to adjudicate claims on the treasure other than the state's. The recent cases are collected in *Sindia Expedition v. Wrecked and Abandoned Vessel, Known as "The Sindia"* (1989) (concerning a vessel 3,000 yards off the beach).

Absent such an assertion of state power, persons who take possession of sunken ships or treasure are entitled either to the rights of finders or salvors—the latter being persons who take possession under federal admiralty law.

Which body of law applies, finders' or salvors', is a muddle. Finders' law has been applied not only when the ship or treasure is on state land, or submerged land, but also when the state waived its Eleventh Amendment immunity from suit, or when the find lay outside of the state's territory. Two courts, using the embeddedness/top of the land distinction, found that the state and federal government respectively, had title to a sunken vessel embedded in their submerged lands. *Klein v. Unidentified Wrecked and Abandoned Sailing Vessel* (1985); *Chance v. Certain Artifacts Found and Salvaged from The Nashville* (1984).

a. Finders at Sea

The elements of the law of finders, though well-established, bear repeating here. This body of law applies when the ship or treasure has been abandoned. An inference of abandonment may arise from lapse of time or non-use of the property. Competing explorers are entitled to enter and search the area where the abandoned property is located and are also entitled to an injunction freeing them of unreasonable interference from each of their number. *Eads v. Brazelton* (1861). The first explorer to take possession of the property acquires title to it and the court releases the property to the finder. *Eads,* op. cit. See also, for those with patience, *Treasure Salvors, Inc. v. Unidentified Wrecked and Abandoned Sailing Vessel, "Nuestra Senora de Atocha"* (1981) (three opinions extending an injunctive order holding that property may be seized under federal admiralty court order and even though property is claimed by the state, suit is not barred by the Eleventh Amendment and that wreck in United States waters is the property of its finder, in continuous possession of wreck-site with intent to control site and vessel). This rule applies to the cargo of the wrecked vessel, as well as to the vessel itself.

b. *Salvage*

A salvor is a person who, without any legal obligation to do so, rescues a vessel or its cargo, in whole or part, from some peril at sea. *Platoro, Ltd., Inc. v. Unidentified Remains of a Vessel, Her Cargo, etc.* (1983). He may also recover it after its actual loss. The typical act is towing a ship in danger of floundering at sea, into port. Such a person may, under maritime law, claim compensation for his adventure. This compensation is called salvage. It is not a claim of title or possession to the vessel or cargo saved, but is rather like a lien on the proceeds of the sale of the cargo or the profits of the voyage.

This compensation is court-awarded. It is intended to be generous enough to encourage heroism and discourage embezzlement in the course of a rescue of life and property. For more on the law of salvage, see the eminently readable treatise by Gilmore and Black, Admiralty 532–85 (2d ed. 1975).

c. Comparing Finders' and Salvage Law

Some comparisons between these two bodies of law reveal important differences. Finders' law only applies when the property has been abandoned and it has as one of its purposes, the re-titling of the property, so that it can be put back into use and service. Salvage law assumes that the title to the property remains with its prior holder, although property cannot be salvaged until subjected to a "marine peril." Thus if finders' law is applied, the property's title goes to the finder; if salvage law is used, the successful salvor acquires a right of possession, but not title, to the property—the salvor's possession being only to the extent necessary to save it.

An intent to save the property, and actually saving it, are the two elements necessary to justify a salvage award and are akin to the elements necessary to a successful finder. Salvaged property is returned to court jurisdiction and, once the court has passed on any disputed claims on the property, it is returned to its true, prior owner and the court then determines an appropriate salvage fee for the salvor.

The finder is a solo operator and his search has an all-or-nothing quality about it: he either is awarded the title, or not. He must possess a higher degree of control to win a judgment. The salvor can act alone and receive an award, but he can also act in tandem with others and share an award with them in proportion to his efforts and accomplishments. *Hernandez v. Roberts* (1988) (pleasure boater found entitled to $500 salvage fee for staying with sinking vessel until the arrival of Coast Guard).

d. *Governmental Claims*

The finder taking possession at sea as well as the successful salvor both take their rights subject to governmental claims. For example, the federal government might (but has not to date) lay claim to property lost in its territorial seas under the admiralty jurisdiction granted it in the Constitution. It has never asserted such a broad claim, but has by statute claimed property abandoned during the Civil War, required permits of those who would search for objects of antiquity, and asserted control over the sub-soil and seabed, and disturbances thereto, within its national zone of interest.

While these are limited, technical assertions of jurisdiction, further complicated matters of treaties and international conventions arise when foreign nationals are involved in disputes over sunken and wrecked vessels. The Law of the Sea Convention, for example, contains both finders' and salvage law provisions. C.F. Newton, Finders Keepers? The Titanic and the 1982 Law of the Sea Convention, 10 Hast. Int'l & Comp.L.Rev. 159 (1986). Under it, finders' rights are qualified, in that consent to them must be obtained from the country of origin of the find.

Similar problems arise for wrecks and cargo found in inland water ways and within the three mile limits of state territorial seas. State statutes protecting sunken antiquities are common in coastal states, particularly in the Southeast and along the Gulf Coast. Searchers for treasure under these statutes apply for permits for specific search areas. Such permits look like leases for the search area, are issued only to archaeologists, and are executed in exchange for a percentage of the treasure and subject to giving state experts an opportunity to study and evaluate the artifacts recovered—even seizing artifacts connected to the state's history and culture. Subject to such controls, a treasure hunter's best hope is to find fungibles in the cargo.

When such legislation is passed, the easiest cases are those where treasure seekers trespass on state-run excavations which are already underway. Harder are cases in which the state seizes artifacts of which the government has no knowledge, but which are found by private citizens, without even compensating them for their time and effort. Such a decision has however been taken. *State of North Carolina v. Armistead* (1973). It can be justified by a recognition that the legislative assertion of title to historical artifacts has as its objective the regulation and control of the methods used to gather them, in an attempt to make sure that those methods represent sound archaeological practice.

V. FINDERS' STATUTES

If a thief buries a stolen chattel on O's land, and F finds it, the thief may have the better right to possess the chattel than the finder. At least this result is consistent with the rule in *Armory.* The thief may get caught and may want to lead the authorities to his cache in the hope of plea-bargaining or in just plain remorse for his misdeeds. Moreover, he knows of the true owner, of whose identity the finder usually hasn't a clue. Nonetheless, the result seems strange, favoring as it does a bad guy over a finder, so that if the finder can be encouraged to live the law's oft-repeated justification for protecting finders' right because this result is likely to protect the true owner's, then the finder should be preferred. Legislation has therefore attempted to encourage the finder to report his find. *Willsmore v. Oceola Township* (1981).

In many states, certainly a third and perhaps now a majority of states, there exist statutes which provide that a finder must, under penalty of the criminal code, report his find to local authorities and deposit it with them. After the publication of notice of the find, or sometimes just after the police have retained custody for a stated period of time (sometimes the period varies with the value of the chattel), the chattel is returned to the finder if unclaimed and the right of the finder becomes absolute. The right of a prior possessor or the true owner to claim it thereafter is cut off. When, however, through the use of these statutory procedures, the chattel is returned to the true owner, these statutes typically make provision for the finder to receive a reward, either fixed at a percentage of the value of the chattel, or at a reasonable amount, otherwise undefined, but related to the level of effort required of the finder, the promptness in reporting the find, and the expenses required to preserve it. See, e.g., McKinney's— N.Y.Pers.Prop.L. §§ 251–258 (1992). However, in the New York statute cited, there are exceptions for negotiable instruments found by a state employee undertaking official duties (they escheat to the state), chattel found on bank safety deposit box premises (the bank takes them), and a chattel found by an employee under a duty to deliver it to his employer. See *Paset v. Old Orchard Bank and Trust Co.* (1978).

Many states provide for a statutory duty to compensate the finder for his expenses; others provide only for a statutory reward for the finder. Such provisions have generally been upheld against the argument that they deprived the true owner of property without due process of law.

Finally, some of these statutes have been held to abrogate the common law of treasure trove, although this view is not without dissent.

A. THE EFFECT OF STATUTES ON THE COMMON LAW OF FINDERS

Many finder's statutes apply to "lost" personal property. Such statutes raise a definitional question whether the word "lost" refers to (1) the popular meaning of the word—as in "lost and found"; (2) the legal meaning of the word, as in a description of one of the four common law categories of personal property—lost, mislaid, abandoned, or treasure trove property. Because these statutes give expression to a legislative policy of encouraging finders to report their finds to public officials or others in a position to locate the true owner, the word "lost" will probably be given a broad enough meaning to permit use of the statute in a wide variety of circumstances. Lay rather than legal definitions will thus be used by the courts. This makes sure that the legislative policy behind these statutes is implemented, and avoids putting the lay finder in the difficult position of being forced to classify his find as one of several types of personal property in order to determine whether the statute applies to him. Avoiding putting the finder in this difficult position will be particularly important if the statute carries criminal penalties.

A Delaware statute requires that the police make reasonable efforts to locate the true owner of money turned over to the police and that such money, after a year, shall become the property of the state police retirement fund if stolen and of its finder if "lost or abandoned." 11 Del.C. § 8807 (1991). The reference to "lost or abandoned property" has been held to encompass all of the common law categories of lost, mislaid, abandoned, or treasure trove property.

Such a statute does not require turning over such money to the police. When turned in, however, the finder of non-stolen money acquired absolute title to it after a year. (If the common law were to apply, he would get only the right to possession.) Also, a court has held that there was no requirement in the statute that there be a good faith turnover of found property (the police had argued that the plaintiff in a replevin suit did not turn over the money in "good faith" because he first avoided them, and when he found the money he was performing undercover work in return for immunity from criminal prosecution); so long as the property came into the "custody" of the police, the statute applied.

Moreover, under the Delaware statute, there is no presumption that property turned over to the police was stolen. Such a presumption would defeat the policy of the statute to encourage people to turn in property which they find. Money being found in a thieves' junkyard, amid other stolen property, in a safe previously stolen, in a large amount, in bundles of small denominations—from all such circumstances it could be reasonably inferred that it was stolen in fact. However, such an inference is not compelled. When only one of the bills was traced (through a police computer check on the serial numbers on the bills) to a specific theft, and further police inquiries with over 100 people failed to link the money with any specific theft, such a failure could reasonably justify, but again does not compel, the inference that the money was not stolen. It is sufficient to avoid the state's motion for a summary judgment. *Campbell v. Cochran* (1980) (cross motions for summary judgment denied in replevin action by a finder for currency turned over to state police).

B. FINDERS' REWARDS

Sometimes a finder is said to have a lien on a chattel for the payment of a reward publicly advertised by the true owner who later refuses to pay it. Certainly the finder has a claim to have fulfilled an owner's unilateral contract regarding the promise of a reward for the finder's act of returning the lost object. Such a contract provides a separate cause of action against the owner, but providing that finder with more than a contract claim by labelling it a lien on the chattel, is to provoke litigation because this lien arises only by giving up possession of the chattel to the true owner and can only be perfected or foreclosed thereafter in court. A contract claim will serve the finder just as well.

Nor is the contract to pay a finder's reward void for an unlawful consideration under criminal statutes requiring finders to report their finds and give them over to the true owner. Only if the finder knows the true owner's identity at the time of finding do these statutes impose an immediate duty to turn over the find to its owner. Otherwise the finder must deposit the find with a public official and then search for the owner. Reward contracts are intended to encourage such searches and so implement and supplement such statutes, rather than supplant a finder's statutory duty. Presumably an owner will take into account the legal duty imposed by such statutes and calibrate the level of the reward accordingly, but the statute need not be read as nullifying all such contracts, particularly when owners seem to find them useful in encouraging finders to comply with the law.

One state's finder's statute entitles the finder to a reasonable reward for the return of the chattel to the true owner, without further defining what amount is reasonable. In one case, the court found thirty percent of the value of the coins returned to be unreasonably large. It considered relevant to the level of reward, the fact that the finder had spent a little more than $1,000 of the more than $8,000 found, although it permitted as a matter of course the finder's expenses in preserving, storing, and safe-keeping the find. In re Unknown Silver Coins (1988). In this state, the contract award would almost certainly be regarded as reasonable in amount. Other states provide by statute that a finder will receive a fixed percentage (say 10%) of the value of the lost and found chattel, but again such statutes should be taken to provide a standard which can either be supplanted by private agreement or construed to set a statutory minimum on the amount of the reward.

However, before the finder can claim a reward, the chattel "found" must indeed have been "lost". For example, supermarket carts scattered around the neighborhood of the market cannot be deemed lost where they had been left by shoppers. When a defendant systematically appropriated various carts where they had been left, held them a few days, and then made a demand for a finder's fee from the market before returning them, he is guilty of larceny and it is no defense that the carts were legally lost because a court found that under these circumstances in fact they were not lost. *People v. Stay* (1971). See also *Michael v. First Chicago Corporation* (1985) (involving certificates of deposit "found" by purchaser of bank's cast-off office furniture).

The *Stay* case brings us back to our point of beginning for this discussion. Where the true owner of a "found" chattel is readily ascertainable from the circumstances of the find, it is not "lost" and not subject to the law of finders. A stock certificate or savings bond with the holders' name and address, travellers' checks with the payor's signature on them, or shopping carts in the locale of the market—all are examples of a rule that says, only the truly lost chattel, can be found. A second rule suggested by examining these statutes is that what is of no value to a finder, cannot be lost within the meaning of the statute. Registered or non-negotiable stock certificates and bonds fall into this category.

C. ESCHEAT

Escheat is a legal procedure, known to the common law as early as the twelfth century, whereby the sovereign acquires title to abandoned property when after a number of years, no rightful owner appears and claims it. Its early applications were limited to real property, but in this country it has usually been applied to both real and personal property. This power exists in the state because it either has jurisdiction over the property or over its last holder. It is a matter of statute in all states, but the dormancy period varies greatly from state to state, ranging from as little as two to as many as twenty years.

D. UNCLAIMED, INTANGIBLE, PERSONAL PROPERTY ACTS

Thirty one states have enacted statutes promulgated by the Commissioners for Uniform State

Laws in 1954, 1966 and 1981 concerning the disposition of unclaimed, intangible, personal property. The need for uniform legislation on this subject has become more pressing in this age of multi-state businesses. One has only to visualize the number of dividend checks issued every quarter in the fiscal year by corporations like International Business Machines Corporation or General Motors and then to imagine the (remote) possibility that all of those checks will reach the owners of the corporate shares represented and that all those checks will thereafter be cashed.

What should be done with the funds deposited to pay the uncashed checks? One resolution is to give them to the state. All the states have escheat laws under which property, including intangible personal property, reverts to the state because no one is available or competent to inherit it. However, it is difficult to make the assumption that because one object of personalty has not been claimed, its holder has no heirs. Some states have statutes dealing with unclaimed bank deposits within their jurisdiction. These laws presume that such property has been abandoned after a statutory period of time, and possession of unclaimed deposits is transferred to the enacting state.

But which state's escheat law should apply? Conflicting claims among the states meant that the holders of unclaimed personal property might be subject to multiple liability if they disposed of the property. In the case of a corporate dividend check, four states might claim the property: 1. the state of incorporation of the corporation, 2. the state in which that corporation has its principal place of business, 3. the state having the most contacts with the payment of the dividend, or 4. the state of the shareholder's last known address.

The drafters of the Unclaimed Property Act have adopted the fourth alternative because this will distribute this property among the states in proportion to the commercial activities of their residents and because it provides a simple rule which is easy to administer.

Unlike the escheat laws, the Uniform Act does not give title to the state; instead the state of the last known address of the lost owner of unclaimed, intangible personal property acts in a custodial manner. The Act in its present and past versions creates a "presumption of abandonment" of unclaimed personalty after the lapse of a statutory period of time. After that time, the property is turned over to the state of the last known address of the lost owner. Because the law abhors a forfeiture, the Act will generally be preferred over the escheat laws. Moreover, the presumption of abandonment is rebuttable, whether the property is in the hands of a private holder or the state.

Unclaimed intangible personal property is defined by the Act as (e.g.) any monies, checks, money orders, traveler's checks, dividends, gift certificates, unpaid wages, unused airline tickets, or stocks; monies deposited to redeem stocks, bonds, or coupons; monies payable under insurance policies, or monies distributable to pay various fringe benefits to wage-earners. Moreover, property covered by the Act must be held by a banking or financial organization, business association, insurance company, public utility, state court, other public agency, trustee, or a debtor or a holder in possession of the property of another.

The holder of unclaimed, intangible personal property is required by the Act to send a notice of its possession to the owner and then to file a report with the state administrator (a public official designated in the Act). This report lists all property unclaimed in its possession and the lost owners' last addresses. The administrator is authorized to take possession of this property, sell any property, not money, and deposit all money and the proceeds of sales in a custodial account maintained by the state for lost owners in perpetuity. Thus the lost owner's rights to a *pro rata* portion of this account are not forfeited under these Acts; rather, the state acts as a conservator of the funds representing the property. However, the property itself may be sold free and clear of a lost owner's claim.

The period of time during which the property must be unused by the owner varies with the type of personalty. The general dormancy period is five years in the 1981 version of the Act. The 1966 version used a seven year period. Various states, in adopting the Uniform Act, have substituted general dormancy periods of between 10 and 20 years.

The trend has been to shorten the dormancy period in the recent adoptions of the Uniform Act. This both increases the chance that the last owner of the property will be located and, more importantly, raises the amount of revenue which these Acts produce for their adopting states.

If another state under its escheat laws or under a claim of abandonment of its own (possibly working through its version of this Uniform Act) asserts a claim for any property held by the administrator, the administrator may pay this claim. A principle of reciprocity is generally used to determine whether a claimant state will be paid.

Other provisions of these Acts detail the procedures for a lost owner to follow in making a claim against this fund and, in the 1981 version, provide for a minimum period of two years during which the state must hold the unclaimed property. (This last provision was added to "address the small but active heir finder's industry.")

Ten states adopted the original version of this Act, promulgated in 1954. In 1966, more detail and coverage for travelers' checks and money orders was added and twenty-one states adopted this second version of the Act. These two versions of the Act tied the enacting state's claim to abandoned personalty to its ability to assert personal jurisdiction over the holder. In 1965, in an escheat case, the United States Supreme Court untied this connection. *Texas v. New Jersey* (1965). To make the Act consistent with the holding in this case, the 1981 version of the Act provides that unclaimed intangible property is payable to the state of the last known address of the owner or, if that information is unavailable, to the state of the holder's domicile.

Litigation concerning these Acts as adopted in the several states has revolved around four types of problems. They are, first, what property is subject to the holder's reporting requirement when held before the date of enactment of the Act. Most of the states adopting the 1966 version have specifically enacted a retroactivity period (e.g., ten years before enactment). Second, there has been litigation over whether the reporting requirement included property for which the relevant statute of limitations has expired. Most state courts hold that, notwithstanding the fact that the statute has run out, the property must be reported and then turned over to the state. Third, some litigation has centered around the question of when the period of dormancy starts to run: what if an offer to settle an insurance company claim is made, to be payable for six months thereafter? Does the dormancy period run from the date of this offer to settle, or has it already started to run based on the underlying insurance policy? (One court holds for the latter.) What if the owner is undetermined; must the owner be determined before the period can start to run? (At least two courts have held not.) A fourth set of cases have involved the constitutionality of the Act, and it has generally been upheld as constitutional.

This type of legislation has several advantages. It protects the holders of unclaimed intangibles against the risk of multiple liability on the same property. It protects the rights of the lost owner. It encourages interstate agreement over the disposition of such property. It allows non-monetary property subject to the Act to be put back into circulation. And finally, it provides a modest source of revenue for the states.

Modest though this source of state revenue might be in terms of a state's total budget, it is none-the-less worth the cost of litigation to obtain or protect. The Uniform Acts do not provide which states are to be given possession of unclaimed property, the subject being too sensitive for such an Act to handle. In 1987, Delaware, the state in which many mega-businesses are incorporated, sued New York, the state in which many corporate accounts are maintained, to recover the unclaimed dividends and interest payments of Delaware corporations. Since 1987, every other state has joined this suit. Delaware v. New York (1992).

Over the years, New York has shortened its dormancy period until it is today three years. Delaware has a longer period—seven years. Thus once Delaware is entitled under its statutes to demand the unclaimed monies in corporate coffers, New York has already made its demand and been paid.

This suit was brought under the federal constitutional provisions conferring original jurisdiction over suits between states on the United States Supreme Court. Its justices will hear this case during the 1992–93 Term. The states (1) in which a corporation's executive offices are located, (2) where its accounts are maintained, and (3) where it is incorporated, are thus contesting the right to a first claim on these unclaimed, corporate monies.

CHAPTER VI

BAILMENTS

I. THEIR NATURE AND DEFINITION

A bailment is rightful possession of a chattel by one who is not the holder of the title to it. This is a minimal definition. It avoids any controversy of whether a bailment is a creature governed by the law of property or of contract.

If the law of property governs, then a bailment is the delivery of possession of a chattel to another who intends to possess it and takes possession, agreeing that his possessory right in it will cease upon a demand by the transferor for redelivery. There must be a delivery and acceptance of the chattel, with an actual transfer of the chattel itself. This definition is akin to a common law conveyance of land by livery of seisin.

If the law of contract governs, a bailment is a transfer by mutual consent of the possession of a chattel for some specific purpose under an express or implied contract to carry out the purpose of the transfer and to return the chattel to the holder of its title once that purpose is accomplished. *B.A. Ballou and Co., Inc. v. Citytrust* (1991).

Does it make a difference whether the contract, the property, or the minimal definition of a bailment is chosen? Indeed it does.

If the contract definition is chosen, there will be cases which will be hard to classify as bailments but which the law has traditionally regarded as such. What if a car, parked in an attended parking lot, is stolen from the lot with valuables inside the trunk? Were the valuables the subject of a bailment when the car was left in the lot, even though the attendant had had no knowledge of their presence? Or how about a purse left in a restaurant by a patron? If it contains valuable jewelry, is the jewelry the subject of a bailment? There is authority in each instance for holding that there was a bailment of the valuables and that the bailee—the owner of the parking lot, restaurant, or shop—assumes the risk that the car or the purse will contain chattel more valuable than he knows.

Because the contractual definition of a bailment will require that there be some notice by the bailor of the chattel delivered to the bailee, that definition will be stretched to the breaking point by these "closed receptacle" cases. The notion of a constructive bailment will either have to be introduced into the law, or the test for whether or not a bailment arises will have to be generalized into a test of whether, considering the attendant circumstances, the bailee could have reasonably expected that the receptacle would contain the valuables

that it did. Thus a hotelkeeper might be expected
to know that some of his guests will arrive with
purses and suitcases containing valuables, or a
parking lot owner might reasonably be expected to
know that some cars left in his possession will have
valuables in their trunks. Similar and perhaps
stronger expectations can be imputed to the bank
which accepts valuables for storage in safe deposit
boxes, even where the bank cannot gain access to
the box without a key in the depositor's possession.

In these cases, the law would probably be better
served if, instead of engaging in the fiction of a
constructive bailment, the courts adopted either
the property or the minimal definition of a bailment. Then the bailee's risk of increased value
arises when the delivery and acceptance of the
receptacle takes place (under the property definition) or when the bailee assumes possession of the
chattel (under the minimal definition). Under either definition, a bailment arises when the alleged
bailee assumes possession or takes control of the
chattel, with an intent to exercise control. (This is
no different from the requirements of possession in
the wild animal cases.) Under either, as well as in
a jurisdiction in which the courts want strictly to
maintain a contract definition, a threshold question is whether the bailment or the contract was
not set in motion because there was no delivery to,
or assumption of possession by, the bailee. This
approach has negated a bailment in cases in which
the chattel is allegedly bailed in an area (say a
cloakroom) set physically and visually apart from

the primary place of business (say a sales floor or the dining room of a restaurant). This factual context of the alleged bailment speaks to the question of whether the shopkeeper, as an alleged bailee, knew of the presence of the chattel on his premises. If the bailee has no knowledge, there can be no intent to possess the chattel on his part and hence no bailment.

However, it may also be important whether the deposit of the chattel left behind by the customer facilitated the transaction in the shop, as where a customer removes his coat in order to try on a new one in a clothing shop. This aspect of the alleged bailment indirectly addresses the question of whether the shopkeeper, as an alleged bailee, should have known of the chattel's presence, whether it was in his sight or not. Note, "Bailments—Delivery—Liability of Restaurant Keeper," 3 U.Pitt.L.Rev. 51 (1936).

Considering both the closed receptacle cases as well as cases in which the knowledge of the alleged bailee is at issue, it becomes obvious that a bailment does not require and does not arise only upon a separate contract, but may also arise when the parties to it deliver and accept possession of the chattel. Yet even this latter conveyancing definition of a bailment may be too detailed, and it might be better to say that for a bailment to arise all that is needed is the consent of the parties to the transfer of possession.

A. FINDERS AS BAILEES

If a minimal definition of bailment is a consensual transfer of possession of a chattel, it must then be asked whether the consent of the parties can in any circumstances be implied, and if so, what those circumstances might be. One circumstance that arises out of the discussion in the last chapter pertains to the law of finders. If F finds O's watch, what obligations does F owe to O? R. Aigler, A. Smith, and S. Tefft, 1 *Property* 47 (1960) suggests the following problems:

a. What if F tires of keeping the watch and throws it in the trash? F had no duty to take possession of the watch in the first instance, but once he decided to keep it, he should realize that he has only the right to possess it, and not the title to it, so that he should keep it safe, and treating it as trash when it clearly has great value, would be gross negligence. *Isaack v. Clark* (1615) ("[F]or at the first, it is in his election, whether he will take them or not into his custody, but when he hath them, ... he ought to keep them safely.").

How will this liability arise? There is no consensual arrangement between F and O to support a contract-based bailment. A bailment on the theory of contract would founder either on the bargain principle of contract law or on the doctrine of consideration.

Neither is this a tort duty imposed on F. The duties imposed by the law on tortfeasors are duties owed to all the world, and F knows that the watch he found probably had but one owner. To that person, F might reasonably expect to have some duty to preserve the watch, but his duty is not owed to the public in general.

F's duty is more particular. It is to search for the true owner and hold the watch until there is no reasonable expectation of the true owner's turning up. Until that time comes and goes, F should not throw the watch away. His duty to search becomes the purpose of a bailment implied by law.

Whether F's period of search for the owner is shorter or longer, will to some degree depend on some assumptions which F can reasonably make about the duration of O's interest in the watch. If it is an inexpensive time-piece, then it may quickly reach the point at which the cost of repair exceeds the cost of replacement and F might reasonably assume that O's interest in the watch will the more quickly wain and F will be able to throw it away sooner. The more expensive the watch is, the longer the period of O's interest in it can be assumed to be and the longer will be the time before F can throw it away. These are rules of reason and of reasonable expectations. Absent circumstances on which reason can work, no definitive answers can emerge.

b. What if F wears O's watch while swimming, has it cleaned or lends it to a drunken man? It is often said that the degree of care required of a finder is slight. This rule of slight duty is inferred from the slight benefit which the finder received from any implied bailment between himself and the true owner of the chattel. A finder is said to be a gratuitous bailee, liable only for gross negligence. The idea of a slight benefit was engrafted onto the law as a method for inferring that some consideration was given to the finder in order to sustain the finder/owner relationship as a contract of bailment, but if it is a contract, it is an implied contract. An implied contract has those terms which can be reasonably expected by the parties to it and so which are imposed by the law. These expectations and terms are modified by circumstances, and if the finder's degree of care is modified by the benefit conferred on him, then it is an overstatement to say that a finder *always* has a slight duty of care. If the find involved a watch set with diamonds, the courts may increase the duty of care for the finder accordingly.

If F were to wear O's watch while swimming and it turns out not to be waterproof and the works were damaged, the question is whether he treated the found watch as a reasonably prudent person would treat his own watch. If so, no liability is likely to attach. It is unlikely that a person would not know whether his own watch is waterproof, so that if a cleaning was necessary because of the dunking which F gave it, F's responsibility is to restore it to its former condition. However, if the watch was in need of a cleaning beforehand and F had it cleaned, the question arises whether the costs of the cleaning, when O turns up shortly thereafter and is benefitted thereby, can be charged to O. O will be in a poor position to deny liability for routine maintenance of the watch, and if that is what this cleaning was, he will be liable for the charges. F can undertake reasonable expenses to preserve the watch and charge them to the owner who later claims it.

If F lends the watch to a drunken man who smashes the watch's crystal while falling on the way home, F will be liable for the decrease in value because F might reasonably expect that if he gave his own watch away in this manner, it would be damaged.

After F's swim he will be able to recover the maintenance and repair charges from a reclaiming O. After the drunken man smashed the crystal, however, because F's negligence made the charges necessary, no recovery by F will be possible against O. That O might be held liable for routine maintenance or maintenance to preserve the watch from harm, is a matter of a promise which the law will imply.

It is unlikely that F could withhold the watch from O until the repair charges are paid; rather, he has a separate suit based on a contract theory of bailment for the amount of those charges.

Where the repairs are necessary to preserve the watch or chattel itself, however, the courts are more willing to entertain the possibility that F can retain possession until such charges are paid by O. Even for the recovery of such repairs, when O continues to refuse to pay, it is doubtful that F could sell the chattel to satisfy his claim. Rather, he can sue O, have his judgment satisfied, and then surrender the possession of the chattel to O.

There is, however, some authority for the proposition that F need not turn the watch over to O before O pays the reasonable expenses which F has incurred in holding the watch. Courts sometimes speak of F"s having a lien on the watch for the payment of the charges. Such a lien, being a creature of the common law, is probably one that permits F to withhold delivery of possession but probably would not permit F to sell the watch to a third party to satisfy his claim.

c. If F found a diamond-encrusted watch and when O claims it, it is damaged or cannot be found by F, what result? If the diamonds are nicked when O claims it and O proves that F, while in possession presented the watch to a jeweler for appraisal in an undamaged condition, then O has at least shifted the burden of proof to F to show that F did not damage the watch. Absent such evidence, the damage may have been done before F found it, and O will have no claim in trespass or conversion for the damage.

If, when O claims the watch, F cannot find it, and O cannot show that F treated the watch negligently, what result? A court might still impose liability on F to deter finders from "losing" their finds when they are claimed, but if O cannot show that F treated the watch other than in a non-negligent manner, F would have no liability. Absent a showing by O that F misdelivered the watch to an unknown or absconding third party, many courts would not indulge in a presumption of mis-delivery.

d. Finally, what procedure should F use to ascertain that O is indeed the true owner if O shows up to claim the watch? Clearly F need not give up the watch on demand. He also need not give in to a demand that the claimant inspect it because that would preclude his satisfying his own duty to ask reasonable questions as to the nature and identity of the watch in order to meet his duty to safeguard it for the true owner. If the questions are answered wrongly and the trier of fact can conclude that the finder has a reasonable basis for refusing to give over the watch, then no action of replevin or trover will thereafter lie against him because he has not yet converted the watch—his questions indicate no act of conversion; they instead show a desire to hold the watch for its true owner, not for himself.

1. The Right to Sue and the Causes of Action

Common law judges, for centuries, debated whether or not a bailor could maintain an action against a person who wrongfully took a bailed chattel from a bailee. So long as the essence of the action against the trespasser was criminal in nature, or sounded in tort, the crime or the tort was committed against the bailee and on this basis the courts held that he alone had the remedy. Likewise, the bailee had the present right to possession, and his duty to deliver the chattel out of the bailment constitutes an interest in the chattel on which to ground his suit. Finally, however, the common law rule came to be that both bailor and bailee could maintain trespass.

Often the bailee is said to have a cause of action against convertors of the property because he is liable over to the bailor. This notion was given the lie in the case of *The Winkfield* (1901), where the bailee was the English postal system and was not liable to its bailors, the persons posting letters. None-the-less, the court decided that the bailee could maintain suit against a ship, *The Winkfield,* which negligently collided with a ship that carried the mail and sent the mail-boat to the bottom of the sea. So the bailee was suing a third-party tortfeasor that negligently interfered with the bailment. The court held that the bailee's possession is good as against a wrongdoer, and that the latter would not have the defense of *jus tertii.*

The history of bailments shows two things: that the bailee has a right to sue where he is liable over, and that he is liable over because he has the right to sue. Which one of these rules has priority in the law, is now difficult, and probably impossible to say. Where the bailee is strictly liable, he arguably should be the one with the right to control the suit against the tortfeasor, trespasser, or convertor of the chattel. When as today he is liable only if negligent, and even then has often limited his liability by contract, this right should be shared—and today's rule is that both have the right to sue on the theory that the one to do so will be the more diligent pursuer of the remedy. Today, in an age in which strict liability has fallen away from the bailee and a bailor's suit against a bailee depends upon the proof of facts and the circumstances of the case, the bailor might as easily run the risks of litigation against the third-party wrongdoer. At the same time, to deny the bailee a right to sue would deny this right to a party who often will have the best access to the facts of the case. The careful conclusion is that today both bailor and bailee should have the right to sue concurrently, but that only one judgment per incident can be obtained between them.

The cause of action used today for the recovery of the value of a bailed chattel is trover. The bailor may bring this action even though he does not have the right to possess the chattel at the time he brings the action. He has a "general property" in the chattel; this consists of his title to the property and a future right to possess it. At the same time, the bailee bringing the same action is said to have a "special property" in the bailed chattel—the right to present possession of it. Both thus have a possessory interest in the chattel sufficient to maintain an action in trover, although if one of them pursues this action to a judgment, the other is precluded from doing the same. *Associates Discount Corp. v. Gillineau* (1948).

Permitting the bailee to sue in trover may at times work a hardship on the bailor, who in the usual case has a greater interest than the bailee in the chattel. The bailee's right to recover damages rests on the hypothesis that he is the bailor's agent and is charged to protect the property entrusted to him. Permitting the agent to sue in trover is in effect a decision to permit the title to the chattel to pass to a convertor once the judgment is satisfied. To have the bailor's rights in the chattel concluded by a bailee who may not have adequate incentive to litigate vigorously, without giving the bailor notice of the suit or any settlement of it, is a situation that begs for some procedural reform. This is particularly true in a jurisdiction in which the bailee has only a limited liability—say for gross negligence only, as would a finder have when sued as a gratuitous bailee. On the other hand, if the bailor has put his trust in the agent-bailee, he should look to him for redress; if the bailor has damages uncompensated by the trover judgment secured by his bailee, he still may have a separate action in trespass for any uncompensated interference with his rights in the chattel and, in any event, the bailee is usually liable over to him for the value of the chattel. If the bailee's attorney is negligent in prosecuting the litigation against a convertor, or if the bailee fails to obtain a full recovery, the bailee is also liable as a fiduciary in an equitable action for an accounting.

Likewise, both bailor and bailee have a sufficient interest in the possession of a bailed chattel to bring an action in replevin.

B. BAILMENTS, LEASES, LICENSES AND SALES

1. Safe Deposit Box Cases

When a customer of a bank "rents" a safety deposit box, the weight of authority holds that the relationship between the customer and his bank is that of bailor and bailee. Some courts have said that this relationship really does give rise to a lease, but when access to the box is obtained by the customer's presentation of identification and the use of one (of two, the latter being in the possession of the bank) keys to unlock the vault in which the box is stored, the transfer of an exclusive possession of the vault and the box necessary for a lease is not present. The vault may be "rented," but where the contents of the box are lost or stolen, most courts hold that the contents of the box have been the subject of a bailment. This result obtains even where the bank did not know the exact contents and value of the chattels in the box; the courts infer that the bank knew of their general nature. And even though the bank may not have exclusive control of the contents, its possession is sufficient for most courts to find a bailment which many courts regard as the best characterization of the legal relationship between the bank and its customer.

As one might expect, however, possession is a relative term, and for other purposes, a bank may not have to disclose or hand over property of a

debtor-bailor in its possession to a creditor even
when a creditor asserts a right under a state statute, although the authority on this question is
split. See *Foster v. Essex Bank* (1821); Lord, The
Legal Relationship Between the Bank and Its Safe
Deposit Customer, 5 Camp. L. Rev. 263 (1983).

2. Parking Lot Cases

The same type of definitional problem arises in
the case of a car left in a parking lot. Where the
lot operator does not provide attendants or guards,
the car stolen from such a lot has not been the
subject of a bailment. The car owner has left his
car in a specific parking space and expects to find
it there upon his return. In this situation, there is
a transfer of the exclusive possession of a definite
space necessary for a lease or at minimum a license which is a right to use the space without
liability for trespass. Both a lease and a license
last for a limited or specific period of time. One
court, although discussing the facts using negligence terms rather than bailment, has found the
equivalent of a bailment in an enclosed, park and
lock, unattended lot for the purpose of making the
lot operator liable for the theft of a car tape deck
and cassettes. *McGlynn v. Parking Authority of
City of Newark* (1981). The *McGlynn* opinion analyzed the indicia of possession and control over the
car left in the lot, as part of its discussion of
whether the lot operator owed its customers a duty
of due care. It discarded what it said were the out-

moded distinctions between bailment, license, and lease formerly used in parking lot cases and distinguished the two issues of the case—the extent of the duty, and whether to apply a presumption of negligence. It found that there was a duty and, on the second issue, said that the operator has the burden of coming forward with evidence showing that it was not negligent when a parked car leaves the lot damaged. On both issues, then, the court reached a result consistent with the law of bailment.

Where the car owner surrenders the keys, the lot operator provides an attendant, and that attendant has the right to move the car from one space to another, possessory rights are given to the operator and a bailment arises. *Allright, Inc. v. Strawder App.* (1984). This makes the operator responsible to take due care of the car if damaged or stolen from the lot and also makes the operator responsible for chattel which he might reasonably expect to find in the trunk.

Sometimes the lot operator will attempt to exculpate himself from liability for loss or theft of the car by language on the claim check given the car owner upon his arrival at the lot. Typically the check is hurriedly given, received, and shoved into the owner's pocket without a reading. In such cases, the owner would not have notice of the limitation of liability, and most courts hold that the bailor is not restricted to the amounts or conditions printed on the ticket. Such a rule works a result preferable to holding otherwise. As Professor Brown notes, however, it places a "disturbing premium" on not reading the claim check. Where a portion of the check is placed on the car, some courts may conclude that its primary purpose may be to identify the car rather than to state the terms of a bailment contract.

When the check is read, most courts will construe it strictly against the lot operator or other party standing to benefit from its enforcement. It may not, moreover, excuse the operator's gross negligence. More broadly speaking, it is hard to see why a person whose business is being a bailee should be permitted to exculpate himself from even ordinary negligence for damage or loss which can be reasonably expected to arise in the course of his business.

Where the attempted exculpation is not total, but limited, and the parties can be found to have agreed to it, the question becomes whether the restriction of liability is out of reasonable proportion to the loss. A reasonable limitation will then protect the operator from loss or damage due to the actions of third parties but not from his intentional conversions of the bailed chattel; it may also set an upper limit on a bailee's liability by an agreement as to the value of the chattel bailed.

A majority of courts hold that a contractual provision which would protect a bailee against liability for his own negligence is void because it is against public policy. Some courts have sustained such exculpatory clauses in situations where the bailee's business does not involve being a bailee for the public; with a public bailee such as a parking lot operator, however, this contractual exculpation is invalid.

3. Photography Cases

The purpose of a bailment is often the performance of a service. When a person brings exposed film to be processed by a photographic laboratory, the relationship between the photographer and the processor is one of bailment. The photographer has title to the film, and transfers its possession to the processor for developing. The bailee does not have the use of the film and must return the negatives and the prints made from them to the photographer, even though the negatives are worth more than the exposed film initially transferred. Whatever profit arises from the use of the images, is the photographer's. See *Carr v. Hoosier Photo Supplies, Inc.* (1981), and noted at 16 Ind.L.Rev. 83, 90; 283, 288–290 (1983).

But not all photographers have complete use of the image on the film he uses. A commercial photographer, asked to make a photographic portrait of a person, may hold either the title to or have the right to permanent possession of the negative produced, but the person hiring him and sitting for the portrait has the right to control the use of the negative. *Corliss v. E.W. Walker Co.* (1894); *Pollard v. Photographic Co.* (1888);

Hochstadter v. H. Tarr, Inc. (1947). Next time you sit for a photographic portrait and want the negative or do not want your black and white portrait colorized, make the arrangements before the shutter clicks.

4. The Bailee's Personal Injuries in the Bailment for Hire

Often courts and writers use the terms lease and bailment for hire interchangeably in situations in which temporary possession of a chattel is exchanged for a consideration, as when a person "rents" a car. Older authorities considered a bailment for hire to be an entrusting of a chattel for safe-keeping with a bailee and the lease as a transfer of a right to use the chattel. This distinction is important in situations in which the chattel supposedly bailed are misdelivered and the bailee seeks to avoid the strict liability that applied to a conversion, but may also be too technical to be useful in tort litigation involving personal injuries to the bailee.

In tort litigation, for example, the locus of the title as between bailor and bailee will not likely prove dispositive of the suit. When the chattel proves defective and the bailee suffers personal injuries, the bailor's liability will be based on and calculated according to the doctrines of negligence or, in a minority of jurisdiction, strict liability. In such a lawsuit, the locus of title is relatively unimportant. Moreover, a personal injury suit may be conducted by first finding an implied warranty in the transaction between bailor and bailee, and in this event, the implied warranty may be part of an implied contract between the parties which has consequences for the burden of proof. In tort, the burden is on the plaintiff-bailee, but if the implied warranty arises in an implied contract, the burden of proof will shift, and once the plaintiff invokes the warranty, it is the bailor who will have to show due care.

5. Negligent Entrustment

In a situation somewhat similar to a bailment for hire, but in a non-commercial context, some states recognize that when a person supplies, directly or through a third party, a chattel for the use of another whom the supplier actually knows or has reason to know, is incompetent to use or operate it, that person is liable to those injured through its use or operation. The incompetence may be due to youth, inexperience, or feebleness of mind or body. Scienter on the supplier's part is a necessary element of the proof of this tort. Supplying an automobile to an incompetent driver is the most litigated context for it. Restatement (Second) of Torts, § 390 (1965). This tort is not one of imputed negligence—in that the negligence of the user is not imputed to the supplier; rather, the supplier's negligence is in supplying the chattel to a person incompetent to use it.

6. Sales Distinguished From Bailments

A bailment is a transfer of possession. It is not a transfer of a consideration given in exchange for possession and title—which would be a sale. If a transferee acquires possession "for approval" or "on trial," no title is yet transferred and a bailment results, although the bailee has an option to purchase the chattel at the end of the approval period. If the option is not exercised, the identical goods must be returned.

On the other hand, if the chattel's possession and title change hands at the same time, a sale results, and the law of sales in the Uniform Commercial Code applies. The Code's § 2–509 rejects the location of title as the test for which party—vendor or purchaser—bears the risk of loss, but the location of the title is still applicable to decide whether a transfer is a bailment or a sale. In a bailment, where the title has not been transferred from bailor to bailee, the risk of loss remains on the bailor if the chattel is destroyed without the fault of the bailee. Under § 2–401 and § 2–509, once the property is identified, title to it and the risk of its loss pass from a vendor to a purchaser "in any manner and under any conditions explicitly agreed on by the parties"; if the parties have no agreement, the title passes if its transfer "completes the vendor's performance with reference to the physical delivery of the goods." U.C.C. § 2–401(1) and (2).

Under the UCC, then, title is still an important concept, but less so. Under it, the title might pass between the parties for some purposes, but not for others. An agreement between the parties may assign the title and so allocate the risk of loss for the purpose of (say) suing a third-party wrongdoer, but not for the purpose of filing an insurance claim for the loss of the chattel.

C. RETURNING THE CHATTEL

The eventual objective of a bailment is the delivery of the chattel's possession to its true owner or prior possessor, the bailor, or to a third party at the bailor's direction. When the time of the bailment for the bailor's sole benefit is indefinite, the law implies a reasonable time within which the bailor may request return of the chattel. In this connection, typically the outer limits of reasonableness is set by the applicable statute of limitations for personal property actions. The bailee who refuses to deliver the chattel, or who cannot deliver it because he has lost it, has committed a conversion of the chattel against the bailor. His duty is to return the chattel, and any other act of dominion over it is a conversion. The bailee who delivers the chattel cannot be held liable for a conversion, except that when the bailee delivers the chattel to the bailor after a true owner has notified him of a claim on it, a conversion may result because the delivery in this instance is a denial of the true owner's right to the chattel. The premise that a finder is a gratuitous bailee is linked to the idea that a bailee cannot refuse to deliver the bailor or true owner's chattel without becoming a convertor.

If the objective of the bailment is by definition the delivery of the chattel to its rightful owner or the bailor, misdelivery is then a risk inherent in a bailment. The courts assume that no bailee will undertake the relationship without realizing this and so a bailee is strictly liable for a misdelivery. So, too, it might be argued, is the risk of third party actions, like theft, or acts of God, or a fire started by lightning. Strict liability for a failure to deliver also discourages a bailee from engaging in fraudulent misdeliveries. This delivery must be of the identical chattel which was bailed in the first instance. If there is no duty in the bailee to return the identical chattel, there is no bailment.

Many cases have arisen in agricultural settings. If, for example, a farmer delivers his wheat to a miller on the understanding that the latter will deliver back one barrel of flour for every four of wheat, the majority of courts hold that there is no bailment because the same goods are not to be returned. If, in the meanwhile, the mill burns and the wheat is destroyed, the risk of loss falls on the farmer, not the miller. That the flour delivered back need not be milled from the wheat delivered to the miller, indicates a payment for a frustrated sale. However, this majority rule is inflexible and ignores the possibility that there was a bailment of wheat, followed by its sale at the time of its milling, so that if the miller had processed some grain and converted the rest, a finding of a bailment is not precluded.

In another group of cases raising a similar issue, there is some authority for the proposition that the provider of seed under an agricultural share-crop contract is a bailor of the crop eventually grown, but it is hard to see how a contract to return some fraction of the crop gives rise to a bailment of the whole of it. Moreover, if the seed and the crop are regarded as different chattel, the rule that there can be no bailment for a chattel not yet in existence will rule out a bailment in this instance. Certainly the person who provides the seed needs to have his interest protected. If the farmer sells that portion of the crop promised to the seed purveyor to third parties, that may be a conversion—an unauthorized exercise of control over another's property—but for this an adequate remedy lies in damages. No court need go further and find that this is a case in which the same chattel was to be returned to the alleged bailor.

On the other hand, if the question was the allocation of the risk of loss of the seed due to drought or other natural occurrence destroying the crop, then the issue of whether identical goods need be returned is squarely raised, and the court can allocate this risk, presumably with the same result as in the milled wheat cases—i.e., that there was no bailment and the risk was on the seed merchant.

1. Fungible Goods

Some chattel are fungible, that is, of such a nature that another object may easily replace it and perform the same function. Money is an example. A bank depositor would not reasonably expect, upon a withdrawal, to get back the same identical dollar bills which he presented for deposit. Grain—that currency of the Midwest—when deposited in an elevator, presents another instance in which the identical kernels will not be returned; instead, the depositor will receive an amount of grain of like quality and quantity. If the grain elevator is destroyed before the return, the risk of its loss falls (under the majority view) on the operator of the silo because a bailment exists in this situation. Similarly, because of the bailment, the operator does not have a mortgageable interest in the grain. It is there for him to return to the depositor or the latter's designee. Thus a bailment can exist in fungible chattel where it normally would not if non-fungible goods were involved.

On the other hand, if chattel are delivered into the hands of another, on the understanding that (as with a herd of sheep) animals of like species, age and condition are to be returned, this may look like a bailment of fungible goods, but the bailor's creditors will not be able to levy on the herd unless they can show that the identical sheep are to be returned. Otherwise the shepherd's ability to manage and increase his flock would be hindered.

Similarly, the risk of loss of the flock falls on the shepherd. Where the alleged bailee is given the power to use the chattel as his own, no bailment results, even if the chattel are fungible.

D. STANDARD OF CARE

The care required of the bailee generally varies according to the totality of circumstances surrounding the bailment. In particular, however, courts emphasize the extent of the benefit received by the bailee through the bailment to determine the standard of care. If the benefit of the bailment accrues to the bailor solely, the care required of the bailee is slight. He will be liable only for gross negligence. A finder is such a bailee, and so is liable for only gross negligence because the benefit of the bailment is the "bailor's" or the true owner's. If the bailment is mutually beneficial to both bailor and bailee, the bailee is required to exercise due care and is liable only if negligent. Where a hotel desk clerk receives a valuable chattel to hold for a guest, a bailment of mutual benefit to both the hotel and the guest is created, as in *Peet v. Roth Hotel Co.* (1934). If the bailment is solely beneficial to the bailee, even the slightest neglect resulting in the loss, injury or destruction of the bailed chattel will be actionable. Any borrower of a chattel is such a bailee.

This three-tiered classification is one that most courts, in Professor Brown's words, "pay lip service

to." However, it requires an initial characterization of the bailment which may go a long way to
deciding the whole case. Moreover, since two of
the three classifications require a finding of *sole*
benefit to either the bailor or the bailee, such
findings will be rare and the bulk of a jurisdiction's
case law will probably fall into the "mutual benefit" type of bailment requiring due care from the
bailee. After all, if I borrow my neighbor's hedge
clippers today, he can borrow my saw—and much
more easily borrow a cup of sugar—tomorrow, so
such neighborliness becomes of mutual benefit to
both parties.

On the other hand, the classifications involving a
sole benefit interpose rules which prevent the
courts from reaching unexpected decisions. An art
museum borrowing a painting for an exhibition, is
commonly thought to establish a bailment for the
bailee's sole benefit because great care of the painting in its possession is reasonably expected, although the painting is likely to gain in value by
being exhibited and if imported for the purpose
may be immunized from seizure by judicial process
by a procedure administered by the State Department. 22 U.S.C.A. § 2459 (1985). In the case of a
bailment of sole benefit to the bailor, the classification allows a court to prevent exposing a finder to
unexpected liability and, in fact, encourages finders to hold onto chattel they come across. Even
here, however, it is difficult to conceive of a find
which is not of some benefit to the finder, who will

get to keep the chattel found if the true owner does not claim it.

Conceptual difficulties, then, with the three-tiered classification of bailments has led some courts to conclude that one standard of care—due care under the circumstances—should be the test. Ease of administration and flexibility commend this uniform standard to the courts adopting it. *Peet v. Roth Hotel Co.* (1934). In determining the due care required of the bailee, the purpose of the bailment is only one of many factors considered by the courts. They will also consider the method of transfer of possession, the terms of any contract of bailment, the type of goods bailed, and whether any consideration was given for it. Some courts have used a standard of care requiring a bailee to safeguard the chattel as if it was *his* own property. Most of the authorities require that the bailee act like a reasonable person. The difference is more than anything else a matter of proof, for evidence that the bailee did not treat the chattel as he would his own requires a showing of his own sub-jective state of mind, while a "reasonable person" standard puts more objective and wide-ranging types of evidence before the court. The more ob-jective "reasonable person" standard is fairer to the bailor; the types of proof which will show a lack of due care encompass the subjective type, but are not limited to such matters which are, after all, within the bailee's knowledge and control.

E. THE BURDEN OF PROOF

1. The Majority Rule

Separate from the question of what standard of care should be applied to the bailee is the question of which party should prove the required negligence. Most states require that the bailor must prove that there was a bailment, that the bailee has failed to deliver, and that the bailee was negligent in carrying it out when the chattel was lost, injured or destroyed. This makes the party alleging the wrongdoing prove it and will deter spurious claims. See *Knight v. H & H Chevrolet* (1983) (an excellent opinion collecting and discussing the cases reviewing this traditional rule and the other rules presented on the next several pages of this book).

2. A Second View

Other states hold that if a bailed chattel is lost, injured or destroyed, a presumption of negligence on the bailee's part arises once the bailor shows that there was a bailment. In defense of this rule, it is said that the bailee will be the person in possession of the facts or at least be in the best position to acquire them. *Nissho Iwai American Corp. v. New England Warehousing & Distribution, Inc.* (1986). Its critics charge that the bailee is here forced to prove a negative—always a difficult matter—but in practice the proof is likely to consist of evidence showing that the chattel was subjected to a prudent regimen or was treated as the bailee would prudently treat his own property and no differently. If successful in this, then sometimes the burden is met and shifts back to the bailor to present further evidence of lack of due care.

The operation of this presumption, however, raises the question of how much evidence the bailee must produce to rebut it. Merely proving that there was a theft or a fire is clearly insufficient. A few states permit him to rebut it by showing that loss or damage was by a fire of an unknown origin or that the loss and failure to deliver was due to the theft of the chattel by someone not under the bailee's control. A majority of states using a presumption of negligence go further and require that the bailee show his due care of the chattel with probative evidence sufficient to win before the trier of fact. *Classified Parking Systems v. Dansereau* (1976).

Imposing the heavier burden on the bailee seems to be the wiser course. First, the policy underlying the presumption is to encourage bailees to take care and the "due care" rule best implements this policy. Second, the "due care" rule places the burden on the party with the likeliest access to the facts, while the minority rule tempts the dishonest bailee to conceal facts relevant to the litigation. Third, the other rule is inconsistent with the presumption of negligence; it permits the trier of fact to draw an inference of non-negligence from the

fact of, e.g., a fire, theft or act of God when through
the presumption, the law has already settled the
legal consequences of the facts the other way.
Knowles v. Gilchrist Co. (1972). Fourth, the other
rule often penalizes a plaintiff's honesty in formulating his pleadings. Often a theft or a "mysteri-
ous stranger" defense arises through a fact alleged
in the plaintiff's pleading, as where the complaint
states that plaintiff saw his watch on the arm of
some unknown party leaving the repair shop as he
entered it or saw his car being driven out of a
parking lot as he approached to reclaim it. The
inference in both cases is that a theft has taken
place. This plaintiff, who knows a little about the
loss, is in a worse position than the plaintiff who
knows nothing or does not plead what he knows.
Finally, the "due care" rule represents a simplification in the system of recovery by bailors for loss
or damage to the bailed chattel.

3. A Third Rule

A third group of states requires that when a
bailor sues in tort, he has the burden of proof that
the bailee was negligent, but if the bailor sued in
contract, the burden is on the bailor to show his
own due care in carrying out the bailment contract. *Thummel v. Krewson* (1989). Here the allocation of the burden of proof becomes the result of
whether the plaintiff has pled his case in tort or
contract. Such a reliance on the pleading gives a
legal advantage to the plaintiff wise enough to hire

skillful counsel rather than to a plaintiff with a good case on the merits. See *Knowles v. Gilchrist Co.*, op. cit. Moreover, the hybrid nature of a bailment makes such facile pleading possible in many, perhaps most, bailment situations.

F. THE MEASURE OF DAMAGES

The usual measure of damages for the complete loss of a bailed chattel is its market value at the time of the loss. For damages to the chattel, the bailee receives the difference between the fair market value of the chattel before and after its injury. Where the lost or damaged chattel has no ready fair market value, courts permit the plaintiff bailor to show its actual value to the bailor. If my bailee loses the incomplete manuscript for this book, I am entitled to the value of my time and labor in replacing it. If I complete the manuscript and the publisher loses it while in the process of publishing it, I will receive its market value. Where a bailor entrusts family papers, portraits of loved ones or photographs of deceased relatives, the fair market value may not be great or even be provable. If the family papers can be reconstructed, the cost of doing so becomes their actual value to the bailor. If the portrait turns out to be the only one of the bailor's dead father, that fact may be considered in assessing its actual value. If the photographic negative of a deceased relative is destroyed, that fact may be considered as well. Courts have split on the question of whether actual value may include the sentimental value of the chattel; on the one hand, sentimental value is speculative and prone to exaggeration after the fact but on the other, the plaintiff's special feelings for a chattel is one factor in any assessment of their actual value because they indicate the lengths to which a bailor will go to repair or replace the object.

Similarly interesting issues have arisen in cases discussing rights in photographic negatives. When a person returns from a trip with several roles of exposed film and delivers them to a bailee for processing, the measure of damages for breach of the bailment for services is not merely the replacement value of the film in its unexposed state. The subject of the bailment being the exposed film with images on it, the damages are measured by the value of the images to the photographer. For a discussion of these issues, see *Carr v. Hoosier Photo Supplies, Inc.* (1981) (enforcing a written limitation of liability). When the bailor has just returned from a world tour and presented films of his travels for processing, he is unlikely to recover the cost of retaking the trip and the photos; the measure of damages is more precisely the value of remembering the trip through the photos, not the cost of the trip itself. Cf. *Hoffman v. Eastman Kodak Co.* (1929) (involving travel pictures, interpreting state statute, and limiting liability to replacement cost of film).

If the bailee has previously recovered an amount more than the bailor proves in damages, the former is not bound to account to the bailor for the difference. A bailment is not a fiduciary relationship and no such accounting as would be imposed on a trustee is necessary because, in contrast to a bailment situation, a trustee would have title to the chattel subject to a trust. *City of Waltham v. Tukay Furs Service Company, Inc.* (1978). Generally, the burden of proof in damages rests with the bailor, as the party with the knowledge and expertise to present this evidence.

G. THE BAILEE'S LIABILITY FOR MISDELIVERY

An ordinary, voluntary bailee is absolutely liable for loss of the chattel if a redelivery is made to some person without a rightful claim to it. In misdelivering the chattel, the bailee has committed an act of conversion, interfering by definition with the rights of the bailor as a prior possessor or true owner.

This liability is not extended to involuntary bailees, be they finders or some person to whom a chattel is delivered by mistake. *Cowen v. Pressprich* (1922). The involuntary bailee who in good faith is trying to return the chattel should not be held liable for making the same mistake—misdelivery—made by the initial deliverer. Indeed, if the attempt to return is promptly undertaken, the actions of the involuntary bailee defeat the notion that he ever agreed to the bailment. Certainly there was no contractual bailment and no acceptance of delivery to make out a conveyancer's bailment. Only the loosest use of the term will sustain the presence of any bailment here.

So the involuntary bailee is not liable unless he is found to have acted negligently in attempting to return the misdelivered chattel. The possibility of a fraudulent misdelivery, as where the bailee claims to have misdelivered a chattel of which he really still has concealed possession, has not persuaded the courts to adopt a different rule. Neither has another con-game. Where a chattel was ordered by a swindler from a plaintiff for delivery to the eventual defendant who then becomes an involuntary bailee and at whose premises the swindler then picks up the goods while claiming to be the agent of the plaintiff, the rule is the same and there is no liability for misdelivery to the swindler. *Krumsky v. Loeser* (1902).

H. BAILEE'S FAILURE TO RETURN CHATTEL

In situations in which the bailee has not misdelivered the chattel, but without excuse fails to return or retransfer it to the bailor at the appointed time, the bailor has an election to make. A demand can be made for the return of the chattel and an action brought for breach of the bailment in contract or tort or, at the bailor's option, the latter can treat the chattel's retention as a continuation of the original bailment. Electing the second course of action would entitle the bailor to recover rent at the rate specified in the original bailment agreement. Some courts however have expressed concern that, when the original agreement is extended to its full term, payment of the rent for the full term may work a hardship on the bailee intending to retain the chattel for a shorter time. See *Bibby's Refrigeration v. Salisbury* (1992) (collecting and discussing the cases).

II. COMMERCIAL BAILMENTS

One certain result of the sliding scale of liability in bailments is that legal results are hard to predict. This uncertainty, producing as it has conflicting results and different classifications of the benefits involved in similar types of bailments, was long seen as a hindrance to commerce. So the Uniform Commercial Code (UCC), Article 7, was drafted for commercial transactions involving bailments to warehousers. A "warehouseman" is defined by the UCC as "a person engaged in the business of storing goods for hire." The business need not be conducted for profit, so state-run and co-operative warehousers are covered by the Code. The warehouser cannot avoid the reach of the Code's provisions by pleading non-compliance with a governmental regulation because his own misconduct does not diminish his responsibility. Still, the warehouser must be "engaged for hire." Storing one's own personal property will not subject one to Code liability.

The other type of commercial bailee for whom the uncertainty of the common law standards of care was unsuitable was a common carrier. Along with inn-keepers, common carriers were subject to strict liability for a failure to deliver bailed goods. They were in effect insurers of the personal property entrusted to them. The receipt issued by a common carrier is called a bill of lading. Under the UCC, § 7–102(1)(a), a bailee subjected to the UCC is "the person who by a warehouse receipt, bill of lading, or other document of title acknowledges possession of goods and contracts to deliver them."

For commercial bailees, then, the tendency in the law in the last several decades has been to make their bailments the subject of state statutes, rather than the common law or any contract (generally in a pre-printed, standardized form). These control the relationship of bailor to bailee and produce in commercial situations a standardized bailment.

A. STANDARD OF CARE

1. Warehousers

UCC § 7–204(1) is declaratory of the common law and appears to change nothing of substance in it.

A warehouseman is liable for damages for loss of or injury to the goods caused by his failure to exercise such care in regard to them as a reasonably careful man would exercise under like circumstances but unless otherwise agreed he is not liable for damages which could not have been avoided by the exercise of such care.

Two slight changes were made in the language of previous uniform acts when drafting this provision. First, the phrase "damages for loss of or injury to the goods" combines prior references to damages as well as to "any loss or injury." A rule *de minimis* seems thus incorporated into this section of the Code. Second, a "reasonably careful man" standard replaced that of a "reasonably careful owner." This shift from a more subjective standard involving the state of mind of an owner to a more universal standard of a reasonable man permits introduction of a wider variety of proof on the question of negligence. So the warehouser must take the care that a "reasonably careful man" would use under like circumstances. The warehouser is not then an insurer of the chattel bailed with him. He must exercise that degree of skill and care which a reasonable man would exercise in the operation of the business in which he engages.

2. Common Carriers

In many states, a common carrier is an insurer of the safe delivery of personal property in its charge; except for acts of God, inherent defects in the goods, the fault of the owner, or express contract, the carrier has a strict liability for nonnegligent loss and misdelivery of the goods. UCC

§ 7–309(1) provides that the UCC "does not repeal or change any law or rule of law which imposes liability on a common carrier for damages not caused by its negligence" and otherwise imposes on a carrier who issues a bill of lading "the degree of care in relation to the goods which a reasonably careful man would exercise under like circumstances," the same standard of care which the public is due from warehousers.

B. THE BAILEE'S BURDEN OF PROOF AND PERSUASION FOR DAMAGE TO THE BAILED GOODS

The warehouser or common carrier under the UCC has, in most states and under the weight of authorities, both the burden of proof and the burden of persuasion as to any of seven defenses listed in § 7–403(1). Two of these defenses pertain to matters already discussed in this chapter.

These lawful excuses which the warehouser or common carrier can use to defend against a failure to deliver to the bailor "entitled to delivery" under the warehouse receipt are (a) "delivery of the goods to a person whose receipt was rightful as against the claimant" and (b) "damage to or delay, loss or destruction of the goods for which the bailee is not liable."

In some instances, the practical difference between holding the warehouser and the common carrier liable for negligence or strictly liable is not that great. This is due both to the propensities of juries and to procedural problems involved in a suit against either a warehouser or a common carrier.

A bailment is an agreement to deliver the bailed chattel to its owner. Under the UCC, the bailee, whether a common carrier or a warehouser, has a duty to "deliver the goods to a person entitled under the document." This is the document's holder if it is negotiable or the person to whom delivery is to be made under its terms if it is non-negotiable. This permits the document to control the bailee's liability for misdelivery, so long as the bailee acts in good faith, i.e., behaves honestly in fact. UCC § 7–404. The adept forgery of a warehouse receipt or bill of lading will not place the risk of a misdelivery on the bailee.

Under the UCC § 7–403(1)

The bailee must deliver the goods to a person entitled under the document ... (who pays the bailee's shipping or storage charges and surrenders the bill of lading or warehouse receipt for cancellation) unless and to the extent that the bailee establishes any of the following:

(b) damage to or delay, loss or destruction of the goods for which the bailee is not liable ... (parentheses the author's)

This makes it clear—clearer than much prior caselaw and the uniform acts that preceded the UCC—that it is the bailee who has the burden of establishing his non-liability for the bailed goods' loss or damage, i.e., that he has the burden of proving that he acted like a reasonable, careful person with regard to the goods. The bailee must, in other words, show himself free of negligence.

An optional clause, which the Code drafters advise can be added just after the quoted language, underscores this point:

... the burden of establishing negligence in such cases is on the person entitled under the document.

The "burden of establishing" is a term of art in the Code for what the law of evidence calls the burden of persuasion, to distinguish it from the burden of proof. (Thirteen states have adopted this optional language in their versions of the UCC).

The burden of proof usually refers to the necessity of adducing evidence to avoid an adverse ruling or judgment, and generally this burden is satisfied if a trier of fact could draw an inference from the fact or facts presented that (say) the bailee was not negligent. By presenting this evidence, the bailee avoids an adverse judgment at an early stage of the litigation. The inference drawn is not the only one possible and, indeed, the trier of fact need not draw it.

There is a second "burden of proof"; that is, after the bailee has produced evidence that a trier of fact could use to infer his non-negligence or due care, what happens if no more evidence is adduced by either bailee or bailor? Four things could now happen. First, the case could be decided at that point (no jurisdiction does this, however); second, the judge could rule that the burden now shifts to the bailor to adduce conflicting evidence of at least equal weight (but wouldn't it be illogical to assign the same burden of proof twice?); third, the judge could rule that the burden never shifts—and that the bailee has to adduce facts from which the trier of fact could infer due care, as well as facts from which the trier of fact could not help but infer due care; or fourth, the judge could rule that the burden shifts to the bailor who has the burden of adducing not only evidence of equal weight but also of adducing facts from which no other inference but the lack of due care is reasonable. In the third and fourth options, the judge has assigned the bailee and bailor respectively the burden of persuasion—of coming forward with facts from which the trier of fact not only could infer but also could not help but infer, the controverted proposition. Allocating this burden carries with it an allocation of the risk of non-persuasion.

The fourth alternative—assigning the burden of persuasion to the bailor—is what the optional language of § 7–403(1)(b) proposes. The "burden of establishing" negligence is in § 1–201(8) defined as "the burden of persuading the triers of fact that the existence of the fact is more probable than its non-existence." This is a clear reference to the burden of persuasion. Unless this optional language is used, the third alternative is preferable and the burden of proof is on the bailee to adduce a fact or facts from which non-liability can be inferred. This burden never shifts and encompasses both the burden of proof (in the sense of adducing facts from which non-liability could be inferred) and the burden of persuasion (adducing facts from which no other or only one inference could be drawn); both are assigned to the bailee. Some courts have held that the allocation of this burden applies in both negligence and contract causes of action.

There is some authority contrary to these conclusions, but it is unlikely that the drafters of the UCC would single out language for optional treatment if they intended the body of the section to accomplish the same result without it.

The negative phrasing of the text ("damage ... or loss ... for which the bailee is not liable") of § 7–403(1)(b) indicates that the drafters intended to incorporate the body of tort law pertaining to these bailment controversies. They did not state what liability is because the standards for finding it vary from state to state, and, not wanting to change state law, they put the bailee's burden in the negative. So in all probability the fourth alternative is not before a court deciding a bailor's claim under UCC § 7–403(1)(b).

An action for loss or damage of bailed goods is premised on an undertaking to deliver the goods up out of the bailment upon its fulfillment or upon demand. The UCC recognizes this undertaking ("the bailee must deliver the goods ..."). A showing by the bailor that 1) the goods were delivered to a bailee in good condition, and 2) that upon demand, the bailee could not deliver, or delivered the goods in a damaged condition, is sufficient to throw the burden of proof as to non-liability on the bailee. (The UCC imposes an additional duty to pay requested warehousing charges and present the warehouse receipt for cancellation as well. UCC § 7–403(2) and (3). However, these code-imposed duties may be futile and unnecessary when the goods are lost.)

This procedural discussion has a substantive result. If the bailor shows that goods were delivered to the bailee and either not delivered back or delivered in a defective condition, this leaves a factual vacuum between these two events. The bailee must fill this void. The Code's requiring him to show non-liability amounts to a presumption that whatever happened to the goods in between these two events was caused by the bailee's negligence, unless he proves otherwise. This presumption arises in the course of defining the cause of action, i.e., deciding what the bailor must put into his complaint. Out of the Code's assignment of the burden of proof in § 7–403(1)(b), then, comes a presumption that the bailee was negligent until he proves otherwise.

The next question is to choose the stage in the judicial proceedings at which to apply the presumption. The earlier it can be applied, the more powerful it is, for a presumption allows a court to single out a particular fact or set of facts and draw a legal conclusion from it alone. (As with, in the context of Chapter IV, the *Armory* rule or the presumption in *Clark* that "possession is *prima facie* evidence of title".) When a bailor shows a bailment and non-delivery or loss, he has made a *prima facie* showing that he is entitled to recover in replevin or trover against the bailee. This result follows pre-Code cases as well as the Code itself and cases decided under it.

Afterwards, when a bailee then comes forward with facts that show that he has no record of a delivery of them, or shows that their loss or damage was due to a fire of unknown origin, has he made a *prima facie* case for his own non-liability? The judge might then allow the case to be decided by permitting the trier of fact to balance the presumption of negligence against the facts which the bailee had adduced. A presumption of either negligence or non-negligence might be permissible in this instance. UCC § 7–403(1)(b), however, requires more. The failure to produce any record of their delivery or a failure to find an origin of the fire causing the loss or damage all have this in common: in each instance, the bailee has shown no more than "loss" or "damage" and § 7–403(1)(b) requires more, that he show "non-liability" as well. Indeed, the warehouser's ignorance is not an excuse and itself suggests fault. Moreover, the bailee has to "establish" his non-liability. "Establish" is the same verb used to define the burden of persuasion, so if the optional language isn't inserted in sub-section (1)(b), the bailee has both the burden of proof and the burden of persuasion. The type of legal presumption then involved here is one that skips from the bailor's *prima facie* case to a finding of lack of due care on the part of the bailee. If this telescoping of the legal analysis of the case were to be put into a substantive rule of law, the rule would be, "non-delivery or delivery in a defective condition is *prima facie* evidence of a bailee's lack of due care." This is a mandatory presumption unless the bailee rebuts it with further proof.

Notice, however, that under UCC § 7–403(1)(b) the bailee is not strictly liable for the bailed chattels. If he were, the UCC's substantive rule might provide: "The bailor's right to a delivery is good against all the world, except those with a better right." Under the UCC, no such strict liability arises.

Strict liability is not the rule in UCC bailments also in part because the bailor's cause of action lies partly in tort and partly in contract law (or, historically, trespass on the case or assumpsit). The plaintiff bailor pleads a relationship with the bailee, but whether his cause of action is premised simply on the relationship itself, on any express or implied contract springing from it, or on the bailee's tortious interference with the bailor's right to a redelivery of the bailed chattel, is unclear. Moreover, it is probably purposefully unclear, so that the courts can have flexibility to decide cases (or submit cases to juries) based on the equities of each case. Bailment is a relationship which is a hybrid of tort, contract, and property law—and in this instance, the last may be itself a hybrid of the first two. This hybrid nature of a bailment is still important, no matter that many aspects of the law have been codified in the UCC, because while the Code in § 7–204 and § 7–403 may state the standard of care and outline the procedures involved in many situations, that does not provide the bailor who cannot recover his chattels with a remedy. For that, he must look to the forms of action in conversion, trover, or replevin—all of which continue to exist independently of the UCC. And in such actions, for loss or damage to chattels, the bailee subject to the UCC has both the burden of proof and the burden of persuasion.

1. Theft From a Warehouse

A bailee, including a warehouser, is excused from his duty to deliver when § 7–403(1)(b) applies, but that section covers "damage to or delay, loss or destruction" and does not expressly cover theft. Of course "loss" may include loss by theft. If theft is included within this term the warehouser will be liable if the theft is caused by the warehouser's lack of due care, and the warehouser must plead and prove his due care, carrying both the burden of proof and the burden of persuasion. If the thief is in the employ of the warehouser, the negligence of the warehouse may include a failure to screen or supervise the thieving employee. However, the common law rule was that the warehouser is not liable for the employee's theft because it was beyond the scope of his employment and so was (obviously) unauthorized by the warehouser.

In this instance, this common rule is probably overruled by the UCC and "loss" should include loss by an employee's theft. First, consider that if the employee were negligent and as a result a stranger stole goods from the warehouse, the warehouser would at least have the burden of showing his due care in supervising the employee entrusted with the chattel and would probably be liable because the negligence of the employee would be imputed to his employer. If an employee's negligence is within the scope of his employment, why should not the more heinous act of stealing be within the scope of the employment as well? Second, the common law rule thwarts the rule of § 7–204(2) of permitting reasonable limitations on liability by allowing the warehouser to escape theft liability altogether. Third, the common law rule also runs counter to the general rule of due care imposed on the warehouser in § 7–204(1). Finally, consider a textual argument: the defenses listed in § 7–403 are an illustrative, non-exclusive list of excuses for a warehouser's failing to deliver; reading "loss" broadly implements the policy of construing the section liberally.

The foregoing two paragraph analysis is suggested by Murray, "The Warehouseman's and Carrier's Liability for Theft by Their Employees in England

and the United States," 39 U.Pitt.L.Rev. 707 (1978), which is well worth reading.

C. MISDELIVERY

UCC § 7–403(1) provides that a bailee, including a warehouser, must deliver the bailed chattels to the person entitled under the document. His is a strict liability for a misdelivery unless he can establish the existence of a valid excuse. These excuses are outlined in sub-sections (a) through (g) of § 7–403(1).

The first excuse listed in § 7–403(1)(a) is that "the delivery of the goods to a person whose receipt was rightful as against the claimant." Under this language, the warehouser who delivers goods to the true owner after their deposit by a thief incurs no liability. Similarly, delivery to a person with a claim of prior possession, never abandoned, would be excused.

Suppose, however, that the true owner is not the first to claim the goods. In any later action by the true owner, the warehouser must show, according to § 7–404, that he made any prior delivery of the chattels "according to the terms of the document" and also that he acted in good faith and according to reasonable commercial standards. A bailee who has delivered chattel to a prior possessor, whose "claim was rightful" as to the bailor, when sued by the true owner, would lose his excuse for a failure to deliver under § 7–403(1)(a). The same result would obtain even if the prior possessor had obtained a court order, although compliance with that order is strong evidence of the bailee's good faith and adherence to reasonable commercial standards. See UCC § 7–404, discussed infra.

Two reasons support these results. Certainly the warehouser has a remedy in a replevin or trover action against the person to whom he misdelivers, except in the instance of a good faith purchase of a voidable title. So he has some remedy available to him. And in the second situation in the last paragraph, were he not to comply with the court order, his good faith and adherence to reasonable commercial standards would be doubtful, particularly if he knows of and seeks to judge conflicting claims.

Under the Code, then, the warehouser acts at his peril if he does not ascertain that the claimant of the goods is entitled under the document. This should be ascertained even when the warehouser does not know of the existence of any competing claims.

D. LIMITATIONS ON WAREHOUSER LIABILITY

UCC § 7–204(2) provides for a limitation of damages in situations in which the warehouser is liable. It does not authorize this type of a bailee to immunize himself from, or contract out of, liability for his own negligence; and indeed, under UCC § 7–202(3), any attempt to contract away his liability for negligence is ineffective. Instead, it permits him to set forth a specific liability per article or item, or value per unit of weight, beyond which he shall not be liable. *Griffin v. Nationwide Moving and Storage Company, Inc.* (1982).

The warehouser cannot limit his liability on a warehouse receipt as a whole. He cannot stipulate that he is liable only up to a certain amount on any one deposit receipted by him. What he can stipulate is that his liability on (say) a deposit of 5000 pounds of fish is limited to 50 cents a pound. The bailor of fungible chattels can thus easily calculate the financial risks involved in the bailment. The bailor of non-fungible chattels is by the same token encouraged to itemize his chattels carefully for the warehouse receipt in order to minimize the impact of the bailee's limitation on his liability. If any items of special or unique value are itemized separately, this type of limitation of liability will avoid the common law's problems with bailments of closed receptacles discussed previously. The limitation's effectiveness is subject to three qualifications. The first one sets up a procedure by which the bailor may increase the bailee's liability by a written request to him. This request must be made within a reasonable time of the bailee's delivery of the warehouse receipt to the bailor. The bailee can charge increased rates for storage based on the bailor's increased valuation of the bailed goods, but a further ceiling on both valuations and charges may be imposed by a lawful limitation of liability contained in the warehouser's tariff, the schedule of charges imposed by governmental regulations. If within the tariff, the bailor's timely request is binding on the warehouser.

The purpose of authorizing such requests for an increased valuation is to prevent the bailee from imposing a valuation below that requested by the bailor, so long as the increase keeps the valuation within any limits imposed by the warehouser's tariff. It has been suggested that the scope of this provision is limited to instances in which the warehouser is under a duty, enforced by governmental regulation, to accept the offered bailment. Otherwise, the bailee's freedom to contract has been limited; the Code would then deny him a right to refuse to accept chattels on the valuation assigned by the bailor.

Other governmental regulations may also have an effect on the validity of a limitation on liability. When a warehouse is not fireproof and governmental regulations call for fireproofing, a tariff limitation on fire losses may be invalid, having been authorized only for warehousers who conform to the regulations. Indeed, where such regulations are proven to embody the standards of "reasonable care under the circumstances," any limitation on liability authorized under UCC § 7–204(2) may arguably be invalid as well.

The second qualification on the warehouser's ability to limit his liability is stated in the last sentence of § 7–204(2): "no such limitation is effective with respect to the warehouseman's liability for conversion to his own use." This is a restatement of pre-Code case law and emphasizes the fact that these sections of the Code define the warehouser's duties without providing specific remedies or affecting pre-existing forms of action. Because a common law conversion is a convertor's exercise of dominion over the chattel, the phrase "to his own use" is arguably superfluous and, if so, any misdelivery of bailed goods would lift the limitation on the warehouser's liability; he would then be strictly liable for his misdelivery. The common law rationale was that misdelivery was an inherent risk of any bailment. The need for the common law rule must be weighed against the canon of statutory interpretation that presumes against the superfluity of a word or a phrase.

A third qualification is the most sweeping. It is contained in UCC § 7–404 which provides:

> A bailee who in good faith including observance of reasonable commercial standards has received goods and delivered or otherwise disposed of them according to the terms of the document of title ... is not liable therefor.

This section applies to both warehousers and common carriers. The bailee who stores or transports chattel when he has knowledge that there is a serious question about the property rights of the person bailing the article with him is liable for its conversion but not otherwise. See generally, Note, Bailor Beware: Limitations and Exclusions of Liability in Commercial Bailments, 41 Vand. L.Rev. 129 (1988).

E.   A FINAL WORD ON INNKEEPERS

At common law, inn-keepers had strict liability for the chattels of their guests; they were an insurer against loss, theft, or damage to these chattels while on their premises. Today that rule of strict liability is eroded by many state statutes which limit the liability of inn-keepers to maximum dollar amounts and require that a guest notify the inn-keeper of the presence on the premises of chattels which might produce liability over the dollar limit; some statutes also require that when the guest notifies the inn-keeper of this extra liability, the guest must deposit the extraordinarily valuable chattel with the inn-keeper for safekeeping in order to make a claim for its later loss.

Such statutes limiting an inn-keepers liability are enacted in all fifty states and the District of Columbia. Besides statutory provisions of the type just described, some states expressly permit an inn-keeper to limit its liability regardless of its negligence. *Associated Mills, Inc. v. Drake Hotel, Inc.* (1975). And regardless of its receipt for safekeeping of chattel worth more than the maximum dollar amount. *Nicholaides v. University Hotel Associates* (1990). In contrast, other state statutes establish a maximum dollar amount, but further provide that this maximum is inapplicable when the guest can prove that the inn-keeper was negligent. In the latter states, then, having proven negligence, the guest can recover the fair market value of the lost chattel or all damages to it. *Shamrock Hilton Hotel v. Caranas* (1972) (holding hotel liable for purse and jewels contained in it).

A final type of inn-keepers' statute is silent on the relationship between the stated maximum amount of liability and the law of negligence. Such a silence is taken by the courts to mean that the issue is left to them to decide, and as might be expected, courts have both enforced the limitation in the face of an inn-keeper's negligence and refused to do so.

Another common provision is to the effect that notices informing guests of the dollar limitation and other provisions of the applicable statute be conspicuously posted. *Terry v. Lincscott Hotel Corp.* (1980) [opinion of Judge Sandra Day O'Connor (now Justice O'Connor)]. As you know, this conspicuous posting is typically done on the back of the door to every guest room. *Skyways Motor Lodge Corp. v. General Foods Corp.* (1979). Often legally effective in this position, this location for the posting has also probably acquired the status of a custom or usage of the hotel industry, giving the location extra effectiveness. However, care must be taken by the inn-keeper writing this notice to inform the guest of the procedures offered for the safe-keeping of chattels of extraordinary value.

CHAPTER VII

GOOD FAITH PURCHASERS

The purchaser of a chattel who gives a valuable consideration (1) paid in the belief that the vendor had a right to sell and (2) parted with in circumstances which would not make him inquire into the vendor's title and right to sell, is said to be a good faith or bona fide purchaser. Another name for such a person is an "innocent purchaser for value."

The initial common law position was not favorable to the good faith purchaser, but the latter has increasingly sought and won the protection of the law, not because his innocence was to be rewarded, but because in some situations he served a commercial function that was growing in importance. He represented the needs of increasingly regional and national markets for sales made without an elaborate investigation of the chattel's title and made in reliance on the putative vendor's possession of the goods.

I. THE PROBLEM

The rise in the legal fortunes of the good faith purchaser has been rapid over the last century. He is part of a legal triad including a chattel's true owner, a rogue, and himself. In skeletal form, the facts producing the litigation in which he has had to engage can be reduced to the following: the rogue acquires a chattel from the true owner and transfers it to a good faith purchaser. The rogue either is judgment-proof or disappears. Later the true owner discovers that the good faith purchaser has the goods and seeks to replevy them or recover their value in trover from the purchaser.

With the rogue gone, a legal problem of some difficulty remains: which of the two innocent parties left is going to suffer the loss occasioned by the rogue's crookedness?

Two commentators have said that other names for a bona fide purchaser are "the law student's 'sad sack'" and a "bona fide dummy," and although this may sometimes be the case, the problem, in its "pure" form, calls for more analysis than any such *ad hominem* could provide. If it is impractical to expect a vendor to inquire into the honesty of the purchasers with whom he deals, is it any more impractical than expecting a good faith purchaser to investigate the title of a vendor? Investigating honesty is an inquiry everyone can undertake, but an investigation of title is a more specialized undertaking. And even if these tasks are conceded to be of equal difficulty, perhaps the law is correct in choosing to favor the party representing the societal interests of trade and commerce. Individual equities being relatively equal, a judge is free to choose an expedient solution. And finally, where both the true owner and the purchaser have been equally diligent in protecting themselves against theft and acquisition of a defective title, the law will need to resolve conflicts among its doctrines in such a way as to give it the discretion to decide sometimes for the true owner and sometimes for the purchaser as the facts of the case tip the equities in the balance now to one side and then to the other. These conflicts will be explained in the ensuing discussion.

The primary justification for protecting a purchaser involves an inquiry into his good faith. With this good faith present, the law needs to carve out an exception to the general rule to the effect that, if a true owner does not intend to transfer title to a chattel to another who nonetheless obtains possession of it, that person acquires no title to it and cannot pass good title to it to yet another transferee to whom its later transfer is made. This is called the "void title rule." If a title was void in the hands of a transferor, its quality does not improve in the hands of the next transferee.

The idea that "one can't give what one doesn't have," in Latin, *nemo dat quod non habet,* underlies the general rule and has a metaphysical ring to it. It implies the commonly-held notion that along with the transfer of the chattel comes a transfer of title. Title here is intended to refer to a basic unit of ownership.

A requirement that possession and title be transferred together is evident in the common law attitude toward the requirement of a delivery in the law of gifts. Moreover, it made sense in local markets in which vendors and purchasers of goods met face to face and transferred the goods in exchange for cash. Besides, in some situations, it is impractical to have the title to personalty pass independently of possession. The rule that no title is passed by a person without title cannot control in the case of money, negotiable commercial paper, promissory notes or bank checks. Even a thief can pass good title to money or negotiable instruments. The needs of capital markets and trade overwhelm the void-title rule here.

In England, certain marketplaces on certain days and all of London's shops every business day were designated by charter to be "markets overt", wherein a good faith purchaser could take good title to chattels to which his vendor had no title. The doctrine of a market overt has never been accepted or applied in the United States. The closest we come to a market overt in the United States is a sheriff's sale of a debtor's property to satisfy a judgment, but the analogy has been rejected and the majority rule for such sales is that the successful bidder at the sale acquires no better title than the execution debtor had going into the sale.

The void title rule is intended to instill an attitude of wariness in purchasers: *caveat emptor*—let the buyer beware. It worked well in local face to face markets but became increasingly questioned in markets which were broader in scope. Indeed, in regional or national markets, the good faith necessary to protect the purchaser tended to be proven, not by a showing of his subjective good faith but by the fact that he entered into the transaction using accepted commercial practices. His business practices conforming to the norm, the court looks less into the matter of his individual good faith.

The void title rule has never been overruled. Courts have rather looked at the type of title transferred and have added a new issue, phrased to protect the good faith purchaser. Under common law (and now under the Uniform Commercial Code § 2–403) the law asked itself two questions: (1) did the true owner of the chattel intend to transfer it to the rogue?; and (2) if the rogue received a "voidable" title, did the rogue transfer the title to a good faith purchaser in whose hands the voidable title becomes absolute?

These questions are addressed seriatim, in the order previously listed. This order is mandatory. If the true owner did not intend to transfer title to the rogue, then the title which the latter receives is void, and a court never inquires into the status of the purchaser.

These two questions will now be discussed in turn.

A. VOID AND VOIDABLE TITLE

To protect a purchaser, then, the law first had to inquire into the concept of title. Its unitary nature had to be made, through a type of legal nuclear fission, divisible. The unit-splitting method of legal analysis, it turned out, was the concept of the true owner's intent to transfer title to a person who, under the general rule, would not be able to pass on any title.

The judge's motivation in litigation over a chattel between a true owner and a good faith purchaser is easily enough seen. Both of the litigants are to some degree innocent parties, but the judge may regard this innocence as a relative matter and think one more innocent than the other for, after all, the owner's innocence can be seen as naivete and as the cause of the good faith purchaser's troubles.

Moreover, the judge is caught between conflicting principles of law. On the one hand, he probably believes, along with his common law brethren, that no owner should be deprived of his property without his consent (e.g., by a thief). This belief will be strongest in cases where the chattel concerned are his possessions—items taken out of the stream of commerce and devoted to his personal use. On the other hand, the judge also probably believes that purchasers need a secure title to the goods they purchase, particularly if the transaction takes place in a commercial setting where the purchaser may want to resell the goods rather than use them himself. As Grant Gilmore has argued, he needs a way of maintaining the void title rule in non-commercial settings while relaxing it in commercial cases in which there is some deviation from normal commercial practice in the true owner's parting with the goods, but no such deviation in the acquisition of the same goods by a subsequent purchaser.

The concept of "voidable title" is an intermediate position for the judge. It allows him to maintain both of his beliefs. It works in the manner described in the next several paragraphs.

The early common law did not distinguish between a transfer of title to and possession of a chattel. However, common use of the executory contract changed all that.

Once a transfer of title depends on more than a delivery of a chattel but takes place when the parties to the contract intend it to take effect, the courts are given discretion to distinguish between various types of transactions in which the true owner surrenders possession of the goods. If for example the chattel is stolen from the true owner, he can have no intention to transfer it to the thief, and the void title rule applies even where the thief later sells the chattel to a good faith purchaser. The same is true when the parties make a mutual mistake when contracting with each other. The title in the hands of the transferee is void.

Likewise, a transfer by a bailee confers a void title on the bailee's transferee. Why? Because the bailor did not intend, when the bailment was created, that there be a delivery by the bailee to any person other than himself; this definitionally is what a bailment involves and unless there has been an entrustment (see section II E *infra*) a void title results.

However, when the true owner is induced to part with the goods through some fraud or misrepresentation by the transferee, one can say that the owner did intend to part with title. The true owner intended to transfer the chattel, even though fraud was used to induce that intent. In such situations, the true owner of the chattel can replevy them upon finding out that the original transaction was fraudulent. In this sense the title of the subsequent purchaser is voidable—liable to being revoked by the true owner or an assignee of his rights. However, this ability to void the title ends when the chattel comes into the hands of a good faith purchaser. At that point, the voidable title becomes absolute.

Thus there are two classifications of title which can be passed on to subsequent purchasers—void and voidable. Which type of title was transferred is a matter of ascertaining the intent of the transferor. The vocabulary of estates can assist in this classification. Where there is no title to give, the courts might regard the transfer document as neither a contract for nor a conveyance of the chattel. It is void *ab initio*. When the title is voidable, the title might be regarded as having been conveyed subject to a condition subsequent; here the transferee acquires an absolute title, subject to the right of the true owner to rescind and replevy the chattel while it remains in the hands of the fraudulent transferee.

A voidable title is a defective title, but it is not wholly defective. It is a title which has been transferred by a deed or contract which one party to the document (generally the true owner) has the power to rescind. The title is then voidable by the person with the right of rescission, but it is not voidable by the other party. The right to rescind is often called the equity of rescission.

Asking a court to exercise this equity is like asking a court to compel the surrender of some right, title or advantage by the defendant. Equity will compel such a surrender only when it is unconscionable for the defendant to retain it. If the defendant acquired title with notice of the equity of the plaintiff, or if he did not pay value (but was without notice), he should surrender it.

All this was first a matter of equity pleading before such rules became incorporated into the substantive law of personal property. This highlights another interesting feature of this definition of voidable title. It has a procedural origin and aspect. Defining any substantive concept in terms of its procedural origins is to leave a good deal of imprecision in the concept. Grant Gilmore has called the concept of voidable title the courts' "happiest discovery" and "a vague idea, never defined and perhaps incapable of definition." G. Gilmore,

"The Commercial Doctrine of Good Faith Purchase," 63 Yale L.J. 1057, 1059 (1954). Its greatest virtue was its capacity for growth.

B. THE GOOD FAITH PURCHASER

When a court reaches the question of whether a transferee qualifies as a good faith purchaser the answer depends on whether (1) he gave a fair or reasonable value for a chattel, (2) in an honestly held belief that he was acquiring title, or whatever rights he bargained for, to it, and (3) under circumstances which would not lead him to question his vendor's right or title.

So a donee would not qualify. A good faith purchaser must advance some new consideration, surrender some security, or do some act which will cause him to be in a worse position if the transfer is rescinded. All these things must be done in advance of any notice to him of the true owner's adverse claim. Likewise, a person who acquires a chattel with either actual or constructive notice that his vendor used any fraud or deceit to acquire possession of it, does not qualify. So someone in collusion with a rogue can never become a good faith purchaser.

Many aspects of the definition of a good faith purchaser are today found in cases controlled by the provisions of the Uniform Commercial Code. See Section II, infra, for a discussion of the UCC.

C. INSURABLE INTERESTS
IN STOLEN CHATTEL

In disputes involving the true owner, a rogue and a purchaser, remember that the issue as between the true owner and the purchaser is one of priority of title. When either of these parties loses, they can still pursue the rogue for fraud. In addition, the purchaser will in some situations, as with the purchase of a stolen automobile, have insured the chattel, and there is no reason to deny that he has an insurable interest in the vehicle even though it turns out he has no title to it. The insurance policy after all will be governed by the law of contract rather than the law of personal property. Even if the law of personal property is held controlling of the determination of whether the insured held an "insurable interest," the void title rule can, for stolen goods, be restated to the purchaser's advantage using the relativity of title doctrine; i.e., that a good faith purchaser of a stolen chattel had a right to that chattel good against everyone save the true owner.

One reason that the insurance company might be interested in the state of the title to the insured object is that the company, having paid the claim made under the policy, will want to pursue the insured's right to replevy or sue for damages for the theft. In the case of a theft, however, this right (of subrogation) will be a hollow one since the rogue will many times have disappeared. If the true owner rather than the purchaser had taken out the insurance policy, the insurer's subrogation right would not be any the less hollow.

Moreover, the doctrine of relativity of title means that there is some right in the purchaser to be subrogated to the insurer. It is not the absolute or "sole and unconditional" (the phrase is from many insurance contracts) interest in the chattel insured. However, if only such interests could be insured, the insurer could ignore many claims in which the insured's right of possession gave rise to his expectation of an interest in the insured personal property. To protect this expectation, the sole and unconditional ownership clause in the insurance policy functions only as a warranty of an insured's good faith belief that the title is in the insured and not as a warranty of facts of which the insured has no knowledge, such as the fact that the chattel was stolen.

Could not the finder of a jewel insure his interest in it? If the courts will allow the chimney sweep in the *Armory* case to recover in an action of trover, it does not make a lot of sense to say that he cannot at the same time have an insurable interest in the jewel. If a watch is left for repair, cannot the bailee repairman insure against its being stolen? Insurance companies will lose a lot of business if an insurance company can require that an absolute title be in its insureds.

Another reason that the insurer wants to be subrogated to the rights of its insured is that it does not want to have to engage any insured who wants thereafter to recover twice, in a race to find the rogue and sue him. The settlement of the claim between the insurer and insured is in effect the insured's foreswearing any further legal action against the rogue; any rights he has are put in the hands of the insurer. So the purpose of the sole and unconditional ownership clause is fulfilled when the insured settles his claim.

There is authority to the effect that a purchaser of a stolen automobile (the main litigation-breeder on this question) does not have an insurable interest in it. *Hessen v. Iowa Automobile Mutual Insurance Co.* (1922). Some recent authorities hold that the purchaser of a stolen automobile has an insurable interest in it, although there continues to be a split in the cases in this area. Dispositive for some courts deciding that there is no insurable interest is the fact that state statutes requiring the public registration of title to automobiles provide also that a transfer of title be accomplished by a transfer of the certificate of title to the vehicle and that transfers not so accomplished are void. Where certificates of title are routinely used, the purchaser who does not require one from his transferor is less deserving of protection, but unless the purchaser did not take in good faith, knew of the true owner's identity or had the means to find it out, the doctrine of relativity of title should be enough to give the good faith purchaser an insurable interest in the chattel.

D. EXTINGUISHING THE TRUE OWNER'S TITLE IN FAVOR OF A GOOD FAITH PURCHASER

If a legislature is going to cut off the right and title of a true owner in favor of a good faith purchaser, it must do so clearly. If, for example, statutes on sheriff's sales for payment and satisfaction of a debt are intended to cut off the true owner's rights, they must clearly state that this is the effect of the statute. Most state statutes on the subject do not so state, and their effect is to provide that the purchaser at the sheriff's sale acquires no more title than the execution debtor had going into the sale. *Griffith v. Fowler* (1846).

In the field of international law, if a foreign government, in a declaration of war or expropriation, cuts off a true owner's rights, such an action normally would be recognized by our courts or would place the owner's rights beyond their jurisdiction. Thereafter, Congress must be clear that it intends to reverse this action in our courts; otherwise any declaration or resolution condemning the action will not have this specific legal consequence. *Williams v. Armroyd* (1813).

The first clear legislative reversal of the void title rule in the United States came with the so-called Factors Acts. A factor is an agent employed to sell goods consigned to him in his own name for a commission. Never uniform among the states, the Acts were none-the-less similar in approach.

They shifted the loss caused by the fraudulent factor from the good faith purchaser to the true owner who, after all, selected the broker, transferred the goods to him and enabled him to accomplish the fraud.

Later legislation, first the Uniform Sales Act, § 25, and now in all states except Louisiana, the Uniform Commercial Code, codified both the void title rule and the void/voidable distinction. The UCC also added one further qualification to the void title rule—the so-called entrustment doctrine. Because of the near omnipresence of the UCC, some extended discussion of its relevant provisions is in order.

II. THE UNIFORM COMMERCIAL CODE (UCC)

The UCC has now codified the general rule and the doctrine of good faith purchaser of personalty in its § 2–403(1), using the following language, first to restate the void title rule:

A purchaser of goods acquires all title which his transferor had or has power to transfer except that a purchaser of a limited interest acquires rights only to the extent of the interest purchased.

Under this language, a transferor with a void title confers nothing on his transferee. However, once a transferor has acquired title through this section (or by later portions of § 2–403 as well), his

subsequent transferees take his rights under the
Code. This is the "shelter" principle of this section. (It is also found in later portions of § 2–403).
A second aspect of this general rule is found in the
language "or had power to transfer." This means
that the law of agency, apparent agency and estoppel, apply to implement the general rule to the
effect that "what title the vendor appears to have,
the purchaser gets." The pre-UCC common law
was moving in this direction. See e.g., *O'Connor's
Administratrix v. Clark* (1895) (replevin of a horse-
drawn wagon).

This section then goes on to state the exception
to the general rule:

> ... A person with voidable title has power to
> *transfer* a good title to a *good faith* purchaser for
> *value*. When goods have been delivered under a
> *transaction of purchase* the purchaser has such
> power even though
>
> (a) the transferor was deceived as to the iden-
> tity of the purchaser, or
>
> (b) the delivery was in exchange for a check
> which is later dishonored, or
>
> (c) it was agreed that the transaction was to be
> a "cash sale," or
>
> (d) the delivery was procured through fraud
> punishable as larcenous under the criminal
> law.

The italicized words are discussed below.

The second sentence provides in (a) through (d) some examples of situations which have often been litigated. Under these subparagraphs, a true owner's transferring of a chattel to a rogue in an "all cash" sale, in exchange for a check that bounces or in circumstances punishable as a violation of the criminal code—a forged check—does not deny a subsequent purchaser the status of a good faith purchaser.

A. TRANSFER

The drafters of the Code do not use the word "delivery." Therefore a question arises as to whether or not a person must first take delivery of the chattel before claiming to be a good faith purchaser of it. The examples which follow in subparagraphs (a) through (d) make plain that delivery will usually be present, but paying value for a document of title is sufficient to "transfer a good title" too. Examples of a document of title are a deed, a warehouse receipt or a bill of lading which a purchaser can thereafter present to a bailee.

B. GOOD FAITH

The common law and the Code protect only subsequent purchasers whose transferor has a voidable title to a chattel and who take title in good faith. A transaction is undertaken in good faith when it is in fact done honestly, whether or not the transaction is performed negligently. If the trans-

feree is a merchant, however, a higher standard
applies. A merchant must observe reasonable
commercial practices for the same or similar transactions. If reasonable commercial practice demanded more care than the merchant observed, he
will be denied good faith purchaser status by the
courts. For example, when a person purchases a
car with a rubber check and resells it to a dealer in
another city, that second dealer should require a
certificate or other customary proof of title to the
vehicle and failing to do so will deny that dealer
good faith purchaser status. Similarly, a transaction between two dealers is judged by higher standards than would prevail in a sale by a dealer to a
consumer; unless required by statute, no certificate of title would be required when a consumer
claims good faith purchaser status. Moreover, as
we shall see in the next section, that a purchaser is
offered a chattel at well below its fair market value
is not enough to put him on notice that his transferor's title is defective or impose on him any duty
to inquire into the state of its title. Again, however, more leeway in this regard may be given the
non-commercial purchaser than is given his commercial counterpart.

C. VALUE

A purchaser for value need not have a suitcase
full of cash to exchange for a chattel. To use the
example in the paragraph above again, when the
thief who buys a car with a rubber check resells it

for one half of its fair market value, a purchasing dealer may be denied the protection of § 2–403(1) because he has not given value. A non-dealer purchaser can, however, pay far less than the fair market value and not be denied the status of a protected purchaser. The reason for this is that courts are reluctant to undo a bargain struck by agreement. Inadequacy of price alone will not deny a person a protected status, unless the price is so inadequate as to "shock the conscience of the court." Moreover, not only can a contract price be paid in installments, but the contract itself can be given in consideration of a preexisting debt of the transferor. Generally under the Code value is any consideration sufficient to support a simple, executory contract or a purchaser's pre-existing claim— that is, any contractual consideration, present or past, is sufficient to support the claim that a purchaser paid "value" under the Code. § 1–201(44) (b), (d). Donees are excluded from protection by the phrase.

D. TRANSACTION OF PURCHASE

This phrase is broader than any fraudulent action enumerated in the subparagraphs which follow it. So it includes any transaction which results in the purchaser therein obtaining a voidable title. Courts have applied a functional analysis to this phrase: if the transaction, no matter that it is denominated a lease, is in reality a conditional sales agreement, the courts will treat it as a "transaction of purchase." They will look to the substance of the transaction rather than to its form.

E. ENTRUSTING CHATTEL

If you leave your watch for repair, should you look around the jeweler's shop to find out if he also sells watches, particularly second-hand ones? The answer today is yes, but at common law, you need not have been so careful. At common law, leaving the watch created a bailment. The true owner intended to pass no title to it to the repairman but instead only wanted to give him its possession for the (limited) purpose of fixing it. If the bailee resells it, his title being void, he transfers nothing to a purchaser, even one with good faith. *Baehr v. Clark* (1891).

Indeed, the purchaser in many jurisdictions committed a conversion of the watch by the very act of purchasing it as his own. Some jurisdictions mitigate the harshness of this doctrine by requiring that the conversion is complete only when the true owner makes a demand for the watch's return and the demand is refused, but this only delays the liability of the purchaser for the conversion.

The true owner's cause of action for conversion by the bailee of the watch survives today; the UCC does not affect it. What the UCC does affect is the true owner's cause of action against the purchaser of the watch—no such action survives the passage of the UCC. Why? Because even though purchasers from bailees are denied the protection of § 2–403(1), § 2–403(2) creates an additional class of purchasers entitled to special protection. They are those who buy "in the ordinary course of business" from one to whom a chattel has been entrusted. In the somewhat cryptic language of the UCC,

> Any entrusting of possession of goods to a merchant who deals in goods of that kind gives him power to transfer all rights of the entruster to a buyer in ordinary course of business.

The next sub-paragraph (3) of this section defines entrusting as including "any delivery and any acquiescence in retention of possession," regardless of any condition placed on the transfer between the parties and no matter that the possessor's disposition of the chattel constituted the crime of larceny.

Delivery is a precondition of an entrustment. So delivery of your watch for repair to the jeweler who also sells second-hand watches may be a statutory entrusting, no matter that you only intended a common law bailment. The particular purpose of the entrustment is irrelevant, so long as it is made to "a merchant who deals in goods of that kind." § 2–402(2). Similarly irrelevant is whether the entrustor was acting in the course of his own business, or just dealing occasionally and for his own purposes: all commercial and quasi-commercial entrustments are treated alike. Likewise, the delivery of a chattel on consignment by a wholesaler to a retailer of such chattel means that a purchaser in the ordinary course of business with the retailer will take free of the wholesaler's rights, even if the wholesaler and retailer agreed that the former would retain title to them. Finally, the entrusting is sufficient to entitle a purchaser to Code protection: the latter need not take delivery of the chattel; a transfer of title to him is enough to cut off the entrustor's rights.

An entrustor's clothing the possessor with the power to transfer is, insofar as the term "power" is concerned, a repeat of a phrase used in § 2–403(1). Presumably it also serves as an incorporation by reference of § 2–403(1) into the terms of § 2–403(2) and (3). The principle involved in the phrase is one of estoppel. The entrustor is estopped to deny the possessor's transfer because he set up the situation in which the buyer in the ordinary course of business relied on the title of the possessor.

The facts of a famous pre-Code case are illustrative. In *Zendman v. Harry Winston, Inc.* (1953), the plaintiff went into an auction house on the Atlantic City, N.J. boardwalk and purchased a diamond ring at auction. The defendant had actually left the ring with the operator of the auction, as he often did, with a memorandum in which the defendant retained title. When the defendant learned of the sale, he demanded the ring back.

In its common law form, estoppel requires proof that the appearances at the auction reasonably induced the purchaser to rely on the title of the auctioneer. Reliance is shown by a subjective belief. The concept of a "buyer in the ordinary course" has the effect of permitting appearances, rather than the state of mind of the purchaser, to control the showing of reliance. It may now be shown by objective facts: if the public could reasonably have expected, from all the circumstances surrounding the auction, that the auctioneer had authority to transfer title to the chattel sold, then the entrustor is estopped.

Common law estoppel is usually a shield, not a sword; it does not give rise to a cause of action, but the positive wording of the entrustment rule in the Code indicates that this is no longer true. Thus the true owner of goods who without protest allows another to treat them as his own so that a third person is induced to purchase them in good faith, cannot replevy them from that person, and the latter has an action to quiet title to the chattel which he was induced to purchase.

In deciding the *Zendman* case, for example, the court concluded that Harry Winston had created an implied authority in the auctioneer to deal with the ring as his own. It also cited the fact that Harry Winston had previously and several times approved sales unauthorized by the title-retention memo which Winston left with the auctioneer. This past practice between the entrustor and the possessor should have no significance to the purchaser unless he knew about it; and of course if he knew of this practice, the purchaser could not have acted in good faith at the auction. The past practice does, however, go to show that the goods were entrusted to "a merchant who deals in goods of that kind." To negate this effect, the defendant would have had to make some effort to notify the public at the auction that the ring entrusted to the auctioneer did not belong to the latter.

The *Zendman* case is pre-Code evidence that the common law was coming to accept something like the concept of the "buyer in the ordinary course of business." The "course of business" referred to is the vendor's, so that a buyer purchasing out of a vendor's inventory of like goods and chattels is most likely to achieve this protected purchaser status. The Code, however, makes no reference to a purchase from inventory. (There is discussion of such purchases in the commentary to § 2–403.) However, although the vendor to the protected purchaser need not necessarily have an inventory of goods similar to those sold, vendors who normally do not own the chattels in their possession will have a hard time sheltering their purchasers under the Code's aegis. Brokers in commodities or other types of personalty are examples. They themselves, when acquiring possession, are not "buyers in the ordinary course," although they may be purchasers with a voidable title under § 2–403(1). Neither will a purchaser acquiring the chattel from them be a buyer in the ordinary course. However, in the instance of the pawnbroker, a purchaser might reasonably expect that the period of pawn has expired before he purchased and so he become a protected purchaser of a frequently pawned item of personal property.

Finally, any rights acquired by a "buyer in the ordinary course" are incorporated into the general rule of § 2–403(1) and provide shelter for his subsequent transferees.

The entrustment sections of the UCC favor and expand the role of some purchasers and commerce at the expense of true owners, so remember that entrustment doctrine does not exclude the possibility of a larcenous merchant conveying a voidable title to a purchaser. G. Gilmore, The Good Faith Purchase Idea and the Uniform Commercial Code: Confessions of a Repentant Draftsman, 15 Ga. L.Rev. 605, 618–619 (1981). Although the choice between two perhaps equally innocent parties is basic and seldom tension-free, probably the true owner deserves more protection than that!

F. RESALE BY A VENDOR IN POSSESSION

The Code treats the vendor-in-possession as a sub-category of entrustment. § 2–403(3). In the instance where a purchaser out of a merchant's inventory leaves a chattel in his vendor's possession and the latter resells it to a good faith purchaser, the UCC provides that the vendor's possession was an "acquiescence in retention" under § 2–403(2) and thus an entrusting of the chattel to a "merchant who deals in goods of that kind." If the vendor was not a merchant, the second purchaser must fall back on an argument from § 2–403(1) that the vendor's title was voidable in his hands and absolute in the second purchasers'. Even though no merchant is involved, there is still an "acquiescence in retention," and so a partial fulfillment of the policies underlying § 2–403(2) would dictate judgment for the second purchaser. Since, however, the drafters do not tell us how crucial it is that a merchant be involved, the outcome of litigation between the two purchasers is hard to predict. If the underlying rationale is the encouragement of trade and commerce via lay-away plans, the first purchaser may win. If the rationale is the encouragement of negotiability of goods, then the second bids fair to win.

III.   THE IDENTITY OF THE FRAUDULENT PURCHASER

Whether a transferor, either the true owner or a subsequent possessor, has been deceived as to the identity of a purchaser, is normally a question of proof. This issue has also led some courts to engage in some very subtle and maybe not so sensible distinctions between various types of fraud. It arises in pre-Code cases and continues to be a problem under the UCC.

The distinction between a thief who obtains a void title and a fraudulent purchaser who obtains a voidable title has been difficult to maintain. First, if the fraudulent purchaser tells the true owner of the chattel that he is the purchasing agent for a corporation that in fact he has nothing to do with and the owner-vendor intended to transfer the chattel to the corporation, the transfer did not pass any title to the purchaser who, in consequence, has a void title. He could convey nothing to a subsequent good faith purchaser. What if, second, the fraudulent purchaser is named O. Poore Byer, a pauper, but presents himself face-to-face to the owner and represents himself to be a person named Rich Byer, a person of wealth? When the owner delivered chattel to Byer, who in turn sold it to a good faith purchaser, Byer here acquired a voidable title: the owner intended to pass title to the person appearing in front of him and that imposter could pass good title to a good faith purchaser. *Phelps v. McQuade* (1917).

Section 2–403(1) provides: "A person with voidable title has power to transfer a good title to a good faith purchaser for value." This language maintains the void/voidable distinction and continues to require that courts draw the line between the two types of title. Such line drawing has produced conflicting results in different states starting from the same statute and has been criticized by several treatise writers. Moreover, the last sentence contained in both the main paragraph and sub-paragraph (a) of § 2–403(1) provides that as to purchased and delivered goods a purchaser with a voidable title can transfer a good title "even though the transferor was deceived as to the identity of the purchaser." This language suggests that the so-called face-to-face doctrine in the second hypothetical in the previous paragraph should at least be extended to impersonations, whether by letter, telephone call, or telegraph. The Code provision is no more than a suggestion, however, since the language of subparagraph (a) requires that the transferor—the true owner or subsequent possessor—be "deceived as to the identity" of the impersonator. There is ample room in that statutory language to permit a court to decide on the facts for either the true owner or the good faith purchaser, but "deceiving" is somewhat broader than impersonating and would seem to cover a broader range of frauds.

The focus for judicial analysis of purchaser-identity problems is the intent of the vendor. On this account, it makes no difference to the result in these cases that the convertor at the time of the impersonation had no intent to deceive but rather developed his bad intent when he saw the effects his appearance had. His fraudulent intent at the time of the sale is, however, evidence that the true owner meant to sell to him and parted with a title voidable in him and absolute in a later good faith purchaser.

The UCC language, moreover, suggests again that if there is a tendency in the law, it is to decide for the good faith purchaser. Such a result enhances the negotiability of goods and promotes trade and commerce. Arguments that § 2–403(1) represents this trend are particularly strong when the vendor with an otherwise voidable title is a merchant who regularly deals in goods of the type purchased by the good faith purchaser.

More generally, however, the very notion of a voidable title suggests that the trend in the case law will favor the good faith purchaser. Consider, for instance, what the true owner can do to recover the chattel while title to it is still voidable. He can replevy it from the rogue to whom he transferred it, but it is unlikely that someone so cagey will stay around to receive service of process in this action. If there is a device for doing so, he can notify potential good faith purchasers, but since he is not likely to know the whereabouts of the rogue, he is even less likely to be able to interdict the later sale to the good faith purchaser. To protect the true owner from the transfer which renders the voidable title absolute, a court is going to have to hold that a notice in the legal advertisements of a newspaper was sufficient to deprive the subsequent purchaser of his "good faith" status. Unless there is something routine about giving and searching out such notices, this result is unlikely.

IV. LIENS

If the owner of a watch leaves it for repair, the common law gave the repairman who improves its value a lien for the reasonable value of his services on the chattel or work so improved. The lien holder could not foreclose this lien and sell the watch; he merely had no duty to turn it over to the owner until his charges were paid. Common carriers and innkeepers, because they had to accept all comers to their carriers and inns, were also possessed of common law liens.

Pre-UCC law recognized several types of security interests in chattels. The simplest was the *pledge*. It is a bailment of a chattel for the purpose of securing payment of its sale price, a debt, or the performance of a duty. The fundamental idea is that the creditor (pledgee) retains possession of the chattel. If the primary purpose of the possession is for security, the possessor has a pledge.

Another security device was the *chattel mortgage*. This did not involve a transfer of the possession of the chattel but was regarded as a transfer of either a lien or title to it. The debtor-transferor transferred the title subject to a defeasance or condition subsequent, giving title back to the debtor when the debt was paid or, in the case of a mortgage lien, terminating the right to foreclose it when the debt was paid. The mortgage was generally given in conjunction with the personal note of the debtor, and both the note and the mortgage had to be recorded in a local public office in the county seat to render the mortgage valid against other creditors and subsequent purchasers. The constructive notice which such a recording gave denied good faith status to a subsequent purchaser or creditor extending funds to the debtor in reliance on the latter's ownership of the chattel.

If the vendor wants to retain title of a chattel being sold because the purchaser of it wants to pay for it in installments, a *conditional sales contract* provides that the title to the chattel will pass to the purchaser when the last installment is paid.

Often the installment will include finance charges and the purchase price will be higher than if the sale were for cash; a close kin to this contract is a lease with an option to buy. When the purchaser defaults in the payments, the contract declares a forfeiture in the purchaser's right to possess the chattel. The vendor then repossesses his chattel. However, he cannot always retain all of the payments made under a conditional sales contract. Only so much of the payments which represent either his lost possession, the lost opportunity to resell, or a reasonable rental value of the chattel, can be retained.

All of these pre-UCC security devices and terms have been abolished and subsumed by the statutory scheme embodied in the Code. Article 9 provides that a *debtor* may give a *security agreement* of whatever type in various types of personal property used as *collateral* to secure a loan. When the loan is made, a *security interest* attaches to the collateral and is effective between the debtor and the *secured party*. The latter can perfect the security interest by *filing* a *financing statement* effective against third parties. This security interest is an "interest in personal property which secures payment or performance of an obligation" [§ 1–201(37)] and is established in place of all the pre-Code devices as a single, unitary interest, held by the only type of security interest holder recognized in the Code—the secured party. The filing is on the public records, usually maintained at the county level. This filing system represents a major

simplification of prior law, which often differed
from state to state, and often too within the various regions of any one state. A single notice
system for perfecting security interests was established. (Recall that a property system depends on
being able to find out simply and cheaply who
owns what, whether through possession or other
informational devices.) The italicized terms are
meticulously defined in the Code.

Article 9 of the UCC applies to all transactions
involving personal property which is intended to
create a security interest in that property or in
personal property which has been attached to real
property and become a fixture. For example, although a transaction is labeled a lease and although (again) a lease with an option to purchase
the goods at the end of the leasehold does not make
the lease a security agreement, a right in the
transferee under the lease to exercise the option
for a nominal consideration will render Article 9
applicable. Likewise, where a baker stocks a supermarket shelf with his goods under a consignment (i.e., a bailment for sale), the consignment
agreement will be examined functionally. If, as is
usual with bailments, there is no duty in the bailee
to purchase the goods, Article 9 is inapplicable. If,
however, there is such a duty, it does apply because
the consignment is intended for security. The
bailor's reservation of title alone is not enough to
create a security interest but, when coupled with a
bailee's duty to purchase, indicates that this "bail-

ment" has been modified to function as a security agreement.

When Article 9 is found to apply, the security agreement must be filed in order to be perfected. Moreover, any reservation of title by the vendor under a conditional sales agreement, is under UCC § 2–401(1) limited to a security interest by operation of law and can be perfected only by an Article 9 filing.

This filing system operates on a first-in-time, first-in-right rule of priority. Behind it lies the assumption that the secured party is going to check to see (1) that the person in possession of the collateral is its true owner, (2) that no prior filings have been made or, (3) when there are prior filings on the same collateral, that it is in fact valuable enough to satisfy the claims of all filers, including his own. This third check can only be made by an inspection and physical evaluation of the chattel. Thus, at root, possession is the ultimate source of information about the validity and value of the security interest. If the secured party trusts the information which possession and the filing system reveals, he need not take possession and can trust the filing system to provide him with rights sufficient to secure his claim later on; he need not take possession now, but must file his security interest instead before he can shift the risk of insufficient security to others—that is, to persons who check the records later and find or should find his interest filed there.

Thus the secured party who either takes possession of collateral or perfects an interest in it by
filing attains priority of title over persons interested in it, but neither taking possession nor filing.
Similarly, a second lien holder or creditor who does
not find the filing of a previous one in the records,
knows that he can rely on his taking possession or
filing to attain rights superior to the previous one.
For a wonderfully concise review of Article 9 and
its problems, see D. Baird & T. Jackson, Possession
and Ownership: An Examination of the Scope of
Article 9, 35 Stan.L.Rev. 175, 179–190 (1983).

Similar conflicts between lien creditors can arise
in the context of disputes over possession of chattels to which similar types of information systems
apply, such as automobiles. See e.g., *Bank of
America v. J. & S. Auto Repairs* (1985) (replevin
action for van between a plaintiff who held purchase money security interest and an auto repair
shop in possession of van and holding a vendor's
lien for auto parts installed in it).

As *J. & S. Auto Repairs* indicates, at the same
time that you strive to understand the scope of
Article 9, you should also remain flexible in your
own mind about who can be a security interest
holder. For example, when a purchaser of personal property pays the purchase price and takes
possession, but later claims statutory rights to rescind the purchase, he can claim to be a secured
party in possession. After rescission, his continued
possession is to protect his lien in the amount of

the price he paid. To simply return the chattel runs the risk of kissing the price and the goods goodbye, while retaining possession bars the risk. When the rescission is formally executed in writing and the vendor of the chattel is notified of the nature of the possession, the purchaser has created a security interest in himself. *Ford Motor Credit Company v. Caiazzo* (1989) (collecting the cases for a counterclaim in the vendor's replevin action).

CHAPTER VIII

GIFTS OF PERSONAL PROPERTY

A gift is a gratuitous transfer made voluntarily by one person to another and made without consideration or payment of any type. It is presently effective and does not take effect at some time in the future. It is not a promise to give a chattel sometime in the future (the law would treat that like an executory contract), and it is not testamentary in character (the law would treat that like a will and require that the transfer comply with the Statute of Wills applicable in the jurisdiction).

There are two types of gifts. Gifts inter vivos (accomplished between living persons) and gifts causa mortis (made by a person contemplating his own impending death). The former are unconditional and irrevocable. The latter are revoked by the donor in fact living through the experience which he previously thought would kill him.

Both types of gifts are accomplished by delivery of the chattel or a deed to it with the intent to complete the gift and acceptance of the chattel or the deed by the donee. For a good dialogue on the law, see P.D. Junger, A Dialog Concerning the Delivery of Gifts, 38 U.Miami L.Rev. 123 (1983).

I. DELIVERY

Delivery is essential to the parol gift of personal property. In the case of *Irons v. Smallpiece* (1819), Abbott, C.J. opined that ... "by the law of England, in order to transfer property by gift there must either be a deed or instrument of gift, or there must be an actual delivery of the thing to the donee." In *Irons,* a son claimed that his father made a verbal gift of two colts some twelve months before his death. The possession of the colts stayed with the father until his death; the latter, however, agreeing (the son said) to purchase hay for them at a certain price which the father would advance and the son would ultimately pay. This agreement was not acted on until over five months later—some three to four days within the father's death.

The son brought trover against the administrator of the father's estate. The plaintiff was nonsuited, the court holding that there was no transfer of possession and the plaintiff acquired no rights on which to base his action in trover. Also rejected was the plaintiff's argument that the agreement to furnish hay was a recognition of the son's rights. Even if that were so, that agreement was never executed except by facts taking place too long afterward to refer back to an agreement "made so many months before."

The holding in *Irons* was reaffirmed in the case of *Cochrane v. Moore* (1890). There the court declined to follow the lead of two intervening cases which suggested that delivery was not an absolute requirement for a gift. In one of these cases, the judge had suggested that delivery was merely evidence of intention and that, in its absence, a court was still free to determine the intention of the donor from the nature of the chattel and the circumstances surrounding the alleged gift. The analysis in *Cochrane* is not so functional. It is rather a long historical inquiry into whether the authorities permitted title and possession to move separately to a donee in a parol gift. The court concluded not.

The issue in *Cochrane* was whether the gift of a one-quarter undivided interest in a race horse was the subject of a constructive trust imposed on a subsequent purchaser of the same horse.

The facts were as follows: Benson gave Moore an undivided quarter of a race horse and several days later informed the stable owner on whose premises the horse was kept of the gift. Benson later sold Cochrane the horse, and when Cochrane was told of Moore's interest, he said it was "alright." When Cochrane wanted to sell the horse again, an interpleader was filed in equity to determine the disposition of the one-quarter interest in the horse. It was held that Cochrane took his title in the horse subject to a constructive trust of which Moore was the beneficiary.

The result indicates that the court was willing to subject the legal title to a chattel, a gift of which could not be accomplished without at least satisfying the requirement of a delivery, to the equitable doctrine of a constructive trust. If, as the equitable maxim says, equity follows the law, it also appears willing to add to the remedies benefiting donees of a legal interest in chattels. This combination of legal rights and equitable remedies softens the harsh results following upon a strict adherence to the requirement that the subject of a gift be delivered manually or that the gift be effectuated by a deed of gift. In *Cochrane,* the letter from Benson to the stable owner is not in form a deed of gift, but appeared to acknowledge that Benson held onto the horse subject to a constructive trust which could also be imposed on later purchasers of the horse.

It is unusual for a court to uphold a gift, in an instance where the delivery requirement is unsatisfied, by means of a trust declared by the donor. Note, "Personal Property—Sustaining an Imperfect Gift as a Trust," 7 Mo.L.Rev. 81 (1942). Equity might be expected to act if a donee were injured financially or a donor were unjustly enriched. Neither situation is likely to be present in a gift, which, although a transfer of wealth, is not an economically productive transaction. So why should equity act here to avoid the legal requirements of a gift? Apparently because both donor and donee relied on the third party purchaser of the horse and a fractional interest in the horse was incapable of actual delivery. If this reliance were justified and the defendant knew of it, then equity will act to carry out the reasonable expectations of both the donor and the donee.

Indeed, the law side of American courts have worked out doctrines to liberalize the harshness of the common law requirement of actual delivery. These are the doctrines of constructive and symbolic delivery with which a later section of this chapter will deal.

A. A DEED OF GIFT

At the time the *Irons* case was decided in 1819, there was some question whether a gift could be accomplished by a deed of gift alone. By the time of *Cochrane,* in 1890, a gift might be effected by deed, and in many states today a gift can be accomplished either by a deed or a delivery of the chattel. In other (perhaps most) states, a deed of gift is effective to accomplish a gift only when delivery is impractical.

At the time of *Cochrane,* a deed was an instrument written under seal. Most state legislatures have since abolished the use of a seal in contracts, enacted statutes which eliminate the difference between sealed and unsealed writings or otherwise curtailed the legal effectiveness of a seal. In the opening decades of this century, many courts decided, on the basis of these statutes, that a gift may be accomplished by an unsealed written instrument.

The seal ensured the donor's deliberation upon the soundness of making the gift while he drafted the writing, heated and applied the wax and impressed his sign upon the hot wax. No comparable substitute has replaced it. Indeed, one-third of the states have neither abolished nor validated the requirement of a seal by statute.

Today, an unsealed deed of gift, to be valid, must use language indicating a present intent to give ("I hereby grant," etc.), must identify the donee and the subject of the gift as well as comply with the requirements of applicable state law.

Judicial analysis of the language used in deeds of gift has analyzed the words of grant for their equivalence with words such as "The donor by means of this deed does now grant and give ...." The court may decide that a present interest was transferred by the deed or that a future interest was presently transferred, but this analysis of the "interest" transferred can get sloppy around the edges and is sometimes, when lay-drafted deeds are involved, no more than a cover for evaluating the intent of the donor. In one case the words,

"I wish to pay [for the comfort and care of my retirement home] ... the sum of $10,000 on demand. This may, however, be collectible against my estate if not demanded sooner, or paid by me,"

were held sufficient for a valid deed of gift. That "I wish to pay" is the same as "I hereby grant," may be open to some question, but the Montana Supreme Court held that these words indicated sufficient donative intent on the donor's part.

Faith Lutheran Retirement Home v. Veis (1970), noted in 35 Mont.L.Rev. 132 (1974). Indeed, this use of common law estates' categories puts a premium on the analysis of language, the consequences of which are often unforeseen by its drafter. The question really is whether the delivery of the deed of gift performs the same functions as the delivery requirement does for parol gifts. Let us turn to an elaboration of those functions in American case law.

B. AMERICAN CASES

American courts have been more inclined than their English counterparts to balance the evidence indicating a present intent to complete a gift against the need for an actual delivery of the chattel, or of a deed to it, to the donee. This tendency makes delivery not an absolute requirement of an undeeded gift but rather of evidentiary value alone. See *Whatley v. Mitchell* (1919) whose facts Professor (later Chief Justice) Harlan F. Stone called identical with *Irons*. H.F. Stone, "Delivery in Gifts of Personal Property," 20 Colum.L.Rev. 197 (1920). At the same time, they have been less inclined to permit a gift to be accomplished by use of a deed alone when physical delivery of the chattel was possible. For them, the deed is evidence of donative intent, but the gift must be completed by a delivery.

The origins of the delivery requirement go back to a time long ago when the handing over of possession of a thing was the only method of transfer—when, as Professor Mechem says, "things were things"; title and possession were then inseparable and the law seemingly could not conceive of their not going hand in hand. Mechem, "The Requirement of Delivery in Gifts of Chattels and of Choses in Action Evidenced by Commercial Instruments," 21 Ill.Law Rev. 341, 345 (1926).

The persistence of some form of delivery requirement in our law is referrable to the idea that a delivery is regarded by lawyers and the laity alike as integral to the idea of a gift. It is so basic as to be a definitional and functional component of a gift. First, it serves to show that the donor formed his intention to give into a resolve to make the transfer. Second, the "wrench of delivery" (again, Professor Mechem's phrase) serves to protect the donor from acting hastily and to impress upon him the finality of his act. Third, it provides evidence of the gift. If these functions can be served without an actual delivery of the chattel, however, American courts have shown a tendency to validate the gift.

Its persistence in our law, however, is especially attributable to its third, evidentiary, function and more particularly to the reluctance of courts to sanction a gift when the only evidence of it is an intention of the donor to make it. Informal and gratuitous gifts are too easy for a donee to fake before a jury. Courts are thus wary of the fraudulent donee, except perhaps in intra-family cases in which the donee is a natural object of the donor's generosity.

Two cases will illustrate this tendency. In one case, a donor signed a document stating "I give this day to my wife, Sara, as a present on her 46th birthday, 500 shares of XYZ company common stock." *In re Cohn* (1919). In this deed of gift, the donor declared a present intention to give and identified the donee as well as the subject of the gift. Unlike a fraction of a horse, however, shares of stock are capable of delivery, so no matter how clear the writing is, the question arises whether it can be used as a substitute for actual delivery of the stock. The court held that it could.

Indeed, another New York case required only that the donor of stock instruct the transfer agent of the corporation to change the owner's name on the corporate books in order to satisfy the delivery requirement. *Matter of Mills* (1916). See Section F, infra, for more on the subject of corporate stock transfers as gifts. The donor, Cohn, went one step further and actually gave the donee an informal written declaration of a gift. The remaining difficulty was that the donor, Mr. Cohn, continued to use the stock for his own purposes up to the time of his death six days after the alleged gift. He was, at the time of the alleged gift, involved in establishing a new business partnership. He was using the gifted stock as his contribution to the assets of the business. So, if he were not to lose the benefits of this new partnership, the possession of the shares was temporarily beyond his grasp. (New York case law had precedent authorizing a donor, unable to get possession of shares in his bank deposit box, to use a deed of gift.) In the circumstances of the case, the donor had done all he could reasonably be expected to do to complete the gift. His writing manifested a present intention to deliver the shares in the future. It was a present delivery of a future interest in the shares.

C. SYMBOLIC AND CONSTRUCTIVE DELIVERY

The rule requiring actual delivery of parol gifts is not inflexible, and "delivery may be symbolical as where the donor gives the donee a symbol which represents possession" in instances where actual possession cannot be transferred. Cohn's writing was just such a symbolic delivery of the shares; moreover, there was no evidence in *Cohn* indicating a revocation of the gift. Indeed, two days after giving his wife the gift, he urged his attorney to complete the establishment of the new partnership so that he could get his hands on the shares.

Cohn thus involved an instance of symbolic delivery—giving a sheet of paper to stand for the shares. In one other instance, that of a constructive delivery, American courts have permitted a donor to give access or the means of obtaining possession of the gifted chattel without delivery of the chattel itself. Constructive delivery is involved when the donor gives the keys to a lock box.

Because the donor has relinquished control over the contents of the box to the donee, the contents may be delivered in this manner when the donor is incapable of actual delivery of the contents or if the chattel is too big or heavy for the donor to lift and hand it over to his donee. In this last situation, the donor might deliver the keys to a bulky wardrobe intending that the delivery of the key be constructive delivery of the piece of furniture, but the key is not intended to stand for the chattel. It only gives access to it.

Although courts often use the terms "symbolic" and "constructive" delivery as if they were interchangeable, they are not. Constructive delivery is permitted when the donor gives up access to or control of a gifted chattel—which is what happens when there is an actual delivery so that the courts require that the end result in cases of both actual and constructive delivery be as close as the nature of the chattel permits.

Symbolic delivery cases, on the other hand, involve situations in which the gifted chattel may be small and capable of manumission but are unavailable for delivery. How unavailable must it be? Must the shares of stock, as in *Cohn*, be in a bank in a distant city from which the donor could order them sent to him? In the same city? The same building? The same room? These are Professor Brown's matters of degree, and no fixed rules apply. Courts inquire into the circumstances. The nearer to the donor, the less likely it is that a court will permit symbolic delivery.

However, even if the shares are close-by, the health of the donor may not permit him to get to them. The donee who is given keys to the donor's bulky wardrobe may acquire that piece of furniture but will not become the beneficiary of a life insurance policy or shares of stock found in one of its drawers. The donee is likely to get only what cannot be actually delivered, i.e., the wardrobe.

What if an elderly invalid (now deceased) gave his nurse a bunch of house keys? Would the nurse become the donee of everything to which the keys gave access? Clearly not, unless it could be shown that the donor had a particular thing in mind when he delivered the keys. So the furniture in the sick-room might be transferred to the nurse, but not the furniture out of the donor's sight in other parts of the house. The key which unlocks the keyboard on the piano in the living room will only be deemed a symbolic delivery of the piano to a donee who can prove delivery. In this case, assigning the burden of proof is tantamount to saying that no delivery had occurred. (This paragraph is based on *Newman v. Bost* (1898)). The distinctions between things in the sick-room and those outside are purely practical ones involving compromises between the heirs of the invalid and the nurse whom the invalid intended in some way to benefit.

A rancher can effectively give cattle on the open range to another rancher by changing his brand on the gifted cattle to that of the donee's. In this case, the fact that the cattle stay on the range means that the donee has access to them thereafter. In the case of an insurance policy or shares of stock of a corporation, just giving the policy to the donee will not make the latter its beneficiary or, in the case of stock, just changing the owner's name on the certificate will not suffice either. Access to the chattel itself is in each instance insufficient to transfer the benefits of the policy or the shares without a deed of gift on which the donee could get specific performance. In the one case, the rancher has given up control of the chattel, but in the other, more is required to give the donee access to it. The corporation's or the insurer's records must be changed. Unless a deed of gift is clear and capable of compelling a change in those records through judicial process, no delivery has occurred.

The same distinction is involved in gaining access to a safety deposit box in a bank. Delivering the key to someone will not provide unfettered access to the box since, if the usual procedure is followed, the alleged donor will have not only to give the donee a key, but also sign him into the vault area in which the box is located. Only with this second step complete can it be said that the donor has provided access to the contents of the box *and* relinquished control over them.

D. STATUTES ELIMINATING THE DELIVERY REQUIREMENT

At least eight states have statutes which provide that a "writing" may be used in a gift of personal property as a substitute for the delivery requirement. The writing must be signed by the donor and is generally taken to mean that the document effectuating the gift may be informal or not under seal. It is in this sense that a "writing" is distinguished from a deed of gift. Comment, "Statutory Treatment of the Requirement of Delivery in Gifts of Personal Property," 7 Wayne L.Rev. 571, 572–79 (1961).

E. GIFTS THROUGH THIRD PARTIES

American courts frequently hold that inter vivos gifts of personal property must be irrevocable and unconditional. If a chattel is given to a donee but is subject to a condition, oral or written, the condition is unenforceable. The rule is the same when the condition is written in a deed concerning the property and for the same reason: the delivery of the chattel takes precedence over any conflicting qualification on the title contained in the deed. This is just another way of reenforcing the requirement of a delivery.

This does not mean, however, that the delivery cannot be accomplished in two stages; first by delivery of the chattel or, where appropriate, a deed to it to a third party who, in turn, hands it to the donee in a second stage of the delivery. By this two-step procedure the donor gains the ability to impose conditions upon the person holding the chattel, the fulfillment of which permit the latter to transfer possession of it or a deed to it to the donee.

Frequently, however, the status of the third party holder becomes unclear, and the question arises whether he is the agent of the donor or the trustee of the donee. If the former, the donor still has the right to recall the gift, as it has not yet become irrevocable. If the latter, then the gift has become irrevocable pending only the donee's fulfilling the condition (if any) imposed by the donor: reaching his majority, graduating from college, marrying, etc.

Clear instructions to the third party can avoid these problems. Where the third party states that he is the donor's agent, this will normally be conclusive. *Innes v. Potter* (1915). The test, however, is the intent of the donor—of which the third party's perception of his status constitutes evidence but is not necessarily dispositive. For all practical purposes, if the donor has not communicated to the third party that the gift is irrevocable, he has a power to revoke it. Only where the donor can show that he did not know that he was possessed of this power should he be regarded as having made the gift irrevocable. For example, a donor might have posted a letter with instructions not to return the chattel to him, but unbeknownst to him, the letter was never received by the third party.

For some types of third parties, moreover, a classification as anything other than the agent of the donor will be difficult. Attorneys of the donor fall into this class because the attorney-client relationship creates a fiduciary duty for the attorney which precludes any representation of a party with an interest conflicting with his client. An attorney could not therefore receive the chattel as the attorney for the donor and at the same time hold it as a trustee for the donee. For an attorney, then, any agency for a client donor arises as a matter of a presumption that the attorney was behaving as he should, i.e., with the limits imposed on his conduct by ethical canons governing the bar.

Applying the agent of the donor/trustee of the donee distinction is usually not so clear-cut and depends rather on the circumstances of the case. A decision on the status of the third party should consider whether the donor or donee paid the third party, whether the donor or donee received any income from the chattel while he held it, whether the donor or donee instructed the third party and whether or not such instructions were taken as binding on him by one or both parties to the gift.

F. CORPORATE STOCK

Shares of stock in a corporation are personal property even if the corporation owns nothing but real property. Transfers of stock are a frequent

source of gift litigation. In order for a gift of
shares to be made, the courts require that there be
a delivery and donative intent; these requirements
are no different from those applied to other types
of gifts. There is, however, another consideration;
that is, whether there has been a transfer of ownership on the books of the corporation issuing the
stock. This aspect of these transfers sometimes
takes the place of the delivery requirement and
sometimes is an additional requirement.

Such a split in the case law arises because of
confusion over what a share of stock is. If it is the
certificate itself, that piece of paper must be delivered to the donee, and the transfer on the books is
superfluous except as evidence of donative intent.
If, however, the shares are a representation of an
undivided fractional interest in the assets of the
corporation or its operations, then the thing is not
capable of manual delivery, and transfer of the
certificate is a symbolic delivery at best while a
transfer on the books is a constructive delivery
giving the donee access to the benefits of being a
shareholder in the corporation; with only a symbolic or constructive delivery possible, the transfer
on the books becomes a substitute for a manual
delivery.

In either event, the transfer of the shares on the
books of the corporation is "of great importance"
but not dispositive in establishing donative intent.

The weight of the authority (although not a
majority of American jurisdictions) holds that re-

placing the donor's name with the donee's on the corporate books as the owner of the shares is all that is required to complete the gift. An additional set of cases reach the same result by holding that the transfer agent is the trustee of the donee, and a third line of authority suggests that the transfer agent is in fact the donor's agent, thus making the gift incomplete without the donor's delivery of the new certificate to the donee.

The weight of authority carries with it the best reasoned rule. Viewing the transfer of names on the corporate records as the completed gift gives rise to a rule which is certain of application, completes the gift at a time when the benefits of shareowning accrue to the donee (record status being necessary for receipt of future dividends on the shares), and best protects the donee from the donor's temptation to retract the completed gift. Moreover, in jurisdictions which view the delivery of the certificate as either a symbolic delivery or transfer on the books as a constructive delivery of a share in the corporation, the transfer on the books provides the best evidence of a completed gift.

Finally, this result conforms to the statutes which in many jurisdictions provide that the legal title to the shares passes to the donee when the name on the corporate register is changed. In other instances of the law as well, registration of title is required to pass title to an automobile or a U.S. savings bond. The policy behind the requirement—such as protecting the motoring public or the government from paying the wrong person the proceeds of the bond—might arguably be defeated to some degree if gifts which did not conform to the registry requirement, were not invalidated.

In addition, according to one case the donee acquires contract rights in the shares upon the name-change on the books because the donee is then the designated third party beneficiary of a contract between the donor and the transfer agent.

Quite often litigation results when the donor regains possession of the certificate, now naming the donee as the owner of the shares, and that certificate is never forwarded to the donee. This happens when the donor has given possession of the certificate to a third party who is not the transfer agent to pass along to the transfer agent. In such situations the courts can inquire into the status of that third party as well as the transfer agent, and the donor has two opportunities to show that *his* agent remained in control of the certificate and thus that it never left his control. *Owens v. Sun Oil Co.* (1973).

In most of the cases in which a transfer on the corporate books has been held not to complete the gift, the donor regained possession of the certificate, and persons executing the transfer have been found to be *his* agents. Where the donor regained possession of the certificate, his long-continued retention of it serves as proof of a failure of donative intent. Then a court has no reason to substitute the transfer on the books for the delivery requirement. Some courts reverse this logic and state that unless a showing of donative intent can be made at the time of the transfer, the gift is incomplete without a later delivery of the certificate.

A middle ground is held by cases holding that the transfer is a burden-shifting event. After the transfer, the presumption is that a valid gift was intended and that a transfer on the books is a *prima facie* showing that such was the case. Thereafter the donor must establish by clear and convincing evidence that no gift was intended.

II. DONATIVE INTENT

To be valid, a gift must be made with donative intent on the donor's part. Judicial analysis of facts adducing the intent of the donor is often a matter of reducing the available evidence to one of several verbal expressions. This is often a dry exercise, taking all of the seeming humanity out of the facts of a case and reducing them to a skeletal form. First, a court may decide that a donor meant: "I give you this thing, but I'm keeping the income or the use of it until my death." The gift is a present one, and the retention of the income or the use is consistent with keeping a life estate in the donor, followed by a remainder in the donee. Both interests in the chattel are simultaneously established at the time of the gift. As to the remainder, the donor has a present intent to establish a future interest. Second, if the court might reduce the evidence of intent to a statement that: "You shall have this thing when you reach 21," then the gift is invalid as one taking effect in the future. The condition precedent to making the gift is a future event. The donor lacks a present intent to make the gift, and it falls afoul of the rule that an inter vivos gift must be unconditional. Third, if the court could reduce the evidence of intent to a statement that: "You shall have this thing when I die," there is similarly no present intent, but the gift falls for an additional reason; i.e., the gift is, in effect, a testamentary one and should be contained in a validly executed will. Its failure to comply with the applicable Statute of Wills thus constitutes an additional reason for invalidating the gift. Fourth and finally, the court might reduce the evidence of intent to the donor's stating that: "I give you this thing, but if I return from the war, I want it back." In this instance, there is a present intent to give the chattel, and the gift is valid but subject to a condition subsequent.

These distinctions, particularly the one between a condition's precedent and subsequent, seem dry (indeed they are) and subject to the evidence being manipulated to fit one pattern or the other. To some extent, then, the courts will be looking to the context of facts in which the gift was made. Whether it is witnessed by others, whether the donee is someone to whom the donor might be expected to make a gift (a parent, a spouse, an offspring, etc.), and whether the transfer looks like a bona fide gift or a tax avoidance scheme could all be important contextual facts; though each is not dispositive by itself, cumulatively they may have great weight.

Establishing the donor's intent is a question of fact. In the case of *Gruen v. Gruen* (1986), the court held that evidence established that a father intended to transfer ownership of a valuable painting to his son, reserving a life estate in it for himself and that letters from father to son were sufficient to establish a delivery by deed of gift. Written for the son's twenty first birthday, the letter said, "I wish to give you as a present the oil painting by [a named artist] which now hangs in the New York living room. Happy Birthday." In an accompanying cover letter, the father said that the son should destroy a prior letter mentioning that the father "want[ed] to use the painting as long as I live." For tax reasons, the father continued: "[t]hough I still want to use it", this should not appear in the letter, and the accompanying letter "will serve the purpose of making it possible for you, once I die, to get this picture...."

These two letters taken together, were sufficient to transfer title to the painting without the right to its present possession. A physical delivery, and redelivery would not serve to provide any better evidence of a delivery, the court said, than the two letters do.

As to the father's donative intent, the court found that while it must be a present intent, it need not involve the transfer of present possession, but only a present transfer of a future interest, such as the remainder interest created here in the donee. Once the gift is made, the donor's status is that of a holder of a life estate. His possession, maintenance, loan, and repair of the painting thereafter is not inconsistent with this status. Title to the remainder vests immediately, with possession postponed to the donor's death.

Moreover, if donative intent can be established by present delivery of a deed of gift or its equivalent, it makes little sense to deny the donor's intent when the gift involves tangible chattel, such as the painting in *Gruen*. Gruen *fils* was turning twenty-one when the gift was made. Say that the son, for example, was going off to law school. (As he was.) In this situation, it would make sense for the father to retain possession for a while.

A. CONDITIONAL GIFTS: ENGAGEMENT PRESENTS

The objective of much of this "interest" analysis is to effectuate the common law's prohibition on conditional gifts. No pre-conditions can be attached to a parol gift. In one situation, however, courts have agreed that a condition can be imposed on a gift; that is, where an engagement gift is given in connection with an ensuing marriage, the donor can sue in replevin or trover for its value or return if the marriage does not take place. Contract theories have also been used to achieve this recovery—mutual recission, mistake of fact, unjust enrichment and restitution, and a failure of consideration are the available theories. *Sloin v. Lavine* (1933). However, the most used theory is that of a conditional gift revoked by the failure of the donee to perform the donor's condition.

Thus an engagement gift is conditioned on the marriage between donor and donee taking place. This condition is seldom expressed but is one implied by law. The gift is presumed to be made with it attached. The easiest application of this presumption comes when the gift, by its nature, relates to the engagement itself. An engagement ring is an example. It symbolizes a pledge to marry and is given on the implied condition that the marriage will take place. *Lowe v. Quinn* (1971); *Lipton v. Lipton* (1986) ("An engagement ring is a gift to which a condition subsequent, the fulfillment of the marriage agreement, is attached.")

The presumption of a conditional gift is, however, a rebuttable one. Where the donee can show that the occasion for the gift was not dependent on fulfillment of the condition, the donor's cause of action will fail. Thus, if the gift was made to celebrate the donee's birthday or a holiday, a valid defense exists. Some courts also distinguish between engagement and courtship gifts. The former are made at the time the marriage is proposed and accepted or thereafter. The latter are made beforehand to introduce the donor to the donee and gain favor. Courtship gifts are not made upon a condition of marriage.

Although some courts look to the time at which the gift is made or the type of property, the intentions of the parties is the controlling test, and in addition to engagement rings, donors have recovered or sued for the value of money advanced, furs, furniture, and automobiles.

Where the engagement is broken by the donor, many courts permit the donee to retain engagement gifts or to sue for their value and likewise deny the donor any right to recover even their value. Conversely, if the donee breaks off the engagement without legal justification or the engagement is ended by mutual agreement, the donor may recover the gifts. A donee would be justified in breaking an engagement where the donor has made some misrepresentation of his marital or financial status. *White v. Finch* (1964). In the same vein, where one party to the engagement dies, engagement gifts need not be returned, neither party being at fault as to the termination of the engagement. And where a gift was induced by a donee's fraud, its recovery can be had by the donor.

Recently, the idea that the concept of fault controls the disposition of most engagement gift cases has come in for criticism. See *Aronow v. Silver* (1987) [calling the application of fault "silly and sexist" in **his** action suing **her** for return of the ring (he wins), transfer of title in a jointly owned condo (he wins there too), and for transfer of stock (the action is remanded for adjustments in their respective interests)]. Some states have eliminated suits based on a breach of a promise to marry by legislation—the so-called "heart balm" statutes.

The purpose of the initial heart balm legislation was to rid the courts of these actions where the "wounded" party appears in court to unfold his or her sorrows before a sympathetic jury. To require a determination of fault in order to entitle one to recover engagement gifts would simply condone this same type of action in yet another form. The result would be to encourage every disappointed donee to resist the return of engagement gifts by blaming the donor for the breakup of the contemplated marriage, thereby promoting dramatic courtroom accusations and counter-accusations of fault.

In truth, in most broken engagements there is no real fault as such—one or both of the parties merely changes his mind about the desirability of the other as a marriage partner. Since the major purpose of the engagement period is to allow a couple time to test the permanency of their feelings, it would seem highly ironic to penalize the donor for taking steps to prevent a possibly unhappy marriage. Indeed, in one sense the engagement period has been successful if the engagement is broken since one of the parties has wisely utilized this time so as to avoid a marriage that in all probability would fail.

Just as the question of fault or guilt has become largely irrelevant to modern divorce proceedings, so should it also be deemed irrelevant to the breaking of the engagement.

Gaden v. Gaden (1971).

Likewise, an action by the parents of an engaged person to recover the expenses incurred in planning the wedding ceremony or the honeymoon, is barred. Such expenses are incurred with knowledge that there may be no wedding and no honeymoon if the engagement is broken on either side. *Aronow v. Silver,* op. cit.

The heart-balm legislation referred to previously has been enacted in about a dozen states. It has been generally construed to apply only to prohibit suits based on a breach of a promise to marry and not engagement gift suits. *De Cicco v. Barker* (1959).

Where the engagement gift has been to a person already married, the gift is unconditional. Allowing recovery of such gifts would encourage the dissolution of a previous marriage. Where a prior marriage of the donee is already in the divorce courts, engagement gifts may be recovered. Such results merely underline the basis of these engagement gift cases in matters of public policy.

Similarly, if the donee is a minor and without the capacity to contract, the result may be no contract to exchange the promise of marriage and the gift and no remedy for the donor to use to recover even the engagement ring. This is a mixture of contract and gift theory, the mixture again indicating that the result is more important than the theory and is based on a public policy having to do with the marriage of minors.

B. PRESUMING DONATIVE INTENT

In some situations, where the alleged gift arrangement is long continued with the knowledge of a donor who acquiesces in the arrangement, a presumption arises that the gift is valid. Where, for example, a donor deposits money in a bank account maintained in the names of both the donor and the donee as joint tenants with a right of survivorship, the transfer of the money into such an account creates a presumption that the donor intended a gift to the donee as the surviving joint tenant. Often such cases involve intra-family gifts, and so the presumption operates in a context in which the donee is the natural object of the donor's beneficence. Such a presumption is rebuttable, however, and if clear and convincing evidence is available that no gift was intended, the presumption is overcome. Usually the evidence used to overcome the presumption concerns the use of and the authority over the joint account, whether the donee thought he had access to the account, whether the account was maintained for the convenience of the donor, and the percentage of the donor's assets held in the account.

Nor is a presumption of donative intent likely to be defeated when the donor obtains some benefit from the gift. In *Gruen v. Gruen,* op. cit., the donor had a tax benefit in mind in making the gift of the painting to his son, and the gift was none-the-less valid. Nor is the failure to establish the intent likely to be affected. In *McCune v. Brown* (1983), noted at 38 Ark.L.Rev. 446 (1984), a parent made a gift of a quarter million dollars worth of gold pieces to his child, in order to avoid subjecting them to his spouse's claims in an up-coming divorce proceeding. After the divorce was final, the parent brought a replevin action to revoke the gift and enjoin the child's removal of the coins from a safe deposit box. The court held that the lack of the donor's clean hands in making the gift in the first place, was irrelevant to the presence or absence of donative intent and that the gift was invalid for lack of such intent. The child, the court found, knew that she was to re-deliver the gold after the divorce.

C. SOME PROBLEMS ON DELIVERY AND DONATIVE INTENT

1. Ambrose, a struggling young writer, wrote a long poem for which he was seeking a publisher. Between visits to various publishing houses, he wrote a letter which said: "Dear Beatrice, Thanks for your support. I know I promised to send my poem manuscript to you, but I'm still hawking it, though I still want you to have it. I wanted to

confirm to you our understanding that you get 50% of the profits from my publishing my poem." Months later, Ambrose died without having executed any contract to publish his poem. Some months after that, his literary executor did execute such a contract, and the executor now has had a request from Beatrice for 50% of the royalties and profits from the publication.

There are at least two valid perspectives on the legal problem present here. The first involves a problem of identifying what was transferred. If it were the profits of publishing the poem, the problem is that no profits and no contract from which they could arise in the future were in existence at the time of the letter to Beatrice. No delivery could take place, the argument runs, because there was nothing to deliver. However, the writing may be a substitute for future profits (and is the subject of a symbolic delivery). It is a present gift of future profits and expresses a clear intent on the part of the donor to give future property. See *Rubenstein v. Rosenthal* (1988) (upholding gift of 10% of profits in land speculation); *Elyachar v. Gerel Corporation* (1984) (concerning gifts of stock income).

A second perspective involves evaluation of the letter as an assignment of a contract right. The assignment of a contract right was void at common law but valid as a gift in equity whether or not the contract right assigned is a present or future right.

However, an instrument of gift is still necessary to evidence a clear intent to give a present interest.

Analogous, early common law cases provide precedent here and validated the transfer of an interest in the foal of a not-yet-pregnant mare.

2. Ambrose also wrote: "I know that I promised to send my poem's manuscript to you, but I'm still hawking it, though I still want you to have it." This second aspect of the confirmation letter involves a quite different problem. This gift of the actual manuscript fails for lack of delivery, although there is evidence of a present intent to give it away. What advice would you give Beatrice when she received this letter? Ambrose's retention of the manuscript for his own purposes is much like Mr. Cohn's retention of the stock for use in his business dealings. In this case, however, Ambrose's hawking it is not inconsistent with his making use of it for Beatrice's benefit when one considers the profit-sharing arrangement which his letter proposes. If Beatrice were to write back and say that "you keep my manuscript and get the best publishing deal you can for me," she would buttress an argument that Ambrose held the manuscript in trust for her. This trust would not be of the self-declared type that courts refuse to use to validate an otherwise invalid gift. Here Beatrice has recognized that she has present rights in the manuscript and she (not the donor) has declared the trust.

3. What if Ambrose, after his rounds of the publishing houses and before he received Beatrice's suggested reply, stopped in a bar, then another, and finally went on a binge in about a dozen bars, losing the manuscript somewhere in mid-binge. Fortunately one of the publishers whom he had visited had photocopied the poem so that it was not lost, and when Ambrose next needed it he called the publisher just before leaving town on a speaking tour at colleges and universities around the country. When the publisher met him at the airport with the copy Ambrose said, while with his family and some friends, "Thanks. You've saved my career. I really need to publicize and read this poem during this trip. If you can find the manuscript, it is yours." The manuscript turned up a few days after Ambrose left town, and a few days after that an airplane on which Ambrose was riding crashed, killing all aboard.

Ambrose made a valid gift of the manuscript to the publisher. This gift revoked the prior, unexecuted gift to Beatrice, and because delivery was impossible at the time, his indication of a present intent to deliver the manuscript is as much as he could do; indeed, if this type of gift were to be found invalid, there would be no manner in which lost chattels could be transferred by gift.*

* The three problems presented in this section are a combination of the facts of two cases: *Speelman v. Pascal* (1961), noted at 11 Cath.U.L.Rev. 115, 13 Syr.L.Rev. 481 (1962) and *Thomas v. The Times Book Co.* (1966).

III. GIFTS CAUSA MORTIS

A gift causa mortis is a gift of personal property
made in contemplation of the donor's imminent
death upon the condition that the donor die as he
anticipates. The gift must also remain unrevoked
before his death takes place. Delivery of the chattel is generally required along with proof of the
donor's donative intent. Proof is often hard to
adduce as the gifts are likely to be made in the
course of hurried and private conversations.
Moreover, the credibility of the proof is a matter
left to the trial court which has the opportunity to
assess the credibility of witnesses and the donee.
Once found valid, such gifts are not likely to be
invalidated on appeal for errors in interpreting the
facts.

A gift causa mortis is a gift revocable at any
time before the donor's death. His surviving the
event from which he anticipated death also revokes
the gift unless he subsequently regains full mental
powers and reaffirms it, in which case the gift is
validated as an inter vivos gift. A later will does
not invalidate an otherwise valid gift causa mortis;
the reason is that the will is not effective until the
death of the donor, and the gift has previously
taken the chattel out of the donor's power to place
it under the control of his executor.

The death of the donor must not be a precondition to the validity of the gift. In the understated
words of the law, the gift becomes irrevocable upon

the donor's death. The best evidence of the donor's intent comes from his own words, and some cases have made much of the donor's words of transfer. "If I die (from whatever death the donor is contemplating), this is yours," places a condition precedent to the gift, but "This is yours so long as I die" (from whatever) places a condition subsequent on the gift. The former phrasing invalidates the gift while the latter gift is valid. This distinction seems dry, especially so in the context of a gift which is only valid if made "in contemplation of death"—not of a lingering feeling of life's mortality but of a specific and reasonably immediate event. In such a context, it is downright silly to expect the donor to find the right phrase at a time when he is expected to be concerned with the innocence of his soul. Evidence of a donor's intent should not at such a time hinge on the words of transfer but should be ascertained more broadly.

The donor's surviving the event from which he anticipated death revokes the gift. It is not necessary that the donor state that he anticipates death from a certain event. His anticipation is inferred from the context. Some cases present the situation in which the donor anticipates death on a hospital operating table, makes a gift, in fact recovers from the incision and the operation, but dies of the disease which the operation was intended to cure. Where there is no evidence that the donor revoked the gift between the time it was made and his later death, the gift will probably stand even though the lapse of time involved many months.

If the sickness induced by disease is on-going, as with a progressive tumor, a cancer or a series of strokes or heart attacks, a context in which the donor might anticipate or contemplate death is established.

On the other hand, gifts by a soldier departing for combat in a war or by a person fearing an assassination which took place the next day, have been held insufficient contextual evidence of an anticipation of death. Neither is the putative donor's death by suicide a sufficient context, although some of these cases are influenced by a public policy against suicide and there is authority to the contrary. See *Scherer v. Hyland* (1976). In this case, a donor's leaving a negotiable check in an apartment shared by the donor with the donee, in a location where the donee would find it, is a constructive delivery by a donor. Moreover, a donor's delivery of the check in the manner just described, is made "in contemplation of death," when the donor then leaves the apartment bent on a suicide which occurred a few hours later. This context is sufficient to sustain a gift causa mortis. Indeed, an increasing recognition of the pervasive effects of mental illness may today put gifts preceding a donor's suicide on the same basis as gifts made in the course of many illnesses which ultimately prove fatal.

In many situations, however, the donor's suicide will be an insufficient context for a gift causa mortis because that context implicitly raises a question as to the donor's mental competency to form a donative intent. A better view is that, instead of invalidating such a gift for an insufficient context or "contemplation of death", a full examination of the circumstances of the gift, including the relationship between the donor and the donee, is warranted.

Analysis of whether the gift was made in anticipation of death often proceeds from the objective context to infer the state of mind of the donor. It does not (with some slight authority to the contrary) start and end with the subjective mind-set of the donor. In this sense, gifts causa mortis are not favored in the law, but that may be, in part, because they were a creation of equity. Their basis is a religious premise that when contemplating an imminent death, a donor will express his true feelings, will settle his debts and will disburse his property so as to ease his soul. For past generations, the flames of hell seemed more real than they perhaps do today and, in consequence, some of the religious basis for such gifts may be slipping away.

Other reasons for the law's dislike of them may be more practical. First, depending to any degree on the subjective state of mind of the donor will make the resulting legal rules difficult to apply. Second, because the donor is no longer around to testify, the donee may be unduly tempted to commit perjury and fraud. Third, unlike the gift inter vivos, the continued possession of the chattel by the donee is less likely to be indicative of the donor's acquiescence in the transfer, and fourth, the validation of gifts causa mortis defeats the policy of the applicable Statute of Wills. In the face of the detailed and formal regulation of a testamentary disposition in such Statutes, the evidence for a gift causa mortis should be clear and convincing so that this line of cases can serve as a judicial corrective to such Statutes and the intestate laws of a state.

One state, New Hampshire, has drastically limited the common law pertaining to gifts causa mortis by providing:

> No gift in expectation of death, often called donatio causa mortis, shall be valid, unless the actual delivery of the property to the donee shall be proved by two indifferent witnesses, upon petition of the donee to the judge to establish such gift, filed within sixty days after the decease of the donor. N.H.Rev.Stat.Ann. 551:17 (1991).

The elements of contemplation or expectation of death and donative intent are unaffected by the statute, but in requiring an actual delivery and raising the evidentiary standard for the delivery well above the common law, the New Hampshire legislature seems to endorse the criticism which some courts and legal writers have leveled at gifts causa mortis.

IV. ACCEPTANCE

Because the donee receives a benefit in having the gift bestowed on him, its acceptance is usually presumed. This presumption is a rebuttable one, and the acts of the donee can show rejection of the gift. What the donor intended as a gift of money can be accepted by the donee as a loan—the donee giving back a promissory note in recognition of this fact. Or, a donee can refuse the gift because he is in bankruptcy and to accept it would put the chattel in the hands of his creditors. Likewise, a donee might refuse for tax reasons.

A gift is normally a bilateral transaction, but where the donee does not know of the donor's donative intent (as with delivery to a third person, to a minor, or to an incompetent person), the law will presume acceptance and validate the gift until the donee has an opportunity to accept or reject it. The gift is presently effective, subject to a condition subsequent giving the donee the power to repudiate it. Thus the presumption of an acceptance functions to implement the donative intent of the donor.

Where the donee does not know the precise intent of the donor in making the gift but learns the bare fact that the gift was made (as where donor and donee are on different sides of a war zone and communication is impossible or sporadic), the donee may accept the gift in trust for the donor. Where this is done, the knowledge of the gift in the donee must be incomplete in some respect, otherwise the ambiguous action might be construed as rejection of the gift.

Similarly, accepting a bill of sale for a chattel but not claiming the goods within a reasonable time shows that the donee has not made up his mind whether to accept the gift.

Comparatively few cases discuss the element of acceptance in gifts. Certainly a donee should be free to reject a gift and its acceptance need not be contemporaneous with its delivery, particularly if after delivery the donor makes statements showing the nature of transaction as a gift. Often the donee's filing suit to enforce the gift is sufficient to show that he thought it of some benefit to him.

CHAPTER IX

JOINT BANK ACCOUNTS

I. CONCURRENT INTERESTS IN PERSONAL PROPERTY

Personal property can be held concurrently by two or more persons using one of two common law estates—the joint tenancy and the tenancy in common. (A third concurrent estate, the tenancy by the entirety, is reserved for married persons, is used in only a minority of states, and is often inapplicable to personal property. See Chapter XII.)

Joint tenancy is the concurrent ownership of a chattel by two or more persons who hold it as a unit. All have the right to reduce the whole of the chattel to possession. This is especially appropriate for many small objects of personal property because it provides the only manner in which they can be used. This unitary approach, however, also means that each joint tenant had to (1) take the same estate, (2) at the same time, and (3) from the same title, as well as (4) hold possession of the chattel together. These are the "four unities" of a joint tenancy—a unity of estate, time, title, and possession—and are today the four aspects necessary to establish this estate.

If present, the four unities mean that each joint tenant is entitled to an undivided interest equal to every other tenant's. This joint possession of the whole leads to another more troublesome feature of a joint tenancy—the right of survivorship—by which the entire tenancy passes upon the death of any tenant to the surviving tenants until, at last, the sole surviving tenant takes the whole in absolute ownership.

If the right of survivorship was not express, the English common law had a presumption in favor of it. This presumption did not apply to a second type of concurrent interest—the tenancy in common, which is joint ownership lacking the right of survivorship.

The English presumption for the joint tenancy was rebuttable, and where an intent not to establish a joint tenancy was shown, a tenancy in common resulted.

The English preference for the joint tenancy was developed for real property and was fostered by a desire to avoid dividing the great landed estates among more than one heir. Where personal property is concerned, there is no comparable social policy to be served and, in any event, the English presumption had hardly gained a foothold in the United States before state legislatures in a few states abolished the joint tenancy entirely or else abolished its right of survivorship or, as in the majority of states today, reversed the common law presumption in its favor. Thus the majority of

American jurisdictions today require that there be an express manifestation of intent to create a joint tenancy before one is established; absent such an intent, a tenancy in common is presumed.

American common law as it developed in this area was applied to both real and personal property. But the affirmative manifestation of intent required in a majority of states to create a joint tenancy may, in the case of personal property, be oral and need not, as with real property, be in writing.

Furthermore, although a majority of states have a statutory presumption in favor of a tenancy in common the courts have not generally required that there be any express statement of an intent to form a joint tenancy in personal property. Little harm arises where a piece of personal property is held subject to a joint tenancy with a right of survivorship. The fact that one tenant's heirs may not inherit his interest matters less in many situations involving personal property. Indeed, few reported cases in this country involve joint ownership of personal property. Perhaps because of this, statutes presuming that a deed to a chattel transferred to two or more persons is a tenancy in common, unless expressly declaring itself to be a joint tenancy, do not require that a right of survivorship be spelled out on the face of the document. Instead, an intent to create a right of survivorship can be inferred from surrounding events and circumstances. However, where each tenant has paid a portion of the purchase price, a pro rata tenancy in common is established with each tenant's share determined in proportion to his contribution to the purchase price.

II. JOINT BANK ACCOUNTS

A joint bank account is one established in the names of two or more persons. Although the rules of law applicable to bank accounts do not always square with those applying to joint tenancies and tenancies in common, the courts refer to such accounts as joint accounts. In particular, they do not require technical compliance with the four unities just because they call such an account a joint tenancy. Statutes of several types help courts achieve or provide for this result.

A. STATUTORY TREATMENT OF JOINT ACCOUNTS

One type of statute provides that a bank may pay any funds on account at the death of one account holder to the surviving holder(s) named in the account's documents and signature cards. This type of statute is present in almost all states. Its purpose is to shield the bank from liability to other parties if the bank pays the surviving account holder in accordance with the terms of the account. However, courts have held that such statutes are not dispositive of ownership rights in the account, although more and more state courts use such statutes in settling disputes over such rights, concluding that such a statute is at least presumptive evidence of a survivorship right. *Dyste v. Farmers and Mechanics Savings Bank of Minneapolis* (1930). Bankers feel the need for such statutes because the probate bar is disposed to litigate the legitimacy of paying the surviving account holder, on behalf of the estate and the heirs of the decedent. (And the estate's money is typically available to pay for such litigation.) Even in the absence of litigation, such statutes may not save the survivors from having to present evidence of a depositor's intent to create a survivorship right. To handle this possibility, some statutes provide that survivors may rely on the signature of a depositor as conclusive of his intent, absent other evidence of a fraud, misrepresentation, or undue influence in signing the card.

Even such a statute will not shield a bank whose officials have knowledge of an actual dispute over ownership of the account. If it has actual notice of what they believe is a good faith dispute over the account, then at minimum it should be protected only when the parties to the dispute execute a release of the bank from liability for the withdrawal.

In twelve states and the District of Columbia, additional statutes provide that accounts established in two or more names become the property of all as joint tenants and that a right of survivorship attaches to the account when it is established.

Note, Joint Bank Accounts as Will Substitutes:
The Homemaker, Widow(er) and the Divorced Under New Jersey's Multiple–Party Deposit Account
Act, 15 Rutgers L.J. 1091, 1100–1104 (1984). Such
statutes sometimes preserve the common law's presumption of a joint tenancy for the special situation presented by bank accounts. Like many presumptions, it may be rebutted by evidence to the
contrary. Other states have, or had before the
effective dates of their statutes, reached this result
by judicial decision; here, as a matter of law,
accounts established "in joint tenancy" create a
joint tenancy with a right of survivorship, regardless of whether a contrary intent is evidenced, and
indeed evidence of a contrary intent is inadmissible.

In nineteen other states, a uniform law has been
enacted for joint accounts. It provides that the
amounts on deposit belong "during the lifetime of
all parties, to the parties in proportion to the net
contribution by each to the sums on deposit, unless
there is a clear and convincing evidence of a different intent." Uniform Probate Code [hereafter
UPC], § 6–103 (1989). It also provides that
amounts "remaining on deposit at the death of a
party to a joint account belong to the surviving
party or parties as against the estate of the decedent unless there is clear and convincing evidence
of a different intention at the time the account is
created." UPC, § 6–104.

In successive waves of legislation, then, these
three types of state statutes become increasingly

clear about the ownership rights created in joint accounts. States adopting a variation of the UPC require that a statutory designation be used to reference the rights created by the Code. A failure to make such a designation runs the risk that the survivorship right in the account will fail, even though its creation was the intent of the account holders. Thus a few states require that survivorship be established by the documents and signature cards used to open the account. See Note, The Creation of Joint Tenancy in Bank Accounts: The Old, the New, and the Uncertain, 44 Ark.L.Rev. 199 (1991).

Such statutes are not a complete answer to the problems that plague this area of the law. When the account documents and signature cards function as a substitute for the four unities requirement for creation of a joint account with a right of survivorship, the question of what those documents and cards need to say about the rights created sometimes arises. Such cards and documents must be clear and often are not. In addition, unlike tangible personal property held in joint names, a joint bank account has a fluctuating value as deposits and withdrawals are made. Common law rules in a jurisdiction may work a dissolution of the joint account's survivorship right at the time of a withdrawal of funds on account, thus severing the survivorship right from the bundle of rights otherwise held by the account holders. Of this problem, more later. Because of this, courts in many states have adopted more flexible rules for a joint bank account than would have been possible if it were just viewed as an application of a common-law joint tenancy. It has been called a gift, a trust, a contract, a testamentary disposition, as well as a joint tenancy.

B. ESTABLISHING A JOINT ACCOUNT

The establishment of a bank account in the names of two or more persons requires that the depositor or depositors and all other account holders sign signature cards at the bank. These cards generally define the type of account being established (e.g., joint tenancy or tenancy in common) by checking off the appropriate box. They also give each account holder the right to sign deposit and withdrawal slips for future transactions concerning the account. This is in effect the transfer of title to personal property to all the account-holders made by those who contribute money to the balance on account. As previously discussed, a transfer of title to two or more named persons will without more establish a tenancy in common in the funds on account so it is at this point—the moment of creating the account—that the statutes previously discussed are first useful and must be consulted.

An optional type of signature card in use by many banks contains gift language to the effect that the signatory parties and the bank agree "that the funds placed in or added to this account by any one of the parties is and shall be conclusive-

ly intended to be a gift and delivery of such funds
to the other signatory party or parties to the extent of their pro rata interest in the account."
Several courts have held that this gift language is
effective to overcome evidence that the account
was a matter of convenience and worked no gift of
the deposited funds. Such gift language on the
signature card will not, however, prevent a court
from looking for the elements necessary for a gift.
Rather, the use of this card is evidence to be
considered in the course of such an inquiry, but it
is not by itself dispositive of the question of whether a gift was made.

Bank accounts are today a widely used method of
holding money in joint ownership. Such accounts
provide instances of the courts (1) formulating flexible rules pertaining to concurrent estates in this
type of personal property, and (2) adapting the law
of gifts to new uses. Legislatures have been reluctant to deal comprehensively with joint bank accounts because they are often used as a "poor
man's will." They also facilitate inter-spousal
transfers of family wealth.

The familial purpose of establishing a joint account is often tax-related—i.e., the avoidance of
gift or estate taxes, or the transfer of the assets on
account from one family member in a high income
tax bracket to another in a lower bracket. Often
too, such accounts function as a wallet shared by
all account holders. The "wallet" and the "will"

functions of such an account will now be separately examined.

C. THE "WALLET" FUNCTION: THE INTER VIVOS RIGHT TO WITHDRAW

In the situation where a bank account has been established in joint tenancy by two or more persons and one of these later withdraws his pro rata share or more of the account than he contributed to the balance on account, what is the effect of such a withdrawal? Many of the statutes previously discussed only deal with the intent of the contributor at the moment the account is established. Different evidence may be available as to his intent at the time of a withdrawal, and so courts may deviate from the rule provided in the statute. Most courts begin their search for a solution by reasoning from the attributes of a joint tenancy. For example, each joint tenant has the "right to possession" of all of the money on account, and from this some courts reason that each has the right to withdraw all the money on account without incurring any liability to the other account holders. Other courts conclude that the agreement to hold the account in joint tenancy was only for the purpose of pooling the funds on deposit, but did not necessarily extend to an excessive withdrawal by any one of the tenants. Such courts look to see if the withdrawal was intended as a dissolution of the joint tenancy, either in whole or as to the withdrawn funds. If it is dissolved, a duty to account for any portion of the withdrawal in excess of his contribution to the account follows the withdrawing account holder and attaches to any property purchased with the withdrawn funds.

A few states take the position that the withdrawal ends the right of survivorship that distinguishes a joint tenancy from a tenancy in common. In the jargon of the common law, the withdrawal severs or ends the joint tenancy and a tenancy in common replaces it. In this event, withdrawal of more than a pro rata share of the funds on account renders the withdrawing co-tenant liable to the other tenants for the excess.

A severance of a joint tenancy account might also occur when one co-tenant pledged the balance on account as security for a loan made to that co-tenant alone. Certainly a severance would occur when the other co-tenants know of and assent to the pledge. If they do not, some authority would still hold that a severance occurred when the pledge was made whether or not the other co-tenants knew of it. Perhaps the better view is that no severance occurs when the loan was later repaid and the security was never needed—the non-participating co-tenants remaining ignorant of the loan all the while. A call on the security would, under any view, work a severance and change the joint tenancy into a tenancy in common thereafter.

Until as recently as 1990, California courts held that a joint tenancy in personal property, like a bank account, could not be severed unilaterally, while a joint tenancy in real property could. Today unilateral severance is possible and an account holder can defeat the right of survivorship by withdrawing funds on account. *Estate of Propst* (1990). Thus was a clear rule forsaken in favor of the common law's flexibility.

In a tenancy in common, the presumption is that the co-tenants contributed equally to the funds on account. This presumption is, however, often a rebuttable one.

Whether the bank account is held in either joint tenancy or tenancy in common, some courts have a presumption that where the contributing and non-contributing account holders are husband and wife, the contributing tenant intended to make a gift of one half of the funds on deposit to the other tenant. This last presumption is used to promote the stability of spousal relations as a matter of public policy and is virtually irrebuttable whether or not a withdrawal turns a joint tenancy into a tenancy in common. In such jurisdictions, neither the fact that the withdrawing tenant had been the sole owner of the funds prior to deposit nor the fact that he removed the balance in the account and used it for his own purposes is sufficient, singly or in combination, to rebut it. Whether the withdrawn funds are still in existence or not, the gift to the spouse was complete upon deposit.

One more distinction worth noting in this area is attributable to different patterns of usage of savings as opposed to checking accounts. The tracking of a contribution through a bank account is often more easily accomplished with a savings account where deposits and withdrawals are less frequent and in larger amounts than would be the case with a checking account where deposits and withdrawals will be more frequent and smaller and tracking that much more difficult. From this difficulty an inference might be drawn that a gift of deposited funds was intended to any checking account holder making a withdrawal in any amount, even one in excess of his contribution. At least one court has refused to impose a liability on a checking account holder for amounts withdrawn in excess of contribution although, if the funds can be tracked through an account, there is no need to make this distinction between savings and checking accounts dispositive of any case. Indeed, modern banking practices and mutual fund money market accounts tend to blur the once clear distinction between these two types of accounts. The pattern of use is one fact from which intent might be determined, but not the only one.

Indeed, it is difficult these days for many to figure out who is a banker. Although this section deals with bank accounts, much said here can also be applied to mutual fund, money market, and stock brokerage accounts in joint names with a check cashing feature. See *First Wisconsin Trust Company v. United States* (1982). In the future, the rules used for bank account cases are likely to be used to decide similar controversies involving accounts held by companies functioning like bankers, though not regulated as such. Also seldom subject to statutory regulation are survivorship disputes involving personal property in jointly held safety deposit boxes; in the absence of statutes, the common law applies in such disputes.

D. THE "WILL" FUNCTION: GIFTS TO SURVIVING ACCOUNT HOLDERS

Absent a statute to the contrary, a gift of the balance on account to a surviving account holder is invalid unless the signature cards establish an express or implied right of survivorship.

The earliest reported cases on survivorship rights were decided under the law of gifts. Where a depositor opened an account in joint names but thereafter retained some control over the passbook, checks, or account records, the question arose as to whether there was a delivery. However, because the same retention could also be construed as a completed gift with a survivorship right, courts often look to the execution of the signature cards as a deed of gift that substituted for a delivery. In other early cases, courts regarded the signature cards as a depositor/bank contract for the benefit of the other account holders as third-party beneficiaries of the contract. So gift and contract theories often exist side by side in a jurisdiction's case law to give surviving account holder's rights in the funds on account.

In some states the signature card which opens an account in joint names creates a presumption that a survivorship right attached to the account. This presumption is rebuttable, but only by clear and convincing evidence. Rebutting evidence generally goes to show that the account was opened for the convenience of the depositor and created an agency relationship between the depositor and the other account holders. In such a case, no survivorship rights will be found where the depositor (1) could withdraw all the funds on account in his sole discretion and (2) was ill and the account was needed to order his financial affairs through an agent. An aged depositor whose illness might require all funds on account, but who opened an account with a nurse who never withdrew funds for personal use, could probably convince a court that his intent was to retain control of the funds during his life. Here, if any right in the account for the nurse is intended at all, it will arise only at the death of the depositor. At this time the agent's authority to use the account is terminated by his principal's death, but the survivorship right may have been given as payment for the agent's services. This arrangement is in effect a joint account in which one account holder, if he has any rights at all, has only survivorship rights. Such a result is less plausible where a depositor is in the same aged and ill condition but is nursed by a spouse to whom many courts would accord more discretion in withdrawing funds on account. However, if the nursing spouse withdrew all the funds a day before his spouse's death, he might still be held to have severed a joint tenancy and would lose half of it to his spouse's estate. If, on the other hand, he had waited a day he would have received the whole account as a surviving account holder. Compare *Estate of Gray* (1965) with *Zander v. Holly* (1957).

No matter what type of statute a jurisdiction has regulating the establishing of a bank account in a joint tenancy, courts will often ignore the literal wording, even of a statute purporting to establish a joint tenancy as a matter of law and permit the parties to a dispute to litigate the question of ownership of the funds on account. When the deceased has deposited all or most of his funds in such an account or the survivor has not contributed his share of the funds on account at the time of the death, the courts look beyond the regulatory statutes to review the alleged transfer of the funds to the survivor(s). The statutes, however, do count for something: they extend the possibility of survivorship rights in account holders who have not contributed to the funds on account, even when the funds are all or most of the corpus of the deceased depositor's estate. While the courts are extremely sensitive to the facts of a case and less so to the statutes and the requirement of the four unities for joint tenancies, courts sustain such survivorship rights (if they do) on one of three theories. The first involves contract law, another trust law, and yet a third involves viewing the deposit as a gift to the survivor.

(1) If the deposit of the money with the bank creates a contract between the depositor and the bank, the surviving account holder who has not contributed money to the bank balance might be viewed as a donee, third-party beneficiary to that contract. It is a transaction between the actual depositor of the money and the bank for the benefit of another account holder. Then a third party need not sign the agreements establishing the account. *Malek v. Patten* (1984) (noting that stringent application of the law of gifts would require the beneficiary's signature, but that "[m]odern commercial practice relies heavily upon contractual theory rather than gift theory.") If the supposed beneficiary has in addition signed a signature card, then the contract is a three-party one. This contract is also enforceable without regard to the law of gifts.

(2) Alternately, the depositor who places his money in a joint tenancy account might be regarded as the settlor of a revocable trust. It is revocable in the sense that the depositor retains access to the balance up until the time of his death. Such a view of the joint tenancy bank account is in conflict with the normal requirement that the settlor of a trust relinquish all title and control over the corpus of the account. A combination of factors may, however, persuade a court to overlook this rule: the convenience of the account, a decline in the adherence to the policy underlying the Statute of Wills, the difficulties of probate, and the bank's account-opening formalities which may impress

upon the depositor the fact that he is giving up total control over the account.

Of course, a deposit may be expressly made "by S in trust for B." These words would constitute a formal declaration of a trust, and when accompanied by other evidence of the settlors' intent to create a trust, such as giving some checks or the passbook to the beneficiary, such trust will be valid. In this case, the courts of some jurisdictions assume that the trust is irrevocable but that the settlor has retained a management power over the balance in the account. Such a trust may, however, still be found in violation of the Statute of Wills, and cases in some jurisdictions have so found.

(3) A third view of the joint tenancy bank account involves the law of gifts. The courts of many states have litigated the question of delivery for these accounts. Arguably, the delivery of the funds to the bank is a delivery to a trustee for the co-depositor donee, especially when the donee acquires a present right to make withdrawals from the account. As to the donor's intention to make a gift, the courts have split in finding such an intent in a situation where typically the donor has given access to the funds to the donee but can himself withdraw them and so has not relinquished total control over the balance in the account. If access through checks or the passbook is provided the donee, many courts have sustained the gift even though the donor has only shared control over the

account. So, in situations where both the donor and donee have access to the account, the holdings of these cases are an exception to the general rule that the donor must relinquish all control over the subject of the gift. Either that relinquishment is inferred from the donor's acquiescence in the donee's access, or else the donor is estopped to deny that the access created a survivorship right in the donee, and thus it is the donee's access to the account that proves dispositive in these cases. It is irrelevant whether or not the right to withdraw was ever used or that the donee only actually used the funds in the account for emergency purposes. Acquisition of access and a potential right to control the account is sufficient.

A gift of the balance to the survivor in a joint bank account is not necessarily testamentary in nature. As a gift, it operates at the time the account is established, that is, during the donor's lifetime.

Some courts have presumed the validity of the survivorship gift without looking more deeply into the matter. Other courts, however, have found that the gift is void for noncompliance with the Statute of Wills applicable in the jurisdiction. Courts have hesitated to make this finding, however, since the co-depositor will then be held to account for any withdrawals he made. Only where such withdrawals are made with notice of a rival claim on the funds, such as might be made by the estate of the nonsurviving depositor, will courts readily impose this liability. Otherwise, the donor's providing access to the funds is evidence of acquiescence by the donor to the gift.

Once the donor is dead, a court may show an increasing reluctance to disturb the joint bank account arrangement. Even when the will of a codepositor revokes the survivorship right in the account expressly, the attempt at revocation is only effective after the survivorship right was supposed to become effective—and that may be enough for some courts. See e.g., *In re Estate of Boldt* (1983) (holding that a survivorship right in a bank account may not be revoked by will). To other courts, this notion of when both the will and the right is effective may seem overly formal when it is contrary to the donor's intent. Because an earlier will can be revoked by a later one, a joint bank account's survivorship right should be revoked by a later will as well. A contract or a trust, for that matter, might be similarly revoked. In any event, a will substitute, functioning in the meanwhile like a wallet, should be treated no differently than an earlier will would have been. And it can be, if courts would only distinguish clearly between the two very different functions served by joint accounts.

This area is by no means crisp. No one should assume that a gift made through the medium of a bank account is valid. That this area of the law is so confused violates the expectations of many people because joint tenancy bank accounts are in wide use and function much an everyman's will.

No matter what legal theory is used, the alleged transfer will be held void upon proof of fraud, duress, misrepresentation, mutual mistake, or incapacity. Such has been the traditional rule in matters of gifts and when a domineering person escorts a transferor into the presence of a third party like a bank officer, it would be inequitable to hold that the same grounds for invalidating the transfer are not available because the theory supporting the transfer has changed and is now contractual or trust-oriented. No matter what the theory, proof of one of these grounds for invalidation shows that the transfer does not reflect the intent of the parties. *Lowry v. Lowry* (1976); *Estate of Bowlin v. Ables,* 766 S.W.2d 193 (1988).

1. The Totten Trust

The idea that a joint bank account can serve as a will substitute, without first being a wallet, is when viewed through the lens of the trust theory, akin to a revocable trust—traditionally almost a contradiction in terms. Nonetheless, a depositor's placing his own funds in a savings account "in trust for" or "as trustee for" another is generally held to establish a revocable or tentative trust during the lifetime of the depositor. Restatement (Second) of Trusts, § 58 (1959). It is revocable at will because the depositor retains access to the funds and because of a judicial policy against self-declared trusts. Title to the funds stays with the depositor, and so it is said that the beneficiaries named in the account have a mere expectancy and not a vested right to them. This trust may be completed by delivery of the passbook to the beneficiary or by any other unequivocal act of the depositor. If not revoked during the life of the depositor, a presumption arises that an irrevocable trust is created at his death. In some states, the title to the funds passes by operation of law to the persons named; this means that no evidence to the contrary is admissible because there is no presumption on which the contrary facts might work. The corpus of this trust consists of whatever funds are on deposit at death.

This tentative trust is often called a Totten Trust, so-called after the case of *In re Totten* (1904). Totten trust funds are generally considered to pass outside the estate of the depositor, now decedent. They can, however, be subjected to claims made on him or his estate by his creditors, although they are not subjected to a spousal right to elect against the will of the decedent. As to creditors, the logic is that if the depositor could have used the funds to pay creditors, the latter should be able to reach the funds by judicial process.

A formal revocation of the tentative trust by the depositor is not necessary. Any action, disavowal, or declaration will do. Any withdrawal of funds by the depositor will revoke the tentative trust as to the funds withdrawn but *not* as to the funds remaining. So will any withdrawal by a person with the depositor's general power of attorney. If the passbook is used as collateral or security for a loan to the depositor, the trust is revoked to the extent of the debt of the depositor on the loan because he has shown an intention to use the funds in a manner inconsistent with the terms of the trust. This is so because the alternative of holding that a trustee of only a tentative trust has violated his fiduciary duty seems unduly harsh. Upon revocation by withdrawal, the beneficiary may not follow or trace the funds or hold the depositor liable for them.

If the beneficiary predeceases the depositor, a Totten Trust is terminated. If the payment of the trust funds to the beneficiary is not to be made at the depositor's death, and instead a successor trustee is appointed, or the payment is conditioned on some event after the depositor's death, such as the beneficiary's reaching a certain age, the trust is not a Totten Trust and the traditional rules of the law of trusts are applied. *Estate of Bischof* (1989).

A residuary clause in a will, stating that "all the rest and residue of my property" go to a person other than the beneficiary of a Totten Trust, will not by itself revoke the trust. However, evidence that a testator intended to revoke it with his will is admissible. *Estate of Bol* (1988) (affirming revocation of Totten Trust).

At the death of the depositor, the money is normally paid out to the beneficiary, although the question of whether or not it should be really involves an interpretation of the terms of the trust.

Since its initial judicial recognition in New York in 1904, Totten Trusts have been adopted in eighteen other jurisdictions. Estes, In Search of a Less Tentative Totten, 5 Pepperdine L.Rev. 21 (1977). Florida and Illinois have good cases doing this. For a recent opinion on the validity of Totten Trusts as a *de novo* issue, see In re *Estate of Morton* (1987) (exempting a Totten Trust from Statute of Wills). In addition, statutes permitting banks to pay out funds on account to surviving depositors, often provide an argument for courts that the legislature would have no objection to the recognition of a Totten Trust. In re *Estate of Adams* (1990) (collecting the cases); In re *Estate of Stokes* (1987). In other states, however, community property statutes may protect the spouse of the depositor and limit the usefulness of such trusts because community funds may not be unilaterally placed in such a trust. In re *Estate of Wilson* (1986) (holding that only one half of the depositor's account passed to the beneficiary of a Totten Trust).

CHAPTER X

ADVERSE POSSESSION OF PERSONAL PROPERTY

The title to a chattel can be transferred by adverse possession. Using this method of transfer, even a convertor who holds the chattel for the requisite, statutory period of time in an exclusive, open and notorious, continuous, hostile—and so generally adverse—manner receives title to it. The passage of time involved in the period of adverse possession bars the true owner's or prior possessor's cause of action in replevin or trover. Authority for these propositions is *Henderson v. First National Bank of Dewitt* (1973).

Each of the elements of adverse possession just mentioned raise issues of fact. Was the convertor in exclusive physical possession of the chattel? Did he hold it for all his neighbors and the world to see? For an uninterrupted period of time? In such a manner as to put the world, including the true owner or prior possessor, on notice that he was holding it so as to bar any other rights in it?

The "open and notorious" element of adverse possession will often provide the adverse user of chattels with the greatest difficulties of proof. This is so because many chattels are just not big

349

enough to make their possession notoriously apparent to all. Thus it is not surprising that many crucial issues in the law of adverse possession of personal property revolve around the question of when the statutory period starts—rather than when it ends. On this question, state statutes of limitation for replevin, trover and conversion, and conversion alone, are seldom helpful.

The typical period for bringing such actions is either three or six years in over one half of the states—and four or five years in most of the rest. For a recent treatment of this subject, see P. Gerstenblith, The Adverse Possession of Personal Property, 37 Buff. L.Rev. 119 (1988). See also, R. Helmholz, Wrongful Possession of Chattels: Hornbook Law and Case Law, 80 Nw.U. L.Rev. 1221 (1986). As we shall see in this chapter, there are two modern deviations from the tradition in the law of adverse possession of examining the behavior of the adverse possessor: one involves the so-called "demand and refusal" element of an action for replevin or trover. New York's case law has examined this. The other is the use of the so-called discovery rule in interpreting the statute of limitations for chattels. New Jersey has used this.

I. ADVERSE POSSESSION AND STATUTES OF LIMITATION

Where do the elements of adverse possession come from? The required exclusivity, openness, continuousness, hostility and adversity are a gloss

on statute of limitations provisions of all state
codes. They are judge-made law. Such statutes
typically provide:

> No person shall commence an action for the
> recovery of a chattel or land, or make any entry
> on land, unless within ... years after the right
> to bring such action or make such entry first
> accrued, or within ... years after he or those
> by or under whom he claims, have been seized or
> possessed of the chattel or premises.

The period of time required to lapse under such
provisions is ten to twenty years for real property,
but often only two to six years for personal property. In one leading case, two counters were installed in a shop. The shop's premises were later
mortgaged and the mortgage included all fixtures
within it (including the counters). Can the vendor
of the counters reclaim them after the statute of
limitations for personal property has run but before the real property limitation period has run?
This was the question of *Chapin v. Freeland* (1886).

Holmes, J., held that he could not, but gave an
answer that made it necessary to determine the
type of property involved. The cause of action
brought by the plaintiff, who purchased the premises at the sale foreclosing the mortgage, was replevin which lies for the recovery of personal property. The defendant had installed the counters in
1867 and had repossessed them in 1881. Once
repossessed and in his hands, what had once been a
real property fixture reverted to being personal

property; the court held that the shorter statute of limitations for personal property applied and had already run at the time of the repossession.

The dissent in *Chapin* takes issue with Holmes' application of the statute of limitations for personal property. It thought that the defendant was entitled to have the benefit of the longer limitations period in the real property statute which had not been tolled at the time of the defendant's seizure of the counters. Since the chattels became fixtures and so part of the real property when installed *by the plaintiff,* the defendant should have the benefit of the limitations period chosen by his opponent.

The counter-argument to this is a practical one to the effect that persons like the plaintiff should be encouraged to modernize and improve their property with personal property permanently affixed to their real estate. To permit the defendant to have the benefit of the longer limitations period for real property would be to weaken the plaintiff's ability to realize the profits of the modernization by subjecting the title to the fixtures to uncertainty for a longer period.

Another advantage of Holmes' position is that it does not encourage self-help. The vendor of a chattel which becomes a fixture on real property must assert his right (if any) to self-help within the period of limitations for personal property or be barred. This, too, will tend to give the improver of property an incentive to modernize by confirming his title to the fixtures all the sooner.

Further, Holmes argues that no repossession or self-help was possible because the statute of limitation was intended to bar the right to the chattel as well as the remedy for infringement of that right.

It is this last proposition to which the dissent in *Chapin* takes exception. Barring the right along with the judicial remedy is the traditional view of the effect of an adverse possession statute concerning real property. The dissent, however, thought that in Massachusetts the remedy was barred, but not the right. In a sense, the vendor still had a right or a title that the courts would not reduce to possession. If the underlying right or title of the vendor survives, then self-help is available to him to enforce his right to the counters.

However, the Massachusetts statute bars "the action for replevin and all other actions for the taking, detaining, or injuring of goods or chattels." This inclusiveness suggests that the actions of trespass, detinue, and trover, as well as the action of replevin, are barred under this statute. With both damage actions as well as those for specific recovery barred, then the personal property statute is the equivalent of a bar to both the tort and property causes of action involved in adverse possession and operates as a complete bar to recovery of the chattel.

Holmes also would seem to have the better of the argument over whether there should be a right without a remedy. His underlying premise is that the courts should not permit a right for which they will not provide a review to prevent its abuse. Self-help might be permitted, he might say, but not to this extent.

A. THE U.C.C. AND CHAPIN

Today, in about one half of the states, the holder of a mortgage or other security interest in fixtures who files his interest on the public record obtains a priority of lien over pre-existing recorded mortgages on the underlying real property under the Uniform Commercial Code, § 9–313(4)(a), 1972 version. This priority is an exception to the usual rule of the recording statutes for real property whose rule is usually "first to record, first in right." For fixture filings, the rule is "last to record, first in right." Such a drastic exception is permitted only because of a strong policy to encourage the modernization and improvement of real property.

The exception to the normal priority is itself subject to an exception, but it is one which reenforces the underlying rationale; that is, the fixturizer's priority of lien is itself subject to a lien for a construction loan on the same property. Because the construction lender energizes improvement of the whole property, a fixturizer, as one who improves only a part of it, takes second place to him. U.C.C. § 9–313(6), 1972 version.

II. THE ELEMENTS OF ADVERSE POSSESSION AS A GLOSS ON STATUTES OF LIMITATIONS

Chapin ultimately makes the point that the elements of adverse possession are a judge-made gloss on statutes of limitations. It is the rare case, however, that allows a judge to delve into the causes of action underlying these statutes, for in many jurisdictions the law of adverse possession will have hidden its statutory roots in a maze of cases. These cases will outline the facts necessary to make out the elements of adverse user for both real and personal property.

These statutes of limitations provide that no person shall commence an action for the recovery of chattels unless they do so within up to six years running from the time his right or title to the chattel first accrued or within six years from the time the plaintiff last possessed the chattel or had the right to possess it. Several of the phrases in this paraphrase are indicative of the present-day elements of adverse possession. First, the idea that the plaintiff must assert his "right or title" suggests that his interest in the chattel must be recognized—i.e., *open* and *notorious*. Second, that his "possession or right to possess" the chattel is at issue suggests that his interest in the chattel must be *continuous*. Third, that a "right to possess" may be considered as well as possession itself, suggests that the interest will usually be an *exclu-*

sive one but may on occasion be constructive or at least as exclusive as custom and usage permit.

Six years was the period of limitations in England for trespass, detinue, trover and replevin actions. A similar period has been adopted in many states in this country. Its passage barred both the title and the right to possession of the true owner or prior possessor when he was out of possession for that period and the adverse possessor satisfied all of the elements of adverse user. As with real property, the good or bad faith of the adverse possessor made no difference—the statute of limitations ran in either case.

Many adverse possession cases involving real property revolve around the claim of title of the adverse possessor: did he evidence his actual possession with acts of legal ownership? Often (probably more often than will be the case with real property) the holder of a chattel will not have a bill of sale or other evidence of a claim of title on the public record or tax rolls. This being the case, some courts have heard with sympathy the claim that when a stolen chattel leaves the jurisdiction or when it is hidden, the statute stops running and starts to run again when the thief holds it openly within the jurisdiction. If he leaves once more, the statute stops running and does not begin running again until his return—and so on, until the statutory period is tolled in fits and starts. Often this result is accomplished by statute, but one court has recently put the rule this way:

The statute of limitations on an action to recover stolen personal property in the hands of one who in good faith purchased the personalty for value, begins to run from the time the latter acquired the possession and not from the time the owner first had knowledge of the whereabouts of the property, provided there was no fraud or attempt at concealment .... However, the action is barred only when the property is held openly and notoriously for two years, so that the owner may have a reasonable opportunity of knowing its whereabouts and of asserting his title ....

Riesinger's Jewelers, Inc. v. Roberson (1978). This quotation makes two points about the law of adverse possession. First, the function of its five elements is to provide the true owner or prior possessor of the chattel with notice that non-assertion of his rights will bar his claim after the statutory period runs. Second, the elements are a judicial gloss on a statute of limitations and as such are intended to mollify the harsh effects of the statute alone; they are meant, in other words, to do justice between the parties to a dispute over a chattel.

The weight of case authority holds that the doctrine of tacking between adverse users applies to personal property which is adversely possessed, just as it applies to real property. Again, however, there are some cases to the contrary holding that a new cause of action begins to run against each successive adverse possessor of a chattel. Although the purposes and the policy of the statute of limitations remain the same for both real and personal property, each successive transfer of the chattel is also a new basis for an allegation of conversion. So the adverse use of a chattel must be open and notorious enough to provide notice to its owners and prior possessors that its present holder is seeking to receive title in himself. Successive transfers are likely to be the most public acts available as proof that the open and notorious elements of adverse possession have been fulfilled. Tacking therefore seems justified.

Once an adverse possessor acquires his title, he is entitled also to all of the rents, income and profits derived from a chattel for the period of time during which he has been running the statute. These are known as mesne or interim profits. In the same manner, one acquires the rights in any off-spring born to adversely-possessed animals, crops grown on land adversely possessed, and any other chattels affixed to land adversely possessed. In these situations, the title of the adverse possessor, once acquired, is said to relate back to the date on which he began to run the statute in his favor.

A. "OPEN AND CONTINUOUS" ADVERSE POSSESSION

Unlike land, a chattel cannot easily be held for all the world to see. Even if it is not secreted away or hidden, it is likely to be in the user's home and unlikely to be on public display. The adverse user of a chattel will thus be subject to the argument that he has not openly used the chattel and so cannot prove all the elements of adverse possession.

A recent and now quite famous case illustrates this point. In 1946, the artist, Georgia O'Keeffe, had three of her paintings stolen from a New York City art gallery operated by her husband. From then until 1975 the paintings were lost, and O'Keeffe, thinking them lost forever, did not report the theft until 1972 when, for the first time, it was possible to report stolen works of art and have them put on an international registry. In 1975, the painting turned up in the Princeton, NJ gallery of a purchaser who did not verify the title of the person who sold him the paintings.

O'Keeffe made a demand upon the gallery owner to return the works. He refused and she sued him in replevin. *O'Keeffe v. Snyder* (1980). For a review of this case, see P. Franzese, "Georgia on My Mind"—Reflections on *O'Keeffe v. Snyder,* 19 Seton H. L.Rev. 1 (1989); P. Gerstenblith, op. cit., 37 Buff. L.Rev. at 141–145.

Since this suit was brought more than 20 years after the supposed theft of the paintings and the applicable statute of limitation was six years, the first issue in the case is whether the statute of limitations has run on this cause of action. What then is it, precisely, that starts a statute of limitations running? The answer is a general one—the accrual of the cause of action. When does a cause of action first accrue? One answer might be that it accrues when the last element of the cause of action falls into place. In the case of replevin, the plaintiff must allege: first, some right to the chattel in the plaintiff; second, the loss of the chattel by conversion—some wrongful taking or detention of it; and third, the defendant's retention of it at the time of the suit, after a demand by the plaintiff and a refusal to return it by the defendant, by which, fourth, the plaintiff suffers damages.

The third element of the cause of action—the retention at the time of the suit—is generally proven by a demand and refusal. The plaintiff demands the chattel back, and the defendant's refusal shows that he retains it in the face of his knowledge of the plaintiff's claim to it. A demand and refusal cannot be made until the defendant is located. In practical terms, this is good for the plaintiff in replevin because he then argues that until the defendant is known to him, his cause of action is not complete and the statute of limitations cannot run against it. At least one state (New York) has cases which accept this point of view. *Menzel v. List* (1967) (third party claim). There the demand puts the innocent possessor on notice of the plaintiff's claim. Thereafter, his possession of the disputed chattel is a knowing interference with the plaintiff's rights. The knowing retention of the chattel completes the conversion underlying the cause of action; indeed, it constitutes an entirely new act of conversion and in some states may start the statute running anew.

However, this view of replevin has limitations. The demand is not, of course, the first time that a bad faith possessor is put on notice of another's rights. He is, presumably, already adversely possessing the chattel, and his possession is a continuous conversion of the plaintiff's chattel.

Making a demand and refusal a necessity for replevin will likely prejudice innocent purchasers more than ones with bad faith. In any event, few defendants will be prejudiced by the absence of a demand, and the plaintiff's bringing suit against them will provide them with notice of his claim in the end. The good faith or bad faith of an adverse possessor is not and should not be dispositive of adverse possession questions; rather, the type of user is.

A more general weakness of the argument that a demand and refusal is a substantive element of replevin is that, whether the defendant is known to the plaintiff or not, the defendant retained the chattel for what is alleged to be the statutory period. So the better view is that the demand and refusal is not a substantive element of replevin; it is merely one method of proof of the third element in this cause of action. In some jurisdictions, it may even be *the* traditional method of proof. But only that. As evidence rather than a substantive requirement of replevin, a demand and refusal is not necessary to the bringing of the cause of action, and the statute runs regardless of whether or not it is made.

Yet, obviously, in states which reject demand and refusal as a substantive element of replevin, the courts remain concerned that the adverse possessor of a chattel not hide it for the statutory period and prevent the true owner from finding it until it is too late. So normally the concealment of a chattel stops the running of the statute. Where the defense to the replevin action is a title in the defendant by adverse possession, the defendant will have the burden of proof to show each of the elements necessary for such possession. In the instance of a concealment, he will fail to show "open and visible" possession. The focus of the court's inquiry will be on the defendant's actions. Ignored will be the need for a secure title in a later possessor and equitable defenses such as laches. To decide whether the statute ever began to run, therefore, some courts examine the plaintiff's actions including, but not limited to, whether he made a demand for the chattel's return.

The *O'Keeffe* court said that the difficulties of applying the law of adverse possession to chattels dictate that the statute not start to run until the discovery of the chattel in the defendant's possession if, in the meantime, the plaintiff has been diligent in seeking to discover its whereabouts. The burden of showing this diligence is on the plaintiff. Running the statute of limitations is deferred only so long as this diligence lasts, and thereafter, it runs and the defendant must show that he satisfied the elements of adverse possession.

Subsequent uses of the *O'Keeffe* case as precedent make plain that in many instances, the true owner of the chattel as a plaintiff is the one to benefit from the use of the discovery rule, in that it extends the time during which an action is available to him. See e.g., *Mucha v. King* (1986) (involving artwork sought by the artist's heir); *DeHart v. First Fidelity Bank, N.A./South Jersey* (1986) (involving conversion of negotiable instruments owned by a bank). See also, *DeWeerth v. Baldinger* (1987) (applying and formulating, wrongly as it turned out—see infra—New York law), noted at 9 Loy. Entertainment L.J. 57 (1989).

Use of the discovery rule in *O'Keeffe* downplays the fact that the defendant was not a bad fellow; indeed, he has some of the traits of a good faith purchaser. Yet the difficulty of establishing what constitutes open and notorious possession of the paintings persuaded the court that the burden of first establishing those elements of adverse possession should not be imposed on the defendant. Rather, the true owner has the burden of showing diligence, although why that diligence is less difficult to show is unclear. Meanwhile—that is, while the true owner is being diligent (if he is)—how is the possessor supposed to learn of this diligence and thus learn of the security of his right to continued possession of the chattel?

The answer is that he cannot know, and so can't be secure in his claim. And this is particularly true of the good faith possessor. The *O'Keeffe* court solves one problem by creating another.

This "discovery rule" has been used in other areas of the law (e.g., torts) to protect causes of action which would otherwise not be brought due to ignorance. It is particularly apt when the plaintiff is injured—or when there is an injury to property not immediately evident—and the defendant is a bad fellow. (Notice, however, that this is not the situation in *O'Keeffe.*)

Another apt use of the discovery rule occurs out West. The true owner of livestock bearing a brand should not be held to have an action in trover or replevin until he knows of their whereabouts. Brands were commonly recorded and branding thus became a sign of diligence in sorting out ownership (particularly on the open range). See Utah Code Ann. 78–12–26 (1987) (predating *O'Keeffe*). Thus could rustlers be pursued in the courts, as well as by a posse.

The use of the discovery rule permits a court to balance the injustice to the defendant (whether through the difficulties of defending a stale suit, his innocence, or the injury which he will suffer) against the benefit to a plaintiff in allowing the replevin action. The discovery rule is flexible. It is an invention of equity and permits the plaintiff to bring replevin when he can show due diligence under the circumstances of the case. Moreover, it considers degrees of due diligence—whether the defendant was blind to facts he should have seen, was intentionally idle, made some efforts, or was faced with an impossible task. It renders the title of a remote possessor that much more uncertain but gives force to the rule that, with stolen chattels, the thief acquires no title and cannot transfer good title to others regardless of their good faith or ignorance of the theft.

Nonetheless, the *O'Keeffe* case has not started any pronounced trend in the courts or legislatures. Although California amended its statute of limitation to reflect it, the New York Court of Appeals rejects the case. *Solomon R. Guggenheim Fdn. v. Lubell* (1990). While stating that, after discovery of the stolen chattel, the true owner cannot unreasonably delay the demand upon the possessor for its return, this court thought that imposing on the true owner the burden of proving due diligence was a retreat from the traditional protection afforded owners in New York. Moreover, the court said, all true owners should not be expected to behave alike, so that crafting a rule of due diligence would become very difficult. Some will not want the notoriety of advertising the theft. Some will think their chance of recovery greater if they don't advertise it. In addition, were the rule otherwise, the court said, the possessor able to hold onto the chattel for three years (the applicable limitations period) would be able to retain possession unless the true owner is able to show due diligence. (That is, the court fears that a procedural rule would quickly turn into a substantive one.) Due diligence, while not irrelevant to this court, is thought best considered by way of an estoppel or laches defense. Thus the Court of Appeals protected the true owner when he is the victim of an art theft, by placing the burden of tracing the title of the art object—or provenance, in the parlance of the art trade—on its purchaser.

The statute of limitations controversy between the holdings in *O'Keeffe* and *Lubell* is inapplicable to the moral rights of artists. Although little accepted in this country, the doctrine of moral right holds that an artist has, even after selling his work, the right to preserve its integrity, to prevent its being exhibited up-side down, or copied in a way that distorts its meaning. This doctrine has been codified in seven states. See e.g., McKinney's— N.Y. Arts & Cult.Aff.L. § 14.03 (1988). The artist's cause of action under this type of statute only arises when the integrity of the work is threatened.

When a museum is the purchaser or donee of a work of art or other chattels, the law of adverse possession is often used as a title-quieting device. Thus, after the delivery as a gift of a collection of historical documents to a museum holding them for the statutory period, the transferor of a heretofore unqualified delivery cannot seek to reacquire them on the ground that the documents were the subject of a bailment or loan. *Wilcox v. St. Mary's University of San Antonio, Inc.* (1973). This decision is based on the rule (discussed in Chapter VIII) that a delivery unqualified on its face cannot be cut back by a condition unstated at the time of delivery or not appearing in the deed of delivery.

This title-quieting function is often seen today in international law, to protect the repose of chattel that is on permanent exhibition in or is owned in one country, but which another country claims as its cultural property. In this context, some present possessors are likely to have to return the artifact; so a dealer should know enough to investigate the title and the export papers for the chattel. *Autocephalous Greek–Orthodox Church of Cyprus v. Goldberg & Feldman Fine Arts* (1989) (involving a mosaic stolen from a church during wartime). A similar fate awaits the heirs of a WW II soldier possessing art objects acquired in wartime and hidden in his basement for the rest of his life. See the situation of Joe Tom Meador: W. Honan, With Stolen Treasures, Generosity Has Its Price, N.Y. Times (March 1, 1992), at § 4, p. 6, col. 1. None of this will prevent the courts of the United States from passing on the clarity and due process accorded in foreign laws asserted in derogation of the rights of United States citizens, but nothing prevents the courts from enforcing those laws either. See e.g., *United States v. McClain* (1979).

A difficult international case involved Hebraic manuscripts about to be destroyed, but smuggled out of Nazi Germany by giving them to a scholar with an exit visa and headed for the United States. See J.D. Bleich, The Controversy Concerning the Sotheby Sale, 8 Cardozo L.Rev. 91 (1986) [arguing that Talmudic law of gifts should control and reporting the arguments in *Abrams v. Sotheby–Parke–Bernet*]. The Talmudic rule is that the possessor of stolen chattel may convey valid title, provided that the victim of the theft has despaired of recovering the chattel—a rule akin to that of *O'Keeffe*. (How is the possessor to know of the victim's despair?) When the chattel is a sacred Hebrew text, it is presumed that despair is not present, because (some Talmudic authorities hold) the text is of no value to a non-Jew and so will be eventually sold back to a Jew—the latter bound to attempt a return to its true owner. However, there are other Talmudic precedents holding that if a conquerer (here the Nazis) were in control of the text, valid title may be transferred, but if not, the true owner may not have despaired of recovery.

To resolve the issues in *Abrams,* return to the chapters on finders and bailments: award the possessor a safekeeping or salvage fee, and permit the true owner to recover the texts on behalf of the Jewish community in Germany seeking their return. Possession may be nine points of the law, but as you know by now, it is not always presumptive of title in the possessor. The smuggling scholar's use of the texts is consistent with a bailment for the period of time the texts were in danger of destruction.

Finally, should the scholar be subject to Talmudic law? That raises anew the issues of custom explored earlier in the case of *Ghen v. Rich* in *Chapter I.*

CHAPTER XI

ACCESSION AND CONFUSION

I. ACCESSION

In an earlier chapter, we saw that the true owner of a chattel could reach down the chain of possession and bring an action in replevin against subsequent possessors of the chattel, so long as the subsequent possessor chosen as a defendant did not assert the rights as bona fide purchaser. There are some limits to his reach, however, and we will now discuss one of them—the doctrine of accession.

Accession is the addition of labor to the chattel of another, without the latter's consent, which so changes the chattel that the title to it is transferred to the laborer. Thus one defense which may be offered in an action of replevin is that the physical identity of the chattel is so changed that it is no longer the same piece of property and that the cause of action should not lie when the identity of the goods was so altered. *Wetherbee v. Green* (1871). This is so because the title to the chattel has, by the addition of labor, been transferred to the laborer.

In *Wetherbee,* the defendant cut timber worth $25. He mistakenly thought that the timber was his to take and, after doing so, made it into barrel hoops worth $700—28 times the original value. The true owner of the timber sued to replevy the wood.

Judge Cooley concluded that a judicial inquiry based solely on the physical identity of the chattel was difficult to apply. He cited the instance of grain becoming malt, coins melted down into a cup, and timber made into a house—all instances of altered identity—and compared them with cloth made into garments, leather into shoes, or trees sawn into timber; all instances in which the alteration was insufficient for the title to be transferred to the laborer. He then decided that the title to the affected chattel should lie with the claimant who had contributed the most value to the final product. Assuming that an appraisal of the components of value is not too difficult, this rule has ease of application to commend it.

This does not necessarily mean that the party who is allocated more than 50% of the new chattel's improved value wins. After all, the labor added in *Wetherbee* made the chattel 2700% more valuable. Later cases have not resulted in a fixed and certain percentage or number, so in some measure this rule of relative value is subject to the same charge which Cooley laid at the door of the physical identity rule. It, too, is hard to apply and uncertain of application.

One limitation on a transfer of title to a laborer often applied is that the labor must be added innocently and in good faith or, in other words, under a belief that the chattel is rightfully his. This limitation arises from the facts and the holding of *Wetherbee* and has been followed in other cases, though not uniformly; there are cases in which a knowing appropriator received title.

In an industrial age, when the addition of labor comes through expensive manufacturing processes, requiring organization and capital on an unprecedented scale, the relative value rule might be expected to have great appeal in many jurisdictions. Such was the case, and after *Wetherbee* some form of the relative value rule quickly became a majority rule in this country.

I say some form of the rule is the majority rule because, as it comes into the law in *Wetherbee,* it could take at least two forms: first, the physical identity rule continues to be the law unless the laborer can show that the work added substantially to the value of the improved chattel. Or else, second, the relative value rule supplants the physical identity rule. The latter possibility seems the more straightforward as well as the easiest to apply. If Cooley meant otherwise, he would not have criticized the old rule as he did.

What if, then, the property falls back into the hands of the prior possessor in its improved, value-added state? Can the innocent laborer recover for the value of his work? What authority there is on this question holds not. If the law were otherwise, a possessor of property could be forced to become the debtor of another acting without his consent.

The debtor-creditor relationship should be established only by mutual consent. *Isle Royale Mining Co. v. Hertin* (1877).

A. CONVERSION AND DAMAGES

When the true owner's writ of replevin is denied, he still is permitted to recover damages measured by the value of the chattel in its unimproved state. *McKee v. Gratz* (1922). This damage action is for the conversion of the chattel. It is not a trover action since that would require the successful original possessor to give over title in a forced sale and this after the accession he cannot do.

Measuring the prior possessor's recovery by the unimproved value is the usual rule, but it works best when the laborer has done no more than innocently converted the possessor's chattel. The possessor is compensated for his loss, and the laborer is not penalized for an innocent action. However, if the laborer's conversion, trespass or other type of appropriation is willful, some authority exists for measuring the possessor's damages by the value of the chattel in its improved state, as if the possessor has been denied the opportunity to improve it himself and is being compensated for the lost opportunity. In natural resource cases, because an action for conversion only lies for damage to personal property, it is additionally reasoned that giving damages based on (say) the trees or other natural resources rather than the timber or other product made from them is to give damages for real rather than personal property. The use of this reasoning would require a measure of damages based on the improved value of the chattel whether the laborer was innocent or willful.

If the improved chattel has been sold by the laborer to a third party, the measure of damages applied when the prior possessor sues the purchaser depends on whether the purchaser acted in good faith and without notice of the prior conversion. If the purchaser acted in good faith, the unimproved value alone will be recovered; if he knew of the conversion, then the improved value is the measure of damages.

B. INCORPORATION OF CHATTELS INTO ANOTHER'S PROPERTY

One might expect that if one person's chattel is incorporated into another's and if the attachments can be removed without damage to what is remaining, the doctrine of accession would not seem to be applicable. The two chattels have not changed into one; rather, one chattel has been attached to another. However, with the advent of the relative value rule, the scope of the law of accession was broadened.

Its new scope can be seen in cases dealing with automobiles. If new tires are purchased for a car owned free-and-clear, they are not permanently attached to the car, but their removal will occasion a loss of value for the car as a whole. It will not run without them, the value of a running car is out of all proportion greater than the value of the tires alone, and so title to the tires is transferred to the possessor of the car. The same might be said of a new clutch, transmission, or engine, but the doctrine of relative value has its limits. As the value of the accessory rises, the likelihood of its being accessed falls: for example, the value of a car's engine is sometimes so great a portion of the car's overall value, that the relative value rule appears inapplicable and results in a contradiction: the greater the utility of the part, the less likely it is to be subject to accession under this rule. As we shall see, however, automobile mechanics and repair shop operators fought against the uncertainties of the rule by using conditional sales agreements for car parts and accessories installed while a car is in the shop.

The limits of the relative value rule can be seen readily when a thief steals three automobiles of the same make and model, using the body of one, the chassis of another, and the engine of a third, in order to construct what becomes then a fourth car. The rule stands helpless in the resolution of such a case. In this event, it is better for each true owner to retain title and follow his part into the newly constructed car. *Atlas Assurance Co. v. Gibbs* (1936) (using this hypothetical).

When, however, there is a chattel mortgage on the car (bought on the installment plan), the pre-existing mortgage holder can obtain, by the same law of accession, title to any accessories added after the mortgage was executed. Typically the same result is achieved in the chattel mortgage by the insertion there of an "after acquired" accessory clause, subjecting later installed parts to the prior lien of the mortgage. The title to such accessories passes to the possessor of the car, and when the possessor has "his" car repossessed by the holder of the mortgage, his title is taken away as well, and since that title includes the added accessories, title to them passes to the mortgage holder. The accessories were presumably intended to become permanent additions to the car. Their removal lessens the utility of the car as a working vehicle and certainly lessens its collateral value as security for the automobile loan. So the lender repossessing the car gets title to its accessories and the former owner loses the right to remove them.

If the accessories are themselves sold under a conditional sales contract, and the title to them does not pass to the possessor of the car, the Uniform Commercial Code § 9–314 provides that a security interest in goods which attaches before installation takes priority over the prior lien on the car, except as to certain types of creditors or purchasers of the whole who take without knowledge of pre-existing liens on the whole. The purpose of such a provision is to encourage maintenance and repair of a mortgaged car, on the assumption that a running vehicle is good for both its possessor and the holder of a prior chattel mortgage on it. The holder of a security interest successfully asserting its priority must, however, compensate the car possessor for any severance damages incurred in removal of the accessory. Instead of occasioning a dispute about title to the accessory, then, the UCC here gives the conditional vendor of the accessories installed or affixed a security interest or lien to perfect.

The retention of title to the part installed by the mechanic under a conditional sales agreement provides its vendor with more than a lien remedy. Relying on the common law in this area, some courts have held that detachable parts to an automobile do not become accessions and so are not subject to the lien of the prior chattel mortgage if the vendor of the part retains the title under the agreement. The logic of this position runs as follows: because the owner mortgagor of the auto does not have title to what was installed, the lien of the prior chattel mortgage cannot attach to it and any after-acquired accessory clause has nothing on which to work. Thus in disputes between conditional sale vendors of parts and prior chattel mortgagees, the vendor has an action for the value of the parts. *Bank of America v. J. & S. Auto Repairs* (1985) (an excellent opinion collecting recent authorities on such disputes).

For purposes of such disputes between two out of possession parties, the definition of what is a "detachable" part is broad indeed. *Clark v. Wells* (1872) (a leading case finding the running parts of a wagon not subject to accession). The relative value rule discussed previously is little used in this line of cases. Even the engine is not subject to an accession.

One must, however, be sensitive to the action brought to resolve such disputes. If the vendor's action is trover and conversion, what is detachable and so subject to trover can be defined broadly because the plaintiff does not want to take the engine out and the question is academic. If the action is replevin, however, one would expect close analysis of whether the part can in fact be removed without injury to the whole. That—"removal without injury"—is what is typically meant by detachable. Conversely, when the vendor has repossessed the part, replevin by the mortgagee will include what remains, but not include the repossessed part because the action affects only the property to which the lien of the mortgage attached. If the mortgagee drafts its complaint for conversion, however, the timing of the vendor's repossession may matter: the vendor will have to act after the owner's default under the conditional sales contract, but before any demand for repossession by the mortgagee, in order to avoid conversion liability.

C. ACCESSION TO REAL PROPERTY

A chattel can occasionally become an accession to real property. For example, suppose a laborer contracts to build a house on one parcel of land and instead builds it by mistake on another. Because the value of the house will be many times more than the value of the unimproved parcel of land, the doctrine of accession implemented by a rule of relative value, if permitted to have its customary effect, would transfer the title to the land to the laborer. However, the law does not work that way. It regards the personal property— the house—as becoming affixed to and part of the real property—the land—with the result that the title to the chattel passes to the rightful possessor of the land. *Sponseller v. Meltebeke* (1977).

Thus at law the title holder to the real property can refuse to pay for the unexpected windfall of the house unless equity intervenes to soften this harsh result. The hardship on the builder itself may justify equitable relief, but other factors enter into such cases as well: the negligence of the builder in not checking the title to the ground on which he labored may be a basis for denying relief or the landowner's conduct leading the builder into the subsequent error may be a basis for granting it. The tendency of recent cases has been to protect the innocent improver or laborer. If the value of the real property is substantially increased by the accession of the added improvement, the hardship created by the doctrine of accession is sufficient for a court to find that the laborer has stated a cause of action in equity.

On the merits, moreover, there is some authority for an equity court to grant relief because of the hardship on the builder, as well as the windfall unearned by the possessor of the land. If the latter attempts to bring an equity action to quiet title to the improvement, he can be made to pay first for the improvement on the theory that he who seeks equity must simultaneously do equity.

II. CONFUSION

Confusion is the intermingling of two or more pieces of personal property so that the property rights in each can no longer be distinguished. Thereafter, no specific identification or separation of the formerly separate chattel is possible. Such an intermingling occurs most often with fungible goods like gas, oil, grain, mineral ore, or unmarked timber.

Where confusion of chattel of the same type and quality occurs, each prior possessor receives a pro rata share of the whole. Each proves what he put in and receives a like amount back again. If no pro rata division is possible, then each receives an equal share of the whole which is thereafter owned by all as tenants in common, each holding undivided fractional shares in the tenancy. Where, however, one of the possessors negligently or intentionally confuses chattels, that confuser either loses his share or has the burden of proof to show what his share was. If he fails to carry this burden, he also loses his share.

Burke, Pers.Prop., 2d Ed. NS—14

CHAPTER XII

COMMON LAW ESTATES
IN PERSONALTY

This is not a guide to common law estates. For that the reader must look elsewhere and to more comprehensive works. However, it may be helpful to summarize in one place the applicability to personal property of some of the rules and doctrines comprising our system of common law estates.

Just to show at the outset that personal property *may* require different treatment than does real property, consider the case of *Scott v. Shuffler* (1973) where the court tossed off the notion that "an item of personal property could not be held in fee simple." Why so? The court must have been thinking that seisin is inherent in the fee simple absolute in realty but does not apply to personalty. If this is so, then no interest to which seisin attached at common law—no freehold interest— could be created in personal property. This would mean no life estate, fee simple determinable, fee simple subject to a condition subsequent or future interest could be established in personalty. Not so. The *Scott* court is technically correct. It is preferable to speak of true or absolute ownership of a chattel, rather than of a fee simple absolute in it.

However, the notion of seisin is now lost in the mists of *stare decisis* and cannot affect many applications to personal property of the common law's system of estates. As noted in this chapter, however, the lack of seisin in personalty serves on occasion to limit the applications of the estate system to personalty.

I. PRESENT ESTATES AND
REMAINDERS

It is therefore harmless error to say, along with many courts, that personal property may be held in fee simple absolute, fee simple determinable, or fee simple conditional (or subject to a condition subsequent). Likewise, there is nothing that would prevent personal property from being held in a life estate followed by a vested or contingent remainder. (*Innes v. Potter* (1915), has a good, short historical discussion of these matters.) However, there is less authority on the use of a contingent remainder and generally there may be some question of the prudence of tying tangible personalty up in this manner; income-producing, intangible personal property may be a more likely subject for such an arrangement.

If the remainder is a contingent one, it could at common law be destroyed by natural termination, merger, or forfeiture; this common law doctrine of the destructibility of contingent remainders has generally been held inapplicable to personalty. This is so because the doctrine evolved out of the requirement of the common law that seisin never be in abeyance after the date of the conveyance or the date on which the devise is effective. Because seisin is irrelevant to questions involving personal property, the doctrine of destructibility is irrelevant as well.

A. THE RULE IN SHELLEY'S CASE

The common law in some instances, as where real property is conveyed "to X for life, remainder to X and his heirs," declared that X took a fee simple absolute in the realty transferred. This result was called "The Rule in Shelley's Case" and is, as a rule of law, inapplicable to personal property. It may, however, still be applicable to a devise or inter vivos transfer of personalty as a rule of construction.

B. FEE TAILS

What if there was a conveyance of personal property "to X and the heirs of his body" or "to X and his issue?" Whether or not any issue or heirs were alive at the time, this would be an attempt to create a fee tail in personalty. This is impossible because the validity of the fee tail depended on the English Statute DeDonis, which, by its terms, applied only to estates in realty invested with seisin.

Whether X takes over absolute ownership immediately, or absolute ownership subject to a condition subsequent if X has no descendents, or a life interest followed by absolute ownership in his heirs, would likely depend on an interpretation and application of a state statute, available in all but a few states, abolishing the fee tail.

C. THE RULE IN WILD'S CASE

If the language in a transfer of personal property were to read "to X and his children," such language would raise the Rule in Wild's Case. In a devise of realty, X has a fee tail at common law if X has no children on the date of the devise, but if X has children, X and his children take concurrently. Such rules apply only to devises of real property and are inapplicable to personal property, whether the transfer is made by devise or inter vivos transfer. If X has no children alive at the time of the transfer of personalty, X has a fee simple absolute or a life estate, followed by a remainder in the children. If there are children alive at the date of the transfer, however, some courts have concluded that X and his children hold concurrently.

D. THE DOCTRINE OF WORTHIER TITLE

This doctrine is fully applicable to personal property in both its testamentary and inter vivos branches. That is, if personal property is the subject of a devise and the devisee is under the law of descent given a same estate as he would take under the will, he is deemed to take by descent and not by devise. If the personal property is subject to an inter vivos conveyance and is thereby conveyed to the transferor's heirs, the estate given to the heirs is void. The testamentary branch of the doctrine makes a difference in estate planning in a few specialized areas, but many authorities regard it as obsolete. Not so for the inter vivos branch: where O conveys personalty to X for life, remainder to the heirs of the transferor, the heirs take nothing. From the date of the conveyance, X's life estate is followed, not by the heir's remainder (which is void under the doctrine) but by a reversion in O. A transferor wishing to avoid the doctrine should specify his heirs by name in his will or conveyance.

II. FUTURE INTERESTS

All five types of future interests—reversion, remainders, executory interests, possibilities of reverter and rights of reentry—may, according to the weight of authority and the Restatement of Property, be created in personal property. However, a future interest cannot be created in consumable personal property and a transfer of such an interest is usually taken to have transferred a fee simple absolute in the personalty. A consumable is an article of personal property which is worn out or destroyed by normal use: crops, farm implements, and hogs ready for the butcher are examples. Dairy cattle, furniture, and a grist mill are non-consumables. The line is probably not firm, nor should it be; nor is the rationale for this exception to the rule that a future interest may be created in personal property firmly established. One writer has suggested that if use of a thing results in its consumption, then ownership must be absolute—or that possession is tantamount to ownership in this case, and a future interest in it would only be a legal superfluity.

A. THE RULE AGAINST PERPETUITIES

The Rule against Perpetuities applies equally to real and personal property. As such, it serves to limit the vesting of future interests in personal property to a period of time extending over lives in being at the time of the transfer plus a period of twenty-one years.

III. CONCURRENT ESTATES
A. TENANCY BY THE ENTIRETIES

There is a split of authority as to whether this estate, limited in any event to property held by legally-married husbands and wives, can exist in personal property. At common law, because the husband became the owner of the wife's personalty, it did not exist for personalty. However, after the Married Women's Property Acts were enacted in all states, a split in the case law developed. Some states held that the Acts made this estate available to husbands and wives. Others held that the Acts did not change the gender-neutral rule that spouses as such could hold personalty only in one of two concurrent forms—the joint tenancy or the tenancy in common.

B.   THE JOINT TENANCY

The overwhelming weight of authority is that a joint tenancy, with its attendant right of survivorship, may exist in personal property.

C.   THE TENANCY IN COMMON

This estate, too, may exist in personal property.

INDEX

References are to Pages

†